The Handbook of Managed Behavioral Healthcare

A Complete and Up-to-Date Guide
for Students and Practitioners

Gayle L. Zieman

Jossey-Bass Publishers
San Francisco

Jossey-Bass books and products are available through
most bookstores. To contact Jossey-Bass directly, call
(888) 378–2537, fax to (800) 605–2665, or visit our website
at www.josseybass.com.

Substantial discounts on bulk quantities of Jossey-Bass books
are available to corporations, professional associations, and
other organizations. For details and discount information,
contact the special sales department at Jossey-Bass.

For sales outside the United States, please contact your local
Simon & Schuster International Office.

Manufactured in the United States of America on
Lyons Falls Turin Book. This paper is acid-free
and 100 percent totally chlorine-free.

Library of Congress Cataloging-in-Publication Data
Zieman, Gayle L.
The handbook of managed behavioral healthcare /
Gayle L. Zieman. — 1st ed.
p. cm. —
(The Jossey-Bass managed behavioral healthcare library)
Includes bibliographical references and index.
ISBN 0-7879-4153-0 (acid-free paper)
1. Managed mental health care. I. Title. II. Series.

RC465.5 .Z54 1988   98-8922
362.2'0425—ddc21

FIRST EDITION
PB Printing   10 9 8 7 6 5 4 3 2 1

CONTENTS

To my mentors—
Gerald Benson and Larry Bloom of Colorado State University and
Laurie Steinberg of Educational Assessment Systems, Albuquerque—
my thanks.

PREFACE

Managed care was not on the minds of most clinicians in 1987. But it took center stage for me on a blustery Sunday afternoon that year when my clinician partners—a psychologist and a child psychiatrist—and I sat around trying to decide what should be the future of our start-up group practice. We knew that Albuquerque was rapidly becoming a bastion of managed care, so we decided that the future for our own group would be brightest with managed care.

That choice has been productive. Our small group practice grew into a large group that accepted capitation contracts (see Chapter Eight) with health maintenance organizations (HMOs) and large, self-insured employers. Today, Mesa Mental Health has become a regional managed behavioral healthcare organization (MBHO). The group manages the behavioral care for nearly three hundred thousand insured individuals in New Mexico and Texas. So, when I describe how an MBHO works and what you should know before you sign up with one, I write from experience.

My first piece of advice—and you will find much advice in the book—is this: whether you, as a prospective clinician or a new member of a managed care organization, think managed care is the best or the worst thing that could happen to healthcare, get used to the idea that it is here to stay. Managed care is the dominant force in U.S. healthcare today.

AUDIENCE FOR THE BOOK

To help readers learn the practical lay of the land in managed care is the purpose of this book. Clinicians and healthcare administrators in training, as well as seasoned clinicians preparing for work with managed care organizations, will benefit from the step-by-step curriculum presented here. This is a pragmatic guidebook for what you will need to know in order to work with managed care—or what you should know if you choose to reject work with managed care insurers. I teach managed care from "the trenches."

OVERVIEW OF THE TEXT

In Chapter One, I show how pervasive managed care is today and describe its evolution. First, I discuss the basic concepts and terms of both managed care and the system that preceded it—indemnity insurance. Managed care is a very different system of healthcare delivery from the indemnity system. As you see how the two systems compare, you will begin to appreciate the radical nature of the change that healthcare is undergoing today.

Chapter Two details the surprising history of prepaid health plans in the United States. You might think that such plans resulted from insurance companies' wish to make more profit. Ironically, physicians pioneered managed care between 1910 and the early 1970s, observing that the fee-for-service system created perverse incentives by rewarding physicians financially for providing treatment but withdrawing those rewards when health was reestablished. The strength of that idea, along with boosts from the federal government and changes in the public perception of managed care, served to reestablish managed care in the 1970s and lead to its phenomenal growth throughout the last two decades of the century.

In Chapter Three, I begin describing the various departments and functional parts of a managed care organization, emphasizing what clinicians need to know in order to work with HMOs and MBHOs. The term *MBHO* refers to a company whose *business* it is to manage the mental health and substance abuse benefits within a complete healthcare insurance plan.

Chapter Four offers invaluable information about what makes a healthcare provider attractive to an MBHO that is hiring clinicians or subcontracting with private practice clinicians. I also tell you what clinicians should find out about an MBHO before signing on as an employee or subcontracted practitioner. In Chapters Five and Six, I get more specific. I show an actual provider subcontract and explain its provisions; this will help you understand what subcontracted clinicians are asked to sign.

In Chapter Seven, I describe the process that occurs simultaneously with new employment or subcontracting with an MBHO: the credentialing of clinical privileges. I also explain recredentialing—a process that usually takes place every two years.

How you, as a clinician, will get paid is described in Chapter Eight. Copayments, discounted fee-for-service, case rates, and capitation contracting are described in this chapter.

The focus of Chapter Nine is the surging demand for report cards and other evidence of quality improvement from managed care organizations that provide general medical insurance and from managed behavioral healthcare organizations. Accreditation standards, outcomes studies, and prevention programs are discussed. No area of healthcare is evolving faster at this time than the push for quality improvement. This chapter is your guide to this critical new area.

Medicare, Medicaid, and TriCare (formerly CHAMPUS, the insurer for the military) are the big gorillas of healthcare. And these government programs are swiftly turning to managed care—a revolution for practitioners, community mental health centers, and hospitals serving the beneficiaries of these programs. Chapter Ten is devoted to teaching you the ins and outs of how managed care has affected these programs and what you must know to work with the "new versions" of these programs.

Chapter Eleven presents profiles of six managed behavioral healthcare organizations; national and regional companies are included. The emphasis of this chapter is on learning from what others are doing. You need to know the operational strategies of these firms.

Nothing may be more critical than the ethical issues discussed in Chapter Twelve. The issues are presented in a straightforward manner, and direct advice on handling them is given. Here's your chance to agree or disagree with me on the most controversial topics in healthcare today.

Your future in managed care is the subject of Chapter Thirteen. What you should plan for and adjust to are covered here. Even where to turn if you wish to avoid managed care is discussed at length. This is must reading for new clinicians and healthcare administrators.

Finally, this text ends with four data-packed appendixes. A thorough managed care glossary (Appendix A), a sample capitation contract (Appendix B), a summary of quality accreditation standards (Appendix C), and an in-depth listing of managed care journals, newsletters, and web sites (Appendix D) are all here. These are the reference materials that will keep you coming back to this text again and again over the years.

BACKGROUND OF THE TEXT

Writing a textbook on managed care is the culmination of my many years spent training clinicians. In the late 1980s I began giving workshops on managed care at the annual meeting of the American Psychological Association. Every year the room was filled with hecklers. Clinicians paid good money to sit up front and confront me. I began asking, in the middle of each workshop, how many wanted a photograph of me for their dart board. In recent years I have given workshops across the country and also at the annual meeting of the American Psychiatric Association. Serious attitudes and questions such as, What do I need to know? have replaced the heckling, but the baseline knowledge of most clinicians still remains far behind what's needed in this evolutionary period in healthcare.

I knew that something more than workshops was needed after a visit to my alma mater, Colorado State University, in late 1996. I was asked to make videotapes on managed care. At the end of the taping sessions, a former professor exclaimed, "We're training dinosaurs!" I left campus committed to writing this text.

Whether you decide that a position within managed care is best for you or not, I have written this book to provide you with sound, practical knowledge and advice that will help you make good career choices. And if you opt for working within this increasingly pervasive system, the information given here is offered as a catalyst to stimulate your adaptation to the rapidly evolving world of healthcare. May you have a prosperous and satisfying career.

ACKNOWLEDGMENTS

No book is produced by an author alone. There is always a supporting cast, without whose assistance the work would never have come to fruition. My supporting cast is a wonderful collection of individuals and groups who have lent expertise and unwavering encouragement for this project.

Foremost, I must thank my wife, Nalini, and my daughter, Larissa, for their enduring patience and support. You encouraged me in my decision to write this text, even though you knew there would be countless weekend and late-night hours when my only interactions would be with my computer. There were; your support persisted. Both of you are a constant source of sustenance and joy.

To my colleagues at Mesa Mental Health, I am forever indebted. You have allowed me to practice and experiment in a business that is evolving with, and sometimes on the leading edge of, healthcare. Foremost is my partner of eleven years, Steve Sehr. We had to learn fast and blaze a new trail. Thanks for being there so we could do it together with a mission and with a steady rudder when the waves came. To Sean McMullan, Carol Furgal, Roger White, and the rest of you on our management team who heartily said, "Go for it" when I said I wanted to do another book: thank you. Many of the exhibits and anecdotes in this text reflect your hard work and the mastery of managed care with which I am surrounded daily. Hats off to our "Can Do Crews" in the customer service, utilization management, intake, credentialing, claims, accounts payable, accounts receivable, network services, human resources, and quality management departments. And special thanks to the many skilled clinicians with whom I have had the opportunity to practice. A decade together has seemed to go by in a flash.

I cannot give enough thanks to my many friends at the Institute for Behavioral Healthcare (a nonprofit organization in the San Francisco area dedicated to bringing together payers, providers, and advocacy groups for dialogue and cooperation). You encouraged my presentations and my writings, and you helped me hang on to my seat in the roller coaster for the wild ride that healthcare has been. Michael Freeman, Tim Harrall, Tom Trabin, Nancy Bechtel, Adam Richmond, Rebecca Theriot, Corey Barrington, and the entire IBH crew—you have my highest praise. Thanks for giving me a place to grow and a forum in which to address behavioral groups from coast to coast.

No group can have a deeper place in my heart than the Council of Behavioral Group Practices. What a go-get-it congregation of colleagues! May the Force remain with you. To my frequent colleagues around the table at steering committee meetings—Leonard Goldstein, Alan Axelson, Bruce Bienenstock, and Kay Swint—thanks for all those great dinner and breakfast discussions. They stimulated this text.

Then, there are my professional pals, Allen Daniels of the University of Cincinnati, Teresa Kramer of the University of Arkansas, and Neil Dickman and Randy Wyatt of Pacific Applied Psychology Associates, Berkeley, California. You've kept my energy high to tackle this and the myriad of other projects we've worked on together. So many ideas, so little time. When's the next conference call?

Special thanks go out to Scott Ries of the University of Cincinnati, Jane Keeports at Lovelace Health Systems (Albuquerque), Judy Barber of Value Behavioral Health (Falls Church, Virginia), Dennis Craff and Don Christianson of OPTIONS (Norfolk, Virginia), Bill Gilbert at Interact (Columbus, Ohio), and Michael Feldman and Greg Winkel of Park Nicollet (Minneapolis). I appreciate your assistance in areas where I was lacking in knowledge.

I also owe a great deal to my editor at Jossey-Bass, Alan Rinzler. Not only were you constantly available, thorough, and knowledgeable but you were correct on many occasions to tactfully advise that I should rewrite a chapter here and there. This text has benefited greatly from your mentoring.

To everyone: you've been a great source of support and encouragement for someone who has desired to straddle the fences between business, teaching, and clinical practice. Thanks!

GAYLE L. ZIEMAN
Albuquerque, New Mexico
March 1998

The Handbook of Managed Behavioral Healthcare

CHAPTER ONE

Managed Care

Healthcare's New Foundation

I don't think we're in Kansas anymore, Toto.
Dorothy in "The Wizard of Oz"

M anaged Care Dominance," declares the cover of the scholarly journal *Health Affairs* (1997). "Managed Care—The Fastest Growing Area of Healthcare," proclaims *The Wall Street Journal,* (Lancaster, 1997). Managed care has become pervasive in America. Observe that

- Over 80 percent of American workers receive their healthcare through managed care (Data Watch, 1997).

- Retired workers are voluntarily flocking into managed care companies that administer Medicare benefits. Participation will increase from 10 percent of Medicare beneficiaries in 1997 to over 25 percent by 2002, projects the Congressional Budget Office (Hammonds, 1997).

- Thirty-nine states by mid-1997 had transferred all or part of their Medicaid programs for the poor to private managed care organizations (State Health Watch, 1997).

- All nine million military personnel, retirees, and dependents have been moved into managed care health plans.

Managed care is well established in U.S. healthcare and continues to grow at a rapid pace. It is no longer an experiment, or an anomaly distinguishing certain regions of the country, or even an emerging trend. Managed care will be the primary mode of insuring Americans into the twenty-first century.

1

Healthcare clinicians now work in a care delivery system that is radically different from that of just ten years ago. There are new rules, new financial payment mechanisms, new methods of managing care, and new incentives for doctors and therapists—incentives that have many clinicians enraged or, at least, confused. Today more than ever, it is crucial for clinicians to thoroughly master the *business of healthcare.* Professional survival depends on it.

BEFORE MANAGED CARE

To comprehend managed care as it exists today and will exist tomorrow, you should first understand the healthcare system prior to managed care and the surprising history of managed care. In this chapter and the next, I will explain the evolution of managed care and the basic concepts and terms of both managed care and the preceding system. Chapter Three begins an in-depth examination of managed care that will help you understand the intricacies of its anatomy and physiology.

Managed care is more than a new form of payment for treatment; it is a new system of healthcare delivery that has turned the previous system upside down. The new system is so different that the insurance system preceding it—indemnity insurance—is often politely referred to as "traditional" or "conventional." Not so politely, many have labeled the previous healthcare system "excessive," "guild-dominated," "perversely incentivised," and, at best, a "cottage industry."

Prior to World War II there was very little healthcare insurance. Most healthcare was paid for by the individual or family receiving the care, which is called "out-of-pocket" today. Although notable examples of early managed care existed before World War II, these nascent managed care plans, which I discuss in Chapter Two, never dominated the healthcare system.

After the war, the prosperity of the 1950s and 1960s nurtured the maturation and almost total dominance of healthcare by indemnity health insurance. Such insurance plans were designed to "indemnify" policyholders, that is, to hold them secure against loss. Healthcare insurance was a financial protection—no more and no less. It paid some or all of the costs but did not become directly involved in treatment planning or decisions (see Table 1.1).

The typical indemnity health insurance policy (contract) stipulated a certain amount per year in health costs (often per person and per family) that the policyholder was responsible for paying. This was called the deductible and was paid before insurance coverage for the year began. After meeting the deductible in any one year, often $100 to $250 per person or several hundred dollars per family in incurred healthcare expenses, the policyholder was indemnified against the majority of healthcare costs. A common arrangement was for the

Table 1.1. Basic Tenets of Indemnity Versus Managed Care Plans.

Areas of Difference	Traditional Indemnity Insurance	Managed Care Insurance
1. Population Served	Not defined. Employer groups or others are managed as individuals having the same benefits covering medical procedures.	Defined as the enrollees of an entire health plan or employer group. Decisions based on how to manage the healthcare needs of the population as a whole, not individuals.
2. Focus of Care	On treating ill individuals. No emphasis is placed on prevention or crisis management programs.	Emphases are on treating ill individuals as well as prevention and crisis-avoidance programs.
3. Care Responsibility	Simply to pay the costs of care, with no responsibility to regulate the quality of the care provided.	High responsibility for ensuring the quality of the clinical programs available to members, along with paying for the costs of care.
4. Provider Responsibility	None. Patients pick their own providers.	Strong responsibility for providing a comprehensive network of providers whose history has been carefully checked by the health plan.
5. Treatment Decisions	No involvement.	High responsibility for directing care to least restrictive alternatives and ensuring the quality of the care.
6. Financial Incentives	If clinical decisions are debatable, encourages overtreatment and excessive costs.	If clinical decisions are debatable, encourages undertreatment and minimal costs.
7. Care Decision Making	None, other than benefit structures (medical procedures and fees covered, for example).	Highly centralized decisions affecting care for the population (such as care protocols).

insurer to pay 80 percent of treatment charges, while the insured remained responsible for 20 percent.

Over time, variations in indemnity arrangements developed, primarily to protect insurers against excessive payments. These variations included

- The *lifetime maximum*—a cap on how much the healthcare insurer would indemnify. For example, a policy might stipulate that the insurer would reimburse the insured up to a maximum of $350,000 in healthcare costs per individual per lifetime, and anything above that amount reverted to out-of-pocket.
- No coverage for *preexisting conditions*—a stipulation in the insurance contract that the insurer was only responsible for medical charges related to healthcare problems that began after the individual began coverage with the particular insurer. A common twist on the *preexisting* clause was that costs related to preexisting conditions would be indemnified, that is, covered, only after a certain time period following becoming insured with the particular plan, often six months or one year.
- *Exclusions*—a list of healthcare procedures or diagnoses for which there was no coverage, for example, cosmetic surgery.
- *Maximum fee schedules* for common healthcare procedures. Under such a schedule the insurer would pay only up to the amount the insurer determined to be the usual and customary charge for a specific procedure or treatment. Usual and customary charge rates were often regionalized, based on surveys of standard clinician fees. For example, in the late 1980s a fifty-minute psychotherapy session by a licensed psychologist might have been reimbursed up to $90 in the Rocky Mountain states but up to $110 in New England.

Indemnity insurance was quite functional for the middle of the twentieth century. Employers saw such plans as a means of protecting and benefiting their workers, whereas employees and labor unions sought ever broader healthcare coverage. One of the sought-after enhancements was coverage for mental health services, which until the late 1960s and early 1970s had remained an exclusion in most healthcare insurance plans. Indemnity coverage also expanded to meet the requests of employers and unions in other areas: richer maternity benefits, inclusion of "alternative treatments" such as chiropractic and acupuncture, and coverage for certain catastrophic health events that generally produced charges beyond the ordinary lifetime maximums— major cardiac surgeries and cancer treatments, for example.

As the benefit structures of indemnity plans grew, however, so did the costs. In an effort to control costs, insurers began to violate or attempt to modify one of medicine's most sacred concepts: all decisions regarding treatment are to be made by the doctor and the patient working together. In the 1980s many traditional indemnity insurers changed their role to include decision making about which services were medically necessary and therefore would be covered.

This monumental change was borrowed from the emerging HMOs of the 1970s and early 1980s. The change brought the introduction of two methods borrowed from HMOs: preauthorization and the establishment of medical necessity. Preauthorization (often called precertification if the healthcare service is in a hospital) is the requirement that the doctor or other clinician (managed care plans call them all providers or practitioners) contact the health plan prior to any major, nonemergent procedure to seek authorization for the procedure to be indemnified. Deciding whether to indemnify the cost of a procedure is based on the determination of medical necessity, that is, deciding whether the procedure is truly required for the acute care of the patient. (A detailed definition of *medical necessity* is given in Chapter Three.) Plans that invoke these measures are hybrids, that is, they represent a cross between managed care and conventional indemnity insurers. These hybrids are known as managed indemnity plans. Almost no indemnity healthcare plans remain today that are not managed indemnity in design.

ENTER MANAGED CARE

Abandoning the sacred axiom that all decisions about treatment must be between doctor and patient laid the foundation for managed care's growth. By 1970 many business-savvy physicians and healthcare economists questioned the efficiency and incentives of a healthcare system that relied solely on individual practitioners to define both the necessity of medical procedures and the quality of the services provided. Specific events in the years surrounding 1970 that led to the questioning of the indemnity-insurance-driven system included

- Annual cost increases in insurance premiums often reaching 20 percent.
- Healthcare as a portion of the gross national product rising from 5 percent in 1960 to 9 percent by 1975 (Wrightson, 1990).
- The national embarrassment that 15 percent of all Americans remained without health insurance.

The Health Maintenance Organization

Although many in Washington called for national health insurance similar to those government-sponsored plans used in England, Germany, Sweden, and Canada, others believed that a complete overhaul of the private healthcare system was the most viable solution. One of those favoring an overhaul of the private insurance industry was, and continues to be, Paul Ellwood, M.D.

Dr. Ellwood worked for many years at the Sister Kennedy Institute in Minneapolis and observed that his hospital was financially rewarded by keeping children hospitalized, even when outpatient services would have been most appropriate medically. He noted that there was no financial incentive for his hospital or physicians to restore health. More treatment led to more insurance payments, and there was no financial reward for curing a patient or using less-intensive treatments. Inspired by what he termed "the perverse incentives of the system," Dr. Ellwood sought to reform healthcare (Belkin, 1996, p. 104). In 1969 he proposed a new form of health insurance which he labeled the health maintenance organization (HMO). (For more about Dr. Ellwood and the history of HMOs, see Chapter Two.)

Dr. Ellwood's efforts regarding HMOs evolved first into several demonstration projects across the country and finally into the HMO Act of 1973. This legislation defined an HMO as having the following characteristics:

1. *Each subscriber (insured person) prepays (usually monthly) for access to his or her own healthcare and for that of any dependents (collectively referred to as members).*

2. *A fixed panel of practitioners (clinicians) is employed by or subcontracted to the HMO to provide the care that members require.* A fixed network of hospital providers is also subcontracted to or owned by the HMO. The members of the plan must choose from this panel of providers when seeking healthcare.

3. *A clearly defined benefit package describes the services and procedures that are covered under the plan.*

4. *A fixed fee schedule defines what providers will be reimbursed.*

5. *Quality assurance standards define service requirements that the providers must meet.* For example, the maximum number of days a patient should have to wait for a first appointment after requesting the appointment is defined.

6. *The financial risk of insuring a population of members is shared with the providers of care.* A common procedure in the 1970s and 1980s was for the HMO to keep a percentage of each payment that was due to a provider (a procedure called the withhold) and, based on the profitability of the health plan at the end of the year, to return a portion of the withhold annually to the providers. (Newer risk-sharing models of case rates and capitation are discussed in Chapter Eight.)

7. *Members pay a fixed copayment, that is, an amount the member pays the provider when service is delivered.* Copayments may vary by type of provider or service, for example, $5 to see the patient's family doctor (the primary care physician—PCP, in managed care terminology), $25 for an hour of psychotherapy, and $200 for a hospital admission.

8. *Premiums charged to members (monthly cost of the insurance) can only be set using community rating.* This was a methodology in which healthcare costs in the community where the members lived (not just members of the plan but the entire community) were used to calculate premiums. The method that was *not* allowed was experience rating—the setting of premiums based on the healthcare costs of the insured population.

9. *The HMO has the right to review medical procedures to determine if they are medically necessary and therefore covered by the HMO for payment.* These reviews, known then as utilization review and now as utilization management, could occur either prior to beginning a treatment (called preauthorization for outpatient services and precertification for hospital admissions), during treatment (called concurrent review), or after the completion of treatment (retrospective review). When the HMO determined that a requested or completed procedure did not fit within the defined benefit package or was not medically necessary, the HMO could issue a denial in which the HMO refused all payment for the procedure(s). These utilization management methods continue unchanged today.

10. *Consumers are to have input into the development of clinical programs and requirements for health education activities.*

11. *The dual-choice mandate can be invoked.* In other words, HMOs had a legal right to insist that any employer in their service area with twenty-five or more employees must offer their employees an HMO insurance option in addition to any other healthcare insurance options allowed. This feature was dropped by federal legislation in the late 1980s.

HMO plans meeting all of these criteria were certified by the U.S. government as federally qualified plans. Being federally qualified was important in the 1970s because it gave a plan, in essence, a governmental "seal of approval," which provided a distinct marketing advantage and also made the plan eligible for government grants and loans.

To build their network of practitioners, HMOs were allowed three models: employed staff (staff model), a network of group practices (group model), and the use of independent practice associations (IPAs). An IPA is a group of independent clinicians who retain their private offices and business structure while forming a broader business entity designed to contract the collective services of the members as network.

HMO plans quickly became known as managed care. Defined provider panels, a rigid list of covered medical procedures, fixed and discounted fee schedules, and the insurer authorizing or denying services for coverage felt extremely *managed* to patients and providers who had been accustomed to the relatively free-wheeling system of traditional indemnity plans.

The Evolution of HMOs

Since their origins in the HMO Act of 1973, HMOs have evolved into a broader array of plan options and services, due primarily to six major amendments to the Act: 1976, 1978, 1979, 1981, 1986, and 1988. These amendments have significantly changed HMOs by eliminating the grant and loan monies for new HMOs, reducing the importance of being federally qualified, removing the restriction against setting premium rates based on experience rating, and allowing plans to contract with individual solo practitioners or small clinical groups as an expansion of the network model. The dual-choice mandate also went by the wayside, as the government believed that HMOs were well enough established to no longer require this protection.

By the mid-1980s, insurers were also allowed to add insurance types beyond indemnity and HMO. First came the preferred provider organization (PPO)—an insurance plan that functions like an HMO but allows members to seek services from providers not on the insurer's list of contracted providers simply by paying a higher copayment to the nonsubcontracted provider. With the PPO, many insurers began offering employers what has been labeled the triple option, that is, the choice between an indemnity plan, a PPO plan, and an HMO. In the triple option, employees are given the choice, usually on an annual basis, of signing up for either of the three options with differing monthly premium amounts ranging from the most expensive—the indemnity plan—down to the HMO.

The latest variation, one that has grown rapidly throughout the 1990s, is the point of service (POS) plan, which is a combination of an HMO and a managed indemnity plan. With a POS plan, members have the option, at any time they need healthcare, to select between staying within the HMO structure or opting out to the managed indemnity-type arrangement. There they may choose any provider and then pay a percentage of the billed charges (usually up to a limit set by the insurer per procedure as the usual and customary charge). A common financial arrangement in the POS indemnity option is for the member to pay 30 percent of the covered portion (that falling within the usual and customary charge) of the bill, while the insurer pays 70 percent of the covered portion. The managed indemnity option often has a yearly deductible amount before the indemnity coverage applies.

At a time when HMOs have been criticized for being too restrictive in the providers available and in directing care, POS plans have become popular due to their preservation of the insured's freedom of choice in selecting providers and the types of payment structure. For example, a family might have one member seeing a psychologist on the HMO's panel of providers and using these services through the HMO structure (with copayments and limits on the number of services per year). That same family member may be simultaneously obtaining treatment from a dermatologist who is not subcontracted to the HMO and who receives payments from the insurer and the family via the indemnity coverage, which has far fewer limits on the number or types of procedures that will be paid by the insurer. Of course, the monthly insurance premium cost for a POS plan is significantly higher than that of a straight HMO plan, but it is still less than a full indemnity plan.

THE IMPACT OF MANAGED CARE

In many parts of the United States, *HMO* has become a household term. Other managed care terms are becoming commonplace, for example, a family doctor or pediatrician is often referred to as a PCP; any healthcare clinician might be called a practitioner. Procedures such as contacting a PCP to receive a referral authorizing speciality care and obtaining preauthorization from an insurer prior to any expensive treatment have become accepted by a growing majority of Americans. Even the venerable concept that all care is to be decided on solely by doctor and patient is rapidly slipping into the pages of medical history.

The word *medical* is now often replaced with *healthcare* because HMOs have been leaders in using clinicians who are not exclusively medical doctors. Almost any HMO has on its panel of providers several nurse practitioners who can prescribe medicines within guidelines. Many also have physical therapists, clinical social workers, psychotherapists, and psychologists. It is no wonder that patients and doctors who experienced the medical and insurance system of the 1960s and 1970s perceive their entire professional world as having been ripped away and replaced by a highly controlled, cost-conscious, and revolutionary system that often seems more like General Motors than a system of medical care.

Nowhere is this better portrayed than in a story told by Dr. Ellwood himself. He reports (Belkin, 1996, p. 106) that he recently required some minor surgery and was surprised to learn that it would be done on an outpatient basis. He also notes, "They told me to bring someone to drive me home. I thought that it was because I would be in too much pain to drive, but then I realized it was because, when they sent me home, I was still coming out from the anesthesia." On the way home in a friend's car he experienced common postoperative complications: nausea, dizziness, and vomiting. Ellwood goes on to joke, "I had to decide whether to go back to the hospital to die or to go on home and die . . . so I decided to come on home to die." He obviously survived and, at his postoperative office follow-up appointment, described these events to his surgeon. Ellwood reports of his surgeon, "The guy got this little smile on his face. . . . Then he leaned in real close and looked me right in the eye [and said] 'Ellwood, it's your own damn fault.'"

Whether in Jackson Hole, Wyoming, where Dr. Ellwood lives, or in New York City, the extent of managed care is such that many healthcare insurers are now dropping all offerings of indemnity insurance, except as a part of a POS plan. Insurers report that indemnity plans have such a dwindling membership that supporting them administratively is a losing proposition. It is true that the growth of managed care plans has been phenomenal since the mid-1980s. (See

Figure 1.1 for an overview of the growth of HMOs.) The growth of PPO and POS plans has been equally astounding.

MANAGED CARE IN GOVERNMENT PROGRAMS

Managed care has even moved swiftly into governmental programs that provide healthcare. As stated at the beginning of this chapter, thirty-nine states have privatized all or substantial portions of their Medicaid programs for the poor to HMO plans. Medicare, which the federal government administers for retirees and disabled individuals of any age, has been targeted by the federal government to sign up large numbers of retirees into managed care Medicare plans. Some HMOs even specialize in Medicare. (Medicaid and Medicare are discussed

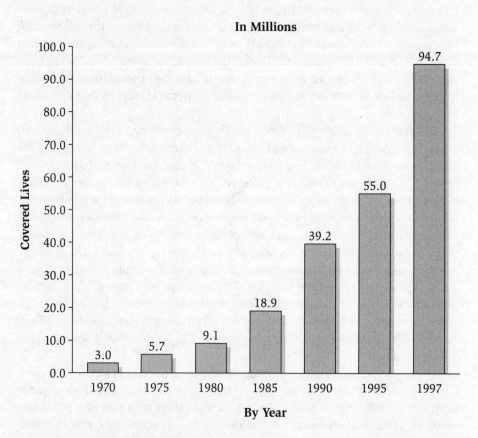

Figure 1.1. Growth in HMO Enrollment.

Sources: Wrightson (1990); *Behavioral Healthcare Tomorrow* (1997); Health Care Financing Authority (1997).

more in Chapter Ten.) Even the U.S. military has adopted managed care plans for its personnel, dependents, and retirees.

Managed care is the dominant healthcare system. It is the industrialization of healthcare nearly a century after the emergence of the manufacturing industry and thirty years after the consolidation of consumer retail businesses such as the corner clothing store, the five and dime, the neighborhood grocer, and the local pharmacy began to flourish. The fact that large medical clinics with employed physicians and hospital-physician joint ventures (called physician-hospital organizations) are popping up all over America is not a fluke or a passing fad. Changes in the financing and foundational axioms of medical care through managed care have promoted a revolution toward integrated delivery systems (IDSs) in which multidisciplinary clinics and networks of providers use HMO concepts to maximize efficiency and convenience in the provision of care. Managed care has changed the very fabric of American healthcare.

Before exploring the details of managed care plans and the realities of providing care and treatment within a managed care environment, it is important to understand further the reasons for managed care and its rise to prominence, as well as what forces will drive it in the future. In Chapter Two, I present the nearly one-hundred-year history of managed care and the forces that are propelling it into the twenty-first century.

Nearly One Hundred Years of Managed Care

A common myth is that managed care was started in the 1980s by insurance companies seeking increased profits. Nothing could be further from the truth. The concepts that define managed care were introduced long before insurers came into the healthcare marketplace. The pioneers of managed care were employers and physicians.

NINE DECADES OF PREPAID HEALTHCARE

The basic concepts of managed care were first developed in the early 1900s as a means of delivering services to employee populations. The earliest such arrangement was in Galveston, Texas, shortly after 1900. The Sisters of Charity created a system to provide healthcare to the spouses and children of sailors who were out to sea. The sisters charged a flat rate per "member" per month, which entitled a sailor's dependents to healthcare at facilities run by the holy order.

The first managed care arrangement with a more formal contractual arrangement was started in 1910 by Drs. Thomas Curran and James Yokum, founders of the Western Clinic in Tacoma, Washington. They contracted to provide all necessary medical care to a group of lumber mill employees for a salary deduction of 50 cents per employee per month. By 1911, another physician, Dr. Bridge, had opened the Bridge Clinic to compete with the Western Clinic. Eventually,

Dr. Bridge established approximately twenty Bridge Clinics in Washington and Oregon, which contracted with employers to provide all healthcare needs to employees and their families.

The Tacoma area also provided the first resistance to managed care—the Pierce County Medical Society quickly organized to oppose the Western and Bridge Clinics and the entire concept of prepaid care. Drs. Yokum, Curran, and Bridge were drummed out of the county medical society.

These early managed care contracts were truly prepaid medical plans and became known in the early decades of the century as prepaid group practices (PGPs) (Mayer and Mayer, 1985; Shouldice and Shouldice, 1978). PGPs flourished in several regions of the country and served the industries of lumbering, mining, transportation, construction, and shipping. In fact, as will be shown, there were numerous variations on the PGP theme. It, like the Tacoma-based clinics, lasted until approximately World War II when indemnity insurance companies were becoming popular.

Of note is how these early PGPs had all the basic features of an HMO today:

- A set of available medical benefits based on the need for care
- Prepayment on a monthly basis
- A fixed panel of providers (doctors and hospitals)
- The assumption of financial risk by the insurer—the doctors in this case—if the cost of services provided exceeded the income from the salary deduction

In 1927 Dr. Michael Shadid of Elk City, Oklahoma, a small farming community, promoted a variation on the PGP arrangement. Dr. Shadid sought a one-time payment from farmers and townspeople through which they could "insure" themselves for healthcare costs over a fixed time period. Dr. Shadid sold shares in the construction of Community Hospital for $50 apiece. Each share entitled the holder to necessary medical care at the hospital. The residents of Elk City enthusiastically supported the plan—but the county medical society did not. As a consequence of selling shares in a prepaid health benefit plan and constructing his hospital, Dr. Shadid lost his membership in the county society and, subsequently, in state and national medical societies as well. He was threatened with suspension of his medical license, and it is reported that for many years physicians seeking to work at Community Hospital had an unusually difficult time obtaining a license to practice in the state of Oklahoma. While embattled in his own state, Dr. Shadid traveled the country speaking about prepaid arrangements, and he is reported to have been the catalyst for other PGPs. Despite the opposition, Community Hospital grew and in 1934 the Farmer's Union took over sponsorship of the program, renaming it Farmer's Union Cooperative Association.

In Oklahoma, Dr. Shadid brought an antitrust suit against the county and state medical societies. Twenty years after filing his antitrust action, Dr. Shadid and his associates settled out of court for $300,000 in a victory that followed previous legal decisions. All court actions contesting prepaid health plans in the 1920s through the 1940s were settled in favor of the prepaid plans.

An example of an employer-driven PGP comes from the early 1930s, when Drs. Donald Ross and H. Clifford Loos of the Ross-Loos Clinic in Los Angeles were approached by the Los Angeles Water and Power Department to establish a prepaid healthcare plan for employees of the department. The plan was so successful that over the next few years other groups of municipal employees were added. Nevertheless, Drs. Ross and Loos were expelled from the Los Angeles County Medical Society.

The Battle over Early Managed Care

The conflict over prepaid plans escalated to a national forum. After a five-year study funded by several large, national corporations, the Committee on the Cost of Medical Care (Falkson, 1980) reported in 1932 that medical care, both preventive and therapeutic, should be furnished largely by organized groups of physicians, and the cost of medical care should be handled on a group prepayment basis. We now call this capitation (see Chapter Eight). Shortly thereafter, the American Medical Association issued a statement strongly condemning prepaid healthcare.

The controversy over prepaid medical plans provided a major impetus for the blossoming of indemnity medical insurance. Social concern that Americans should be protected from devastating healthcare costs ran high following the onset of the Great Depression and the federal programs of the New Deal. Indemnity insurance was ultimately viewed as the best solution because it protected workers from disastrous medical costs yet preserved the tradition of physicians being paid a fee for every service they provide.

As a result, a school teachers' insurance plan offered by Baylor University was transformed in 1929, with the help of the American Hospital Association, into Blue Cross of Texas, the first major indemnity insurer. By 1945 Blue Cross and Blue Shield plans insured twenty-one million Americans (Hammonds, Schiller, Stodghill, and Harris, 1996).

The initial growth of indemnity medical insurance, however, did not immediately slow down the development of prepaid plans. In 1937 the Group Health Association (GHA) of Washington, D.C. was started by the Home Owner's Loan Corporation as a means of preventing mortgage defaults caused by large medical bills. After the District of Columbia insurance commissioner claimed authority over GHA and tried to close it down, a court battle ensued, with the resulting legal opinion that prepaid plans did not constitute medical insurance and therefore were not regulated by the insurance commissioner. Next, the District of Columbia Medical Society attacked GHA—impeding physician recruitment, limiting hospital privileges, and threatening GHA physicians with expulsion from the society. GHA took the medical society to court. Four years later the U.S. Supreme Court decided in favor of GHA. The District of Columbia Medical Society was then indicted by a grand jury for restraint of trade.

Continued Growth

In the late 1930s a major boost to prepaid plans was launched on the West Coast. Physician Sydney Garfield began medical practice at a construction site in the southern California desert where an aqueduct was being built to divert Colorado River water to Los Angeles. Dr. Garfield built a ten-bed hospital on skids, which was pulled along as construction on the aqueduct progressed. Dr. Garfield convinced the project managers that he could treat all patients using a salary deduction arrangement.

Industrialist Henry Kaiser, who had connections to the aqueduct project, was impressed with Dr. Garfield's prepaid program and asked his help in establishing a similar arrangement for workers constructing Grand Coulee Dam in Washington State. After success at Grand Coulee, the prepaid program—called the Permanente Health Plan—was expanded in 1942 to Kaiser's ninety thousand ship-building employees in San Francisco, Oakland, and Portland. The end of World War II, however, resulted in a sudden loss of ship-building employees to support the Permanente Health Plan. Threatened with ruin, the plan was opened to public enrollment. It was immediately successful as Kaiser-Permanente Health Plan, now the largest managed care organization in America.

The Palo Alto Medical Clinic in northern California was another early pioneer in managed care. Originally a partnership between Drs. Thomas William and Russell Van Arsdale, the growing clinic employed physicians, in direct contrast and competition to the predominant solo practice model of the time. In 1947 the Palo Alto Medical Clinic began prepayment when it entered into a contract with Stanford University to provide complete medical care to students on a prepaid basis. Soon, the clinic held contracts for prepaid care with several other local groups. Today, the Palo Alto Medical Clinic continues to serve prepaid health plans.

During the 1940s and 1950s several other prepaid medical plans developed across the country. Encouraged by Mayor Fiorello La Guardia, the Health Insurance Plan of Greater New York began in 1944 to serve municipal employees. Stimulated by a visit from Dr. Shadid of Elk City, Oklahoma, consumers in Seattle formed the Group Health Cooperative of Puget Sound in 1947. PGPs were also founded by the Teamsters Union in St. Louis (the Labor Health Institute Plan), the United Mine Workers in Pennsylvania, Ohio, and West Virginia (called

Table 2.1. Some Early Prepaid Healthcare Plans.

Plan	Date First Accepted Payment	Sponsor
Group Health Association, Washington, DC	1937	Cooperative between practitioners
Kaiser Foundation Health Plan, Oakland, CA and Portland, OR	1942	Industry
Miners' Clinics, nine plans in PA, OH, and WV	1946	United Mine Workers Union
Group Health Cooperative of Puget Sound (formerly Medical Securities Clinic), Seattle, WA	1947	Originally medical partnership, now a cooperative
Palo Alto Medical Clinic, Palo Alto, CA	1947	Medical partnership
Health Insurance Plan of Greater New York (city)	1947	City, physicians, and community
Foundation for Medical Care, San Joaquin, CA	1954	Independent practice association
Group Health Plan of St. Paul, MN	1956	Indemnity insurance company
Columbia Medical Plan, Columbia, MD	1969	Connecticut General Life Insurance, Johns Hopkins University, and the Rouse Company
Harvard Community Health Plan (now Harvard-Pilgrim), Boston, MA	1969	University

Adapted from Wrightson (1990), pp. 28, 29.

Miners' Clinics), and the United Auto Workers in Detroit (the Community Health Association Plan). Table 2.1 shows other early prepaid healthcare plans.

In 1956 a role reversal occurred when the Group Health Mutual Insurance Company, a traditional indemnity insurer serving rural Minnesota and Wisconsin, built a prepaid clinic attached to their new corporate headquarters. This started Group Health Plan, which by 1984 had become the largest HMO in the Minneapolis-St. Paul metropolitan area.

The establishment of independent practice associations (IPAs) as prepaid groups began in 1954 when the Medical Society of San Joaquin County, California, established the Foundation for Medical Care. The foundation linked solo and small-group practitioners into a network under one business structure that contracted to provide prepaid care.

Years of Decline

In 1967 the National Advisory Commission on Health Manpower, a federally funded blue-ribbon panel, released a report concluding that prepaid group healthcare was a superior means of delivering cost-effective care (Falkson, 1980). Despite the panel's conclusions, President Lyndon Johnson was not convinced that prepaid plans were to be encouraged. By the 1960s indemnity insurance had grown to be the dominant insurance mode in the country. Additionally, medical associations and labor unions (unions that two and three decades before had sponsored PGPs) were successful in establishing strong negative connotations regarding prepaid plans, especially in labeling them "socialized medicine." With the McCarthy years of hunting communists and socialists a recent memory and the Cold War in full swing, anything that even hinted at a socialistic approach was frowned upon. Hence, prepaid health plans were not adopted by President Johnson as a part of his Great Society legislation that brought Medicaid and Medicare into existence.

By 1970 there were only about thirty PGPs in fifteen states covering fewer than three million lives. In 1976 the Western Clinic in Tacoma stopped offering prepaid healthcare after almost seven decades as managed care's pioneer.

Legislation Revives Managed Care

As noted in Chapter One, Dr. Paul Ellwood struggled in the late 1960s with the paradox of competing incentives in healthcare. Ellwood observed that good medicine resulted in less hospital usage—an outcome that directly opposed the financial needs of his institute. He concluded that the existing fee-for-service system created perverse incentives in rewarding the provision of treatment but withdrawing financial rewards for the reestablishment of health. He concluded that the healthcare system had to incorporate incentives for the prevention and restoration of health. Finding no way to do so within indemnity insurance models, he turned to studying prepaid group plans. Ellwood concluded that PGPs offered a better model for the alignment of incentives. By the late 1960s Ellwood had developed the concept for a new form of prepaid health plan: the health maintenance organization (HMO).

By chance in 1970, Dr. Ellwood met a well-positioned member of the Nixon administration on an airplane and began explaining his plan. The administration was then groping for a healthcare policy in response to public concern about rising healthcare costs. President Richard Nixon had been elected without a healthcare program in the Republican platform, and by 1970 his administration was desperate to oppose a Democratic proposal calling for national health insurance. Seizing onto Ellwood's HMO ideas, the executive branch quickly turned them into proposed legislation. In February 1971 President

Nixon gave a formal health message to Congress in which he outlined a detailed proposal for HMO development. The plan declared that HMOs should be developed with federal aid and eventually be made available to 90 percent of the U.S. population.

The Federal Boost

Two years of political wrangling ensued. Finally, a compromise was reached in Congress, and in December 1973 President Nixon signed Public Law 93–222—the Health Maintenance Organization Act of 1973. The act established a plan for HMO development but had been so weakened by two years of political debate and compromise that the rapid establishment of HMOs was impossible. The bill provided for federal assistance to establish demonstration projects, created loan programs to stimulate the emergence of HMOs, and prescribed a broad set of requirements for plans to receive the federal government's seal of approval by becoming federally qualified (see Chapter One). The law also mandated the dual-choice provision, which required companies with twenty-five or more employees to offer an HMO option to employees along with standard indemnity plans, if so requested by a local HMO. The law required HMO plans to provide up to twenty outpatient mental health sessions per year but did not require benefits for inpatient psychiatric care; most plans, however, offered such coverage.

The original act was so restrictive and the resistance from established medicine so fierce that by 1977 only 183 plans were available nationally and covered fewer than seven million Americans (Mayer and Mayer, 1985). Six amendments later (1976, 1978, 1979, 1981, 1986, and 1988), the HMO Act was so modified that the rigid fiscal and business incorporation rules hindering HMO start-ups had been removed. New HMOs sprouted across the country in the 1980s. The relaxed business requirements, along with the scaling back of federal grant monies to seed new HMOs, meant that most new HMOs were formed by private investors or existing healthcare corporations without an attempt to become federally qualified. Network-model HMOs using a broad panel of solo and small-group practitioners were allowed after the amendments. The original act had permitted only staff, group, and IPA network panels. And the dual-option provision granted to federally qualified plans was no longer necessary for most HMOs to compete successfully in the marketplace. By the mid-1980s most state governments had enacted basic regulations applying to managed care plans. These typically included state Department of Insurance regulations specific to HMOs regarding monies that must be kept in reserve, ongoing solvency requirements, marketing regulations, and reporting mandates. Direct consumer requirements as a part of state regulations did not become common until the mid-1990s.

As did the HMO Act of 1973, the 1974 Employment Retirement Security Act (ERISA) stimulated the growth of prepaid plans. Although ERISA was designed primarily to modify rules related to pension plans, it contained a provision allowing self-insured groups to be exempt from state laws pertaining to health insurance. This exemption inspired many large employers and organizations such as labor unions to underwrite their own managed care health plans, often with an existing insurer administering the plan (known as a third-party administrator, or TPA). Self-insured groups blossomed in the 1980s, often substantially reducing per-employee health insurance premiums by setting premium rates based on the healthcare cost history of their employees (known as experience rate setting), as opposed to federally qualified HMOs that still had to base rates on the entire community (known as community rate setting). Non-federally qualified plans, however, could compete with employer-sponsored plans by having premium fees set by experience rating.

The Growth of Managed Care

With strong federal support, managed care health plans began to form in the late 1970s and proliferated in the 1980s, especially in urban areas. Certain regions of the country became early focal points of growth: along the Pacific coast, the southwestern states (including Arizona, Colorado, and Utah, but not Texas), the north central states of Minnesota, Illinois, and Wisconsin, southern New England, and metropolitan Washington, D.C. Only in the 1990s have managed care plans become common in the South, the northern Rocky Mountain and plains states, and the Midwest. Rural areas are viewed as major new markets for managed care plans in the late 1990s (Grobman, 1997).

The Economic Catapult

By the late 1980s, HMOs and PPOs had come into the spotlight as cost-saving methods for financing healthcare. Although reducing costs was not a primary objective behind the original development of prepaid group plans or the HMO Act of 1973, the economic efficiency of managed care plans pushed them to the forefront. Managed care plans, especially HMOs, are now touted as economically viable vehicles for controlling costs and allowing healthcare coverage for all Americans. Cost control has brought government to favor the transition to managed care for retirees receiving Medicare, TriCare (for military personnel), and Medicaid, the program for poor Americans.

Concern over the costs of healthcare insurance was well founded in the late 1980s and early 1990s for the following reasons:

- In 1969 healthcare costs accounted for approximately 6 percent of the gross national product but well over 14 percent by 1993 (Geisel, 1993).

- Healthcare insurance premiums between 1986 and 1993 rose at five times the rate of wage increases for nonsupervisory workers (Major, 1994).

- Insurance premiums between 1986 and 1993 increased over three times faster than the inflation rate (Major, 1994).

- The average annual cost per employee for mental health and substance abuse benefits alone almost doubled from 1987 to 1991, going from $163 to $304 (Block, 1992).

In the battle to demonstrate cost control, HMOs and PPOs have done well. As shown in Table 2.2, healthcare yearly increases have slowed dramatically during a period of increasing dominance by managed care. Additionally, the average cost of an individual employee's healthcare insurance premium has remained lowest for HMOs. Figure 2.1 shows 1997 premium costs for different types of plans.

Economic forces continue to encourage healthcare delivery systems that are integrated across specialities and are capable of working with fixed, monthly prepaid dollar amounts to serve a population of beneficiaries. Today, the business of healthcare increasingly rewards the concepts pioneered by Drs. Yokum and Curran in 1910 and their competitor, Dr. Bridge.

OPPOSITION TO MANAGED CARE

As I noted earlier, there has been opposition to managed care concepts since their inception in 1910. In the 1980s and 1990s, however, the resistance has not revolved around the claim that managed care is socialized medicine but rather that managed care

1. Restricts members' rights to select their own clinicians

2. Provides inadequate treatment

Table 2.2. Average Health Plan Cost Increases.

	1991	1992	1993	1994	1995	1996	1997
Employees: Private Industry	14%	11%	11%	6%	2%	4%	3%
Health Insurance: Cost per Hour Worked	$.59	$.69	$.77	$.87	$.93	$.95	$.99
Consumer Price Index Increase	4%	3%	3%	3%	2%	3%	2%

Source: U.S. Department of Labor, Bureau of Labor Statistics (1991 through 1997).

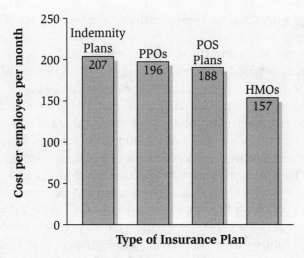

Figure 2.1. 1997 Average Insurance Premiums by Type of Plan.
Source: McCue (1997, p. 25).

3. Structures benefits so as not to provide care for chronic diseases such as personality disorders in mental health

4. Restricts providers from revealing their financial incentives to patients if the incentives are to provide less care

5. Rewards clinicians financially for undertreating patients (the exact opposite of the charge that Dr. Ellwood leveled against indemnity insurance; see Chapters Eight and Twelve for more detailed discussions)

The strongest opposition has always come from physicians and other health-care clinicians. Providers see managed care as removing both their autonomy and the consistent increases in income that they experienced in the 1960s through the 1980s.

I have experienced the opposition of providers, in my case friends and colleagues, at different times when my group was bidding for contracts with local HMOs to become the manager of behavioral services. I have been bitterly confronted with accusations that I was joining the enemy, aiding a plan to reduce their incomes, stealing their patients, and bringing about the death of solo practice. I acknowledged their concerns and asked whether, if my group withdrew, managed care would go away or whether managed care in Albuquerque would just be run by national rather than local companies. Although the issues remain valid, managed care has so engulfed Albuquerque (several national managed care firms have moved in) that clinicians now see our group and me more as stabilizers of the business environment than as threats. And their incomes, autonomy, and solo practices have been far less reduced than they had feared.

Throughout the 1980s and 1990s, various professional associations and societies have bitterly opposed managed care plans, especially HMOs where the loss of professional autonomy is the greatest. The opposition has been so vehement that the American Psychiatric Association has maintained a well-publicized toll-free hotline for practitioners to phone in complaints about managed care insurers. The American Psychological Association also focused major resources toward espousing the evils of managed care and providing consultations to large employers on how to avoid using managed care health plans. The presidents of both APAs in 1997 were elected on anti–managed care platforms.

The APAs, along with the National Association of Social Workers and the National Community Mental Health Council, have vigorously lobbied Congress and state legislatures to enact more laws regulating managed care. The expanded legislation commonly sought includes bills requiring managed care plans to

• Make public their criteria for treatment decisions (called utilization review criteria or, more commonly today, utilization management criteria).

• Open their clinical networks to any willing provider. Statutes mandating any willing provider require that any clinician meeting the health plan's professional credentialing requirements and accepting the plan's fee reimbursement schedule must be allowed to join the plan's provider network. At the beginning of 1997, twenty-eight states had any-willing-provider statutes, but only five—Arkansas, Idaho, Indiana, Kentucky, and Utah—include mental health providers (American Managed Behavioral Healthcare Association, 1996).

• No longer be allowed to include in provider subcontracts gag clauses that restrict clinicians from discussing certain treatment options or healthcare financial incentives with patients. Twenty states have passed legislation banning such gag clauses (Stauffer, 1997).

In general these legislated regulations have had a positive effect on the function of managed care and relations between managed care and providers as well as consumers.

Consumers have also resisted the growth of managed care (Church, 1997). Typically, consumers have reacted negatively to restrictions on whom they can choose as their doctors. They have also perceived managed care as an outside force intruding on their doctor-patient privilege. Additionally, consumers have been influenced against managed care by knowing that the major professional organizations representing clinicians oppose it. Consumer opposition is generally strongest in a city or region until managed care becomes well established (as along the West Coast and in Minneapolis, for example). The most prominent consumer organizations opposing managed care have been labor unions (who once encouraged prepaid group practices). But national patient-advocacy groups have also been strong opponents. Groups such as Parents of Behaviorally Different Children and the National Alliance for the Mentally Ill have fought bitterly to preserve Medicaid as a state-administered indemnity plan rather than see it become privatized by managed care organizations, as is occurring in almost every state.

Individual consumers and concerned groups across the country have staged local protests to prevent the adoption of managed care by employers and government agencies. An example of successful resistance to managed care came in 1995 and 1996, when a public outcry over minimum maternity benefits brought about passage of maternity benefit mandates in over half of the states, followed by the 1996 federal Newborns' and Mothers' Health Protection Act. Prior to this, HMOs and PPOs had often only precertified maternity stays of up to twenty-four hours for uncomplicated births. Despite the absence of scientific evidence showing that mothers and babies who had less than twenty-four hours in the hospital did poorly, public perception prevailed (Gazmararian and others, 1997). Health plans are now compelled to offer maternity hospitalizations of at least forty-eight hours.

The courts have also become involved in reviewing and regulating managed care. Typically, court actions have come in response to civil liability suits charging that a managed care plan member was inadequately treated or that a health plan was negligent in providing competent clinicians on their provider panel.

The well-publicized case of *Wilson* v. *Blue Cross of Southern California* illustrates the claim that benefit restrictions and utilization management activities can result in inadequate care. In this prominent healthcare case, Wilson's attending physician requested precertification beyond the initial authorization of ten days for inpatient psychiatric care. The physician believed further hospital care to be clinically necessary. The insurer judged Wilson to be stable enough for discharge and denied authorization beyond ten days. Reluctantly, the physician discharged him on the tenth day. Shortly after discharge, Wilson committed suicide. His family sued, claiming that the insurer was responsible for his death due to an improper limitation on care. The jury found Blue Cross of Southern California to have acted in bad faith. However, because the bad faith was determined not to be of a malicious or oppressive intent, no damages were awarded to the family. Additionally, the court noted that Wilson's physician was responsible for providing adequate treatment in line with his own clinical judgment, regardless of what the insurer would cover (Jackson, 1992).

Boyd v. *Albert Einstein Medical Center* illustrates a case of alleged negligence by an HMO. In another wrongful death suit, Boyd's husband charged that his wife had died due to negligence in treatment by her primary care physician (PCP) and that the HMO was responsible because the subcontracted PCP was an agent of the HMO. The Pennsylvania Superior Court ruled that the HMO's subcontracted providers were agents of the insurer and the HMO did have a responsibility to ensure competence and appropriate treatment in its provider panel.

The managed care industry asserts that accusations against managed care have been sensationalized and not supported by data. Paul Ellwood calls this "attack by anecdote" (Belkin, 1996, p. 70). Substantial research efforts analyzing managed care are only now beginning to produce solid data reports. These data are discussed throughout the coming chapters.

The result of court rulings, legislative actions, and protests by consumers and professional groups has been many positive modifications in managed care practices such as outlawing gag rules, mandating legislatively that utilization management criteria be made public, and providing for openness in financial disclosures (for example, the Virginia law mandating that providers disclose their financial arrangements with insurers).

Managed care has adjusted to these accusations and changes while continuing to grow and maintain the basic quality of services.

SOCIOLOGICAL EVOLUTION

A variety of sociological changes since the 1970s have aided the growth of managed care. For example, perceptions of prepaid healthcare have changed dramatically. From being considered an un-American way of providing treatment, managed care health plans have moved into a position of being desired by many Americans, especially by those who have received healthcare through a managed care plan.

Another example of the change is the growing satisfaction with managed care from the 1980s through the 1990s. A 1986 survey supported by a number of private foundations and government sources that was only published in 1993 in the *Journal of the American Medical Association,* polled almost eighteen thousand people and found that 65 percent rated the care given by solo practitioners (primarily through indemnity insurance coverage) to be "excellent," whereas only 49 percent so rated the care provided by physicians in large HMO clinics (Rubin and others, 1993). In contrast, a 1993 survey of over twenty-four thousand employees using the Employee Healthcare Value Survey (EHCVS, sponsored by the Xerox, GTE, and Digital Equipment corporations) found that HMO members were more satisfied with their care (Woolsey, 1994). In addition, the EHCVS tracked employees changing health plans during 1993. The rates of annual disenrollment (not renewing enrollment in a specific health plan) for the twenty-four thousand employees were as follows: HMO (group model), 6 percent; HMO (IPA model), 11 percent; POS, 10 percent; and indemnity, 37 percent. Similarly, a later survey of managed care enrollees (Ciba-

Geigy, 1996) found that 62 percent of HMO members reported that they were "very" or "extremely" satisfied with their health plan, whereas only 55 percent of POS members (those with more choice in selecting their own doctors and clinicians) were so satisfied.

In addition to increasing familiarity with managed care, more positive attitudes toward managed care appear to coincide with other social changes. As the pace and urbanization of American life have increased, our society has begun to expect from healthcare the same qualities demanded of other service industries: speed, efficiency, flexibility, low cost, and convenience. Prepaid plans have offered the public many of these attributes through integrated delivery systems in which care from many specialists is rendered in a single office or network with fixed copayment amounts and expedient access to care. In patient satisfaction surveys, convenience, lower cost, efficiency, and fast access to care are rated "very important" by consumers.

The structure of managed care plans has also become a positive feature for many members. Fixed copayments are popular with consumers, as opposed to the more complicated indemnity system of deductibles and splitting fees by a percentage due from the insurer and the insured. Centralized telephone systems for healthcare advice, selection of a primary care physician, and access to specialty care providers are in high demand. And having a defined list of healthcare providers who have been credentialed and scrutinized by the health plan has also become increasingly acceptable as the norm for how medicine works.

QUALITY IMPROVEMENT: THE FUTURE OF MANAGED CARE

Assuring quality has become central to American industry but until recently, healthcare remained outside the quality movement. Today, the terms *total quality management* (TQM), *quality assurance* (QA), *quality improvement* (QI), and *continuous quality improvement* (CQI) are all buzzwords in healthcare. There is no substantial difference among the four terms and their function within a healthcare system. Each refers to measuring events or procedures that are believed to be indicators of quality service delivery. The data are then used as feedback to initiate change wherever processes or treatments can be improved. Quality improvement as a catalyst for change is rapidly becoming mainstream to the practice of medicine from the reception counter to treatment protocols for common conditions. (See Chapter Nine for a more detailed discussion of quality activities.)

Employers, patients, and insurers now demand demonstrable evidence that quality is being measured, maintained, and improved. Data, statistics, outcome measures, policies and procedures, standards of care, and clinical algorithms for specific diseases are now mandated. As we prepare for the twenty-first century, demonstrating quality is challenging cost control as the major task confronting healthcare.

Performance standards for HMOs, POSs, and PPOs, both for administrative functions and clinical care delivery, are now in place through the National Committee for Quality Assurance (NCQA) and the Joint Commission on Accreditation of Healthcare Organizations (JCAHO). Insurers and large care delivery systems across the nation are scrambling to meet these performance standards in order to obtain formal accreditation from one or both of these organizations, much as hospitals have in recent decades sought accreditation by JCAHO. In 1997, NCQA even released specific standards for behavioral health (National Committee for Quality Assurance, 1997; see Appendix C).

The future will bring further reliance on quality improvement data and change initiated to improve the quality of services to patients and their families. Insurers, group practices, networks, and integrated delivery systems that can meet quality requirements will be in high demand. In the next five to ten years the emphasis on quality assurance and improvement may become as important in advancing managed care as legislative actions and economic pressures have been.

Next, Chapter Three discusses the functional parts of a managed care organization. I will emphasize what clinicians need to know in order to work effectively with HMOs, PPOs, and POS plans.

Anatomy and Physiology of a Managed Care Organization

Before I dissect a managed care organization into its functional parts, a bit of clarification is needed. What is the difference between the terms *managed care organization* (MCO), *managed care plan, managed care payer,* and *managed care insurer*? For all practical purposes, there is no difference. In some cases the terms *MCO* and *managed care payer* refer to a subentity to the actual insurance company (for example, a contracted company to administer healthcare benefits) that does not hold the insurance license in the particular state but that handles all operational functions. From a clinician's perspective, organizations described by any of these four terms appear the same, so I will use them synonymously for the rest of this text.

Where does the term *managed behavioral healthcare organization* (MBHO) fit into the list of names? *MBHO* is a specific reference to the business of managing the mental health and substance abuse benefits within the complete healthcare benefit structure. Often, an MBHO is a separate corporation that the full MCO has retained on contract to administer behavioral benefits (both for mental health and substance abuse). *MBHO* may also refer to a fairly autonomous department within an MCO that handles the administration of behavioral contracts and care. Given that this text is entirely about the behavioral functions of an MCO/ managed care plan/managed care insurer or payer, I will use the term *MBHO* when speaking specifically about the management and care delivery systems of the organization for mental health and substance abuse services.

To add to the convoluted variations in how MCOs organize services for the full continuum of healthcare needs, relatively distinct parts of healthcare benefit packages (commonly behavioral, dental, and vision care) may be carved out (*carve out* is the noun) or carved in (*carve in* is the noun).

To *carve out* means that the purchaser of the insurance, typically an employer or a government entity, has bought insurance for general medical benefits from an MCO but has chosen to separately purchase specific benefits, often behavioral, from an entirely different MCO or MBHO. In the carve-out scenario, the general medical and the carved-out benefit programs run in parallel.

To *carve in* means that a single MCO is responsible for both the broader medical services and the distinct piece of the benefit package (behavioral services, in this case). In the carve-in scenario, the master MCO directing general medical services may have a behavioral department—their MBHO—to administer mental health and substance abuse benefits or may subcontract behavioral services to an external MBHO that has specific experience and skill in managing these benefits. In either case, the carve-in method results in the general medical and the behavioral services being overseen by one MCO and working in concert, not in parallel. As an example of common usage of the terms, an accurate statement regarding Medicaid is, *New Mexico chose to have mental health and substance abuse services carved in, whereas all other states up until 1997 had gone with behavioral benefits as a carve out.*

An appropriate question at this point is, Where do the various types of managed care plans described in Chapter One fit into this picture? Health maintenance organizations (HMOs), preferred provider organizations (PPOs), and point of service plans (POSs) are only variations in the healthcare benefit package and in how fees for services are paid. They do not represent different business structures, as in a carve in or a carve out. Any of these three plan types, or a combination, may be offered by a single MCO or MBHO. Most large MCOs sell and administer all three product lines. For example, one might refer to a specific HMO, say All-American HMO, when in fact All-American HMO is a single product line offered by All-American Plans for Health, Inc., which has state licenses in multiple states to insure groups under HMO, PPO, and POS arrangements. Independent MBHOs that exist only to administer the behavioral portion of healthcare benefits typically also manage all three types of benefit structures.

ORGANIZATION STRUCTURE

In addition to knowing the terminology, clinicians must understand the basic organizational parts of any MCO or MBHO (the parts are the same, just smaller in an MBHO). To function smoothly with one or many managed care plans, you must have a working knowledge of the various departments and divisions with which you will come into contact. See Figure 3.1 for a generic organizational chart that is used to outline the departments and subdepartments described in this chapter.

For large MCOs with covered lives in multiple states, there are frequently state or regional divisions that have their own organizational structure and functions, much as in Figure 3.1.

Medical Director

As a clinician, the top office within the business structure with which you will most likely interact is that of the medical director. The occupier of the position is also commonly called the chief medical officer or chief clinical officer. For large MCOs there is usually a master medical director, with an associate medical director or two, followed by submedical directors for the major specialties such as behavioral health. In behavioral health the position is typically held by a psychiatrist, but there are precedents for psychologists holding this job.

The office of the medical director is not involved in just one department but is usually an active resource to the health services and quality improvement departments. Within health services, the appropriate medical director oversees all clinical aspects of utilization management and intake. All clinical authorizations for care and all denials for clinical reasons are his or her ultimate responsibility. For example, the medical director and his or her designees deny approval for a patient to receive payment for continued hospital days or additional outpatient sessions due to no longer meeting medical necessity criteria.

Denials that are administrative in nature (for example, the requested service is not covered by the benefit package or the patient is no longer a member of the health plan) usually do not involve the medical director but are handled by member services.

With regard to intake, the medical director is responsible for the clinical aspects of the procedures for the triage and referral of patients to care. Common here are clinical protocols for assessing risk factors with new referrals and procedures for handling urgent and emergent clinical situations.

For provider relations, the medical director usually has some authority over which clinicians or group practices are added to the provider panel, either in a network, group, or staff model system.

For the quality improvement department, the medical director plays a very active role in directing the development of prevention programs, treatment protocols, outcomes studies, and clinical tools for use in auditing the charts of network providers for clinical appropriateness of the care provided. Additionally, the medical director is involved in the credentialing and recredentialing processes (descriptions of these functions follow). Often, the medical director

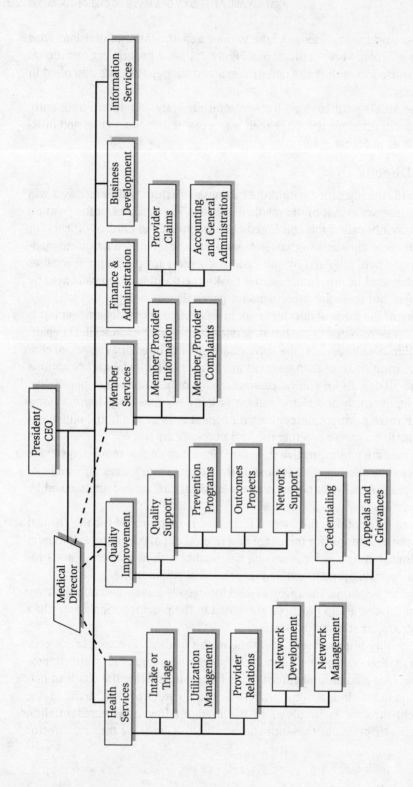

Figure 3.1. Generic MCO/MBHO Organization Chart.

chairs or appoints the chairperson for the credentials committee. When a provider must be given temporary privileges to meet immediate service needs before the entire credentialing process can be completed, the medical director (or his or her designee) reviews the clinician's background and determines whether or not to grant temporary credentialing.

Health Services

The department with which most clinician interactions occur is health services. This department, which is also frequently called clinical services or just utilization management, manages the assignment of patients to care and any authorizations for continued care.

Intake. The intake division is where patients are initially assessed for referral to a clinician or clinicians for service. This division may go by other names such as clinical triage or member advocacy.

With most managed care plans, members must contact the intake department of the MBHO before accessing behavioral care. They may request care in two ways:

• *Calling to seek authorization to go to a particular clinician,* often based on a referral from someone such as their primary care physician (PCP). In most cases this request will be honored if the provider is credentialed by the MBHO for the type of service that is appropriate for the member and the service meets the criteria discussed below for medical necessity.

• *Calling the MBHO to request services and a referral to an appropriate clinician.* This option is strongly encouraged by MBHOs and is very commonly used in areas where managed care is well established.

Health plan members are usually given a local or toll-free number to the intake department at their MBHO, which they are told to call if they need behavioral services. Having made the call, the prospective patient usually talks with a behavioral health worker (a person with a bachelor's degree and special training who has a licensed therapist as back-up), or they may talk directly with a licensed clinician. The intake staff have protocols for conducting triages with prospective new patients. The triage usually follows these steps:

1. Gathering basic demographic data from the caller (and about the prospective patient if the patient is a child or other dependent).
2. Asking for a description of the presenting problem(s).
3. Checking to make sure that the prospective patient has a primary care physician referral for behavioral services (this is for plans requiring the patient's PCP to serve as a *gatekeeper* to all specialty care). If such a referral is needed but the patient does not have it, the intake staff person advises him or her as to how a referral may be obtained. In emergency cases the need for a PCP referral is waived.

4. Comparing the member's name and health plan ID number against the plan's enrollment files to make sure that the caller is truly covered by the named health plan.

5. Advising the member of any pertinent restrictions in coverage (for example, if the member has a higher copayment for substance abuse than mental health services or if the person is calling for marital therapy and it is not covered by the plan). Many MBHOs stop at this step, and for covered services simply preauthorize two to six sessions for an evaluation by a clinician, who must contact the utilization management department if ongoing treatment services are needed.

6. Making a preliminary assessment of whether the criteria for medical necessity are met. If not, then the intake process is stopped at this point and a letter explaining that the requested services are not medically necessary is sent to the patient and the patient's PCP. Generally, in the case of not meeting medical necessity, the patient will be given options to obtain the requested care by paying out-of-pocket or from a mental health source offering appropriate assistance (a community support group, for example).

7. Conducting a brief risk assessment to screen for suicidality, self-injury, physical or sexual abuse, and homicidality. If any of these appear probable, then the patient is treated as an urgent or emergent case. MBHOs typically have a standard that urgent cases are to be seen within forty-eight hours, whereas emergent cases must be provided with immediate assistance.

8. Referring the member to a clinician or facility that is well prepared to meet the member's apparent clinical needs. When the MBHO has staff clinics, the first appointment is often made at this time.

9. Preauthorizing a certain number of initial outpatient treatment visits, or days in the case of facility-based care, before the treating clinician or facility is required to contact the utilization management department if further services are needed. Initial outpatient authorizations are usually for two to six visits. Different types of problems (bereavement or an apparent eating disorder, for example) are often authorized initially for different amounts of treatment. If the authorization is for facility-based care (inpatient, for example), the authorization is called a precertification.

10. Mailing letters to the patient, the PCP, and the assigned clinician or facility defining the authorization for services and advising how an appeal can be lodged if any of the three believe that the initial authorization for services was in error.

Given that the triage results in an initial preauthorization or denial of care, it is truly the first step in utilization management (called a prospective review in utilization management terms). When seen as the beginning of utilization management, the intake department in many MBHOs is often simply made a part of the utilization management department.

Most managed care health plans have the requirement that for services to be covered, the specific condition for which care is sought must meet medical necessity criteria. Although *medical necessity* is not a highly objective term, the definition for mental health and substance abuse services is usually something like this: a service or treatment is medically necessary if it meets the following four criteria:

- The condition is a distinct mental disorder as defined by the latest version of the *Diagnostic and Statistical Manual of Mental Disorders,* published by the American Psychiatric Association; V codes are not accepted as a mental disorder.

- The disorder is likely to show sustained improvement from treatment, or crisis intervention is necessary to prevent harm.

- The treatment is provided in the least restrictive setting possible for appropriate care (called the principle of parsimony).

- The treatment meets community and national standards for appropriate care.

The initial triage results in a broad determination of medical necessity according to the criteria. If the intake staff member is unclear about whether the criteria for medical necessity are met, then the patient is typically passed to a supervisor for a determination, or a referral is made to a clinician for an evaluation prior to a decision.

Utilization Management (UM). Once a patient has begun treatment, the treating clinician must determine if treatment can be completed within the number of sessions and types of treatment (medication management, for example) preauthorized at intake. If further treatment is necessary or if services from another provider (medication from a psychiatrist, for example) are needed, then the clinician must complete a treatment plan form and submit it as a request to the UM department. (See Exhibit 3.1 for an example of a typical treatment plan form.) In cases of urgent or emergent need, the request for additional or other services can be handled by telephone.

Note should be made here regarding a special provision that some MBHOs have for providers with a history of high treatment efficiency, sound clinical outcomes, and very good patient satisfaction. These providers, once they have an established track record with an MBHO, may be offered status as a preferred provider. Often, providers in this category are exempt from close utilization monitoring and may not be required to submit treatment plans as often as regular providers, if at all.

The UM department tracks all insured members who are in treatment and is the data source for utilization statistics. Typically, a large portion of the staff in

Exhibit 3.1. All-American Behavioral Health, Extended Treatment Authorization Request.

Date
Patient Name: Date of Birth: PCP:
Insurance: Subscriber ID: Group Number:
Provider:

DSM Diagnoses	Risk Assessment: Suicidal Homicidal Abusive (victim or perpetrator)	
I	**High** — Ideation with accompanying plan / Prior Attempts / Substance Abuse	Comorbidity / Chronic illness/Pain / Availability of Means
II		
III		
IV	**Moderate** — Ideation with vague or no plan / Good premorbid functioning	Lack of means / Good social support
V	**Low** — No serious ideation or risk	

Precipitant for this treatment episode:

Progress since Initial Assessment/Last session (if little or none, why?)

If a chronic condition, please state the expected benefit from goal-oriented therapy:

Symptoms that are the focus of treatment (please list and rate in severity, 1 being least severe; 10 being most severe)

Symptom	Highest Level of Functioning Past Year	Initial Assessment Last Review	Current
1)	1)	1)	1)
2)	2)	2)	2)
3)	3)	3)	3)
4)	4)	4)	4)
5)	5)	5)	5)

Treatment Plan including goals (be specific):

Current Psychotropic Medications:

Prescribed By: _____

Please authorize _____ additional hours. Number of hours used this year _____.
Expected number of hours for entire treatment episode _____ .
[ ] I have consulted with the patient's PCP regarding the case.
[ ] I am coordinating care with another All-American provider (please specify):

TO THE PROVIDER:
Please complete all information indicated, this is necessary for processing. Extended Treatment Requests will be reviewed and authorized or denied within 5 working days.

All-American Behavioral Health
Utilization Management Department
Anywhere, USA

UM are psychotherapists and psychiatric nurses with master's degrees. Their task is to review requests for additional services with regard to meeting medical necessity and urgency requirements. For routine outpatient cases, this is done using the data from forms like the one shown in Exhibit 3.1. More urgent cases are done via telephone or fax with the provider and, occasionally, with the patient. With questionable requests, the UM staff may telephone the provider to discuss the case or may ask to see the provider's reports and progress notes regarding the patient.

For hospitalized or other facility-based patients, the review for continued stay is generally by telephone and fax, but in urban areas a utilization management staff person may actually go to the hospital and review patient charts directly, as well as discuss cases with the hospital staff.

Conducting utilization management (previously called utilization review) while the treatment being reviewed is ongoing is called concurrent review. Cases that are pended for more information or otherwise reviewed after treatment has occurred are said to be undergoing retrospective review.

Provider Relations. The last major functional area of health services is provider relations. Given the broad nature of this division, it is often a separate department.

The provider relations department is responsible for identifying a full network of clinicians who can meet the needs of the MBHO for clinical services. Once identified, the provider relations staff must assist potential providers in understanding the subcontract with the MBHO and must see that contracts are signed and that the credentialing process is started (see the section to follow). Even in a staff model MBHO or MCO, there are still provider relations tasks with subcontracted providers. Staff clinics can seldom meet all needs for clinical service. Overflow during busy periods, the need for specialists in highly focused clinical areas, the need for providers in geographically distant regions, and the necessity of having clinicians to handle special cases (employees of the MCO, for example) necessitate at least a minimal network.

Once a provider network is established, there are ongoing demands for network development that fall to the provider relations staff. These needs include ongoing education of the providers in how to work with the MBHO or larger MCO in resolving any problems that might arise in provider-MBHO relations.

Quality Improvement

MCOs and MBHOs are under a great deal of pressure from employers and contracting agencies to become accredited by, and maintain accreditation with, either the National Committee for Quality Assurance (NCQA), the major quality accrediting body for MCOs, or the Joint Commission on Accreditation of Healthcare Organizations (JCAHO), which accredits treatment facilities and

MCOs. Both organizations require that a wide array of quality functions and monitors be in place if they are to give accreditation. Prevention programs, outcomes studies, locally selected clinical studies, and strict policies regarding patient treatment records are all items that an MCO or MBHO must have in place to seek accreditation. This is especially true for MBHOs now that there are specific guidelines for behavioral healthcare (National Committee for Quality Assurance, 1997). The details of these standards are discussed in Chapter Nine and are listed in Appendix C.

Quality Support. To sustain the resources and organization required to achieve and maintain accreditation, every MBHO has a substantial quality improvement (or quality assurance) department. Every quality improvement department has a written and highly detailed quality plan, with annual reviews showing quality program results for the previous year and recommendations for the next year.

MBHOs must include, and have cooperation from, a large number of providers in their network in order to collect and report on the necessary quality data. The quality program must actively monitor and provide feedback for improvement regarding many clinical functions such as prevention programs, focused clinical outcomes information, patient satisfaction, and appropriateness of individual patient treatment plans. Additionally, physical inspections of providers' offices are required, along with quality audits of patient charts in network providers' offices.

Clinicians subcontracting with an MBHO will find a clause in their subcontract requiring them to cooperate and participate in the quality improvement (QI) programs of the insurer (see Chapter Six). Usually, the MBHO collects data from the more active providers and groups in their network rather than attempting to engage every subcontracted clinician, even if they treat very few patients for the particular MBHO. Clinical outcomes data most often include information from surveys that are completed by either the patient or the clinician and returned to the MBHO. Patient chart audits are generally conducted by an MBHO staff member who comes to the office of the provider for an audit of clinical records regarding members of the particular health plan.

Office site visits, chart audits, participation in prevention programs, and clinical outcomes assessment tools to fill out are time and energy consuming for network providers as well as the MBHO. But without them the MBHO or MCO would no longer be competitive with other managed care payers. Large employer groups and governmental agencies expect a thorough "report card" from all contracted MCOs and MBHOs. Clinicians must expect ever-increasing demands on network clinicians to be involved in QI activities if they wish to keep frequent referrals from a particular MBHO. On the positive side, if the data collected are fed back in a timely and usable manner to the providers, they can be a gold mine of useful information that providers can use to improve their practice patterns.

Credentialing. Completing a credentialing application similar to the one shown in Chapter Seven is a beginning step for any clinician to become a network provider for a MCO or MBHO. Even in staff clinics owned by an MBHO or MCO, the employed clinicians must complete such applications and go through credentialing just as network providers do.

The details of the credentialing process are discussed in Chapter Seven, but for purposes of this chapter, it is important for all clinicians to know that work with an MBHO begins by obtaining an application form from the provider relations department or the credentialing division within the QI department. The application then takes two to six months to fully process before a provider is accepted to provide professional services in his or her speciality. In cases of an urgent need to add a clinician to the provider panel, a temporary credentialing mechanism is usually in place, despite the fact that temporary credentialing is frowned upon by accreditation agencies.

Credentialing is a quality activity because its primary purpose is to verify that clinicians meet the standards the MBHO has set for providers in their network (for example, state licensure and ongoing continuing education participation) and that the clinician has no untoward events suggesting a liability risk in referring patients to them (such as a history of several malpractice claims).

Recredentialing is usually done every two years; NCQA mandates that it must occur at least every two years. In recredentialing, network providers are asked to update their credentialing application. Any changes in professional status are verified, and routine checks are again done with state and national authorities for malpractice claims and licensing board sanctions. At this stage providers who have not been perceived by the MBHO to be good network providers (for clinical, ethical, or business reasons) may simply be dropped from the provider panel by not being offered a chance to recredential or have their subcontract extended.

Appeals and Grievances. The UM department works with the quality improvement department regarding appeals by patients, providers, or PCPs who believe that the care authorized or not authorized was mistakenly done. Appeals are sent as written requests for a formal second review. All MCOs and MBHOs have a detailed policy and procedure (almost always open to any patient, provider, or PCP for inspection) for how appeals are handled. Most often a UM committee in conjunction with the quality improvement department must review appeals within a fixed time frame and render a judgment.

When a patient, provider, or PCP continues to be dissatisfied after the appeal process, there is a separate procedure for filing a grievance. The grievance procedure is typically paralegal in its nature and usually is conducted at a hearing involving staff from the full MCO, patient and/or provider representatives, and MBHO staff who were not involved in the judgments made at the triage or appeal levels.

Member Services

Health plan members and contracted providers very often have questions about which benefits are covered, what copayments are due, and what the status is of payments to providers. The member services department, also frequently called customer services, is where inquiries are handled for such matters. Typically, member services provides a toll-free number and extended hours (7 A.M. to 7 P.M. is common) for both members and providers with questions. Along with the intake department, member services is an area where quality standards regarding access and turnaround time are critical. NCQA mandates that a member calling for information (or to request services from intake) must be able to speak with a live person within thirty seconds of calling and that at no time shall the percentage of callers who hang up before speaking with someone exceed 5 percent. NCQA also mandates that policies and procedures must be in place defining how calls will be handled. Time frames must be established regarding how quickly questions requiring investigation will be processed and the caller given a response.

In addition to being an information source, member services is also where patient or provider complaints are accepted. Member services staff typically talk with patients or providers about their complaint while assimilating information on a complaint form or screen. After receiving a complaint, the staff member informs the patient that he or she will receive a response and any appropriate consideration within a time frame set by the MBHO's policies and procedures. For the resolution of complaints, the member services staff relies on designated supervisors in their respective areas and the quality improvement department. For example, if a patient complains of poor clinical care the complaint is usually forwarded to the medical director (or designee) for investigation and resolution.

Complaints by providers are typically handled through provider relations or the utilization management division. If the complaint is about payment issues, it is handled by the finance and administration department in coordination with the quality improvement department.

Finance and Administration

This department serves both the providers and the internal functions of the MBHO or broader MCO. The internal services provided are managing the administrative and clerical needs of the company, along with the financial accounting infrastructure required to run an insurance firm.

Provider Claims. Whether for employed staff clinicians or network clinicians, behavioral services provided to members must be financially accounted for in a systematic way. The process goes through the following steps:

1. Intake enters a preauthorization into the claims computer system at the time a referral of a patient is made to a clinician. The authorization is usually for a maximum number of visits or sessions during a fixed time period (usually sixty or ninety days after the intake call). The services the patient can receive (for example, psychotherapy) will be specified and entered into the computer. Service types are entered by CPT code (current procedural terminology of the American Medical Association). Examples of codes are 90847 for family psychotherapy, 96100 for psychological testing, or 90862 for medication management.

2. The preauthorization details are computer-merged into a form letter and sent to the patient and the receiving provider. Most staff model MBHOs also send these form letters to their employed staff to specify the care authorized.

3. Once the provider has seen the patient for a few treatment sessions or has terminated care within the initial authorization, a standard HCFA 1500 billing form is sent via mail or electronically to the MBHO requesting payment at the rates agreed to in the provider subcontract. This method of payment is called discounted fee-for-service because the fees are per service and the rates are usually below the provider's full billing rate. (See Chapter Eight for other payment methods such as case rates.)

The HCFA (pronounced hic-fa) 1500 form is a federal form developed by the Healthcare Finance Administration for use in submitting claims for services under Medicare and Medicaid. It has been adopted by virtually all private insurers for medical claims submissions. Clinicians employed in MBHO clinics do not send in HCFA forms; their standard office superbill or encounter form, which is processed by reception when the patient checks out, is usually sent on to the provider claims department. These individual session claims are then processed as in the following item.

4. If the HCFA 1500 form is completely and accurately filled out (called a clean claim), it is processed against what services by CPT code, provider, and time frame have been authorized in the claims computer for the particular patient. All services that match will be paid. In insurance terms the claim has then been *adjudicated*. Network providers receive a check and an explanation of benefits (EOB) form, also called a remittance advice form, which explains the charges, payments, and any reasons for denying payment, such as that services were not of the type authorized or not within the time frame specified. Many MCOs and MBHOs also mail the patient a copy of the EOB. For staff model clinicians no check is sent; internal accounting credits the clinician and clinic with a "payment" from the claims department.

5. If the provider believes that the patient needs more treatment or a different type of care than was preauthorized, a treatment plan (as shown earlier in Exhibit 3.1) must be submitted to the UM department for consideration of additional treatment sessions. Approval of extended services starts the financial process over at Step 1.

Business Development

Clinicians are likely to have little contact with the business development department. This department, often called marketing, sells the MCO's or MBHO's insurance product lines to employers and government agencies (Medicaid, Medicare, or government employers).

Marketing is done by keeping in ongoing contact with the human resources (HR) managers for large employers and governmental agencies. In preparation for open enrollment (a time period, often annually, when employees or recipients can reconsider which insurance plans available to them they wish to keep or change), the HR manager must decide if the company or agency should add or delete insurance choices available to their population. If there is a decision to offer different insurers, a request for proposal (RFP) listing the requirements of the employer or agency is often let to all interested insurers. In response, the business development staff for each interested MCO or MBHO writes a very detailed proposal. Each proposal describes how the MCO or MBHO can meet the service needs of the company or agency, and at what cost. Every department discussed in this chapter is described in a proposal.

As a personal note, I can attest to the detail required in MCO and MBHO proposals. I helped write a state mental health carve-in proposal for Medicaid that, with the general medical parts, filled seven, four-inch binders.

Once the proposals are submitted, a procurement committee from the employer or government agency reviews all proposals and then offers a contract, called the award, to one or more of the insurers. It is not uncommon for the losers of very large contracts, especially government contracts, to file protests that the award was done unfairly. Many legal cases have been brought around managed care insurance awards, especially those for state Medicaid contracts.

Information Services

This department supports all others with an integrated computer system. MCOs and MBHOs require complicated hardware and software that can connect and support intake, UM, credentialing, quality support, member services, claims, and the general financial needs of the company. These systems are so complex that it is common for major changes or upgrades in the computer system to take four to nine months for all system and reporting capabilities to become fully functional.

Now that you have been introduced to the maze of managed care departments that form a managed care plan, it is time to point out the clinical skills, attitudes, and behaviors that make mental health clinicians attractive to MBHOs. This is the goal of the next chapter.

CHAPTER FOUR

What Managed Care Plans
Look for in Clinicians

The clinical skills and business understanding necessary to function smoothly within a managed care setting are somewhat different from those required by indemnity insurers. For example, the acceptance of utilization management oversight is unique to managed care. The payer and treating clinician must share information about the patient and jointly reach consensus on what is necessary care.

A variety of team skills are necessary to work with managed care insurers and their associated MBHO, even for the solo practitioner. MBHOs administer health plan benefits and a delivery system; they are not simply payers for a collection of clinicians who treat patients. I will discuss the specific skills sought by managed care plans in both individual clinicians and group practices in this chapter. These skills will be useful to you in any of the following situations:

- Meeting with a provider relations representative from an MCO or MBHO

- Completing a managed behavioral healthcare organization credentialing application

- Providing ongoing clinical services to members of a managed care plan

INDIVIDUAL CHARACTERISTICS

MBHOs are looking for mental health clinicians who possess certain skills and attributes, whether the MBHO is part of a network model in which the health plan contracts with individual providers or small group practices or is in a staff model plan that employs clinicians. Although in some cases, especially when a network must be formed quickly, a provider panel is created using any willing provider, over time the providers to whom patients are actively referred become those demonstrating the skill levels and personal attributes desired by the MBHO. Now let's take a look at the most commonly desired characteristics.

Openness to Managed Care

Even though this might seem to be an obvious requirement, many practitioners seek to join managed care panels, even when they are not receptive to basic managed care operational procedures. But unless a clinician is badly needed for a provider panel (for geographic coverage, for example), an MBHO will not contract with or retain for any length of time a clinician who resists the periodic treatment plan reporting associated with utilization management or is not timely in responding to requests for credentialing or recredentialing data.

In most communities, the experience of MBHOs is that there are more mental health clinicians requesting to be on their provider panel than are actually needed. Consequently, many managed care plans flatly declare that their panel is "closed" and have no reservation about removing uncooperative providers. (Note that removal most often means simply stopping the referral of new patients and not attempting to recredential the provider. It is fairly uncommon for a managed care plan to cancel a provider's contract prior to the time for recredentialing, which is usually every two years.) As mentioned in the opening of this chapter, managed care clinicians must be comfortable sharing clinical data with the payer of the service. In every managed care plan, the members, at the time of signing up for health insurance, give authorization for their clinical records to be reviewed by the insurer for the purposes of determining medical necessity or of collecting data for quality improvement activities.

Managed care is, by its very nature, a team endeavor. Whether you are a solo practitioner subcontracted to an MBHO or a staff clinician employed in a clinic, a cooperative, flexible attitude is necessary. Integration and cooperation are rewarded, not independence.

Acceptance of Accountability
and Quality Improvement Activities

Cooperation in quality initiatives is another core requirement for remaining active within a managed care plan. The 1997 NCQA Behavioral Healthcare Standards (National Committee for Quality Assurance, 1997) specify that every managed care plan offering mental health services must

1. Conduct member and provider satisfaction surveys
2. Have active quality improvement clinical programs that track outcomes and clinical effectiveness
3. Develop prevention programs
4. Conduct provider office site visits
5. Conduct audits of providers' clinical charts for completeness and the appropriateness of the care rendered
6. Mandate that all behavioral clinicians participate in these activities

Although quality improvement (QI) activities are very time and resource consuming, and no one gets paid more for doing them, they are a reality in healthcare today. Every health plan and major clinical facility is being mandated by regulation and sociological forces to have an explicit report card. For providers who work with multiple managed care plans, participation in several different QI programs can be a burdensome aspect of daily practice. Avoiding work with managed care in all its forms may limit a clinician's need to participate in an increasing number of quality improvement activities, but total avoidance is unlikely. Even clinicians in forensic, school, and correctional settings not involving managed care are being asked for hard data that can be used as a report card to the consumers and payers of the services.

Along with mandated participation in QI initiatives comes the need to accept the accountability associated with hard data. Mental health clinicians can no longer rely on anecdotal evidence that they provide excellent care and have very satisfied patients.

Providers typically fear the individualized use of quality data for what is called provider profiling. As QI activities build warehouses of data, individual clinician data are available for tracking things like clinical practice patterns, patient satisfaction, and clinical outcomes. Managed care plans already routinely profile and compare clinicians on utilization data (for example, the average number of psychotherapy sessions used for patients with panic disorder or the cost of psychotropic medications prescribed by physicians treating major depression). Although comparisons based on utilization and costs may be scary, clinicians especially worry about judgments based on patient satisfaction, chart completeness, appropriateness of treatment plans, and clinical outcomes. The rapid approach of managed care plans using these data to select the best providers is very real and is becoming another fact of clinical practice. Every graduate training program should prepare graduates for scrutiny based on clinical outcomes, patient satisfaction, and cost data.

On a positive note, well-run QI programs provide excellent feedback to clinicians about their practice patterns in comparison to local and national benchmarks. Perceptive and astute clinicians use these data for ongoing internal improvements in their daily clinical functioning. Perceptive and astute clinicians are already highly valued by MCOs and will remain so.

Brief, Problem-Focused Treatment Orientation

Practitioners must remember that, generally, managed care benefits contracted for by members, insurers, and the insurance purchaser (usually an employer or government agency) are not for long-term treatment or therapies focused on chronic problems. The only significant exceptions are benefits for the severely mentally ill (SMI) that are covered by managed care Medicaid plans (see Chapter Ten). Consequently, clinicians must be skilled in and oriented toward short-term therapies in which *short term* most often refers to outpatients routinely treated with fewer than twenty sessions of psychotherapy per treatment episode and medication management in fifteen- or thirty-minute sessions, with stabilized patients returned to their PCP for medication follow-up.

The focus must be on removing immediate functional impairments rather than long-standing issues. For example, a treatment plan that describes psychotherapy to resolve childhood abuse issues may well be denied as not medically necessary or as outside the benefit package. However, a treatment plan designed to deal directly with current anxiety impairing marital functioning, whether or not the anxiety symptoms are related to a history of abuse, will probably be approved. Although symptoms are important in the assessment of the patient, managed care benefit plans focus on the degree of impairment before, during, and after treatment. Addressing functional impairment is most important when interacting clinically with an MBHO about authorizations for care.

Regarding hospital care, managed care benefits are also acute care–oriented, focusing on stabilizing patients so that they may benefit from outpatient programs. Inpatient care delivery within a managed care benefit package is designed to provide only the treatment necessary to establish safety for the patient and receptivity to other, less-restrictive forms of care such as partial hospital care, intensive outpatient programs, or standard office-based visits. For example, a denial for psychological testing services will likely result if a psychiatrist requests a battery of neuropsychological tests to assess functional impairments of childhood origin in an adult patient hospitalized for acute schizophrenia. The

MBHO utilization management staff are likely to tell the psychiatrist that the testing may be considered as an outpatient, neurological procedure after discharge but should not done in the hospital where logistically it might lengthen the hospital stay authorized to stabilize acute psychosis. Across the country most inpatient stays for adult, privately insured patients with an HMO plan last three to five days (Zieman, Williams, Daniels, and Kramer, 1997). Clinicians comfortable with active, short-term hospital treatments are highly desired by managed care plans.

Rapid Access and Responsive Emergency Coverage

MBHOs are required by NCQA behavioral standards to offer

- Routine office appointments to patients within ten days of requesting care
- Appointments for urgent situations within forty-eight hours
- Immediately available emergent services, which can be offered through a hospital emergency room

To meet these standards, MCOs seek clinicians who are flexible in appointment scheduling and who do not shy away from urgent cases.

In most employee groups, emergent daytime psychiatric cases represent about 1 percent of calls, whereas urgent cases represent about 9 percent. These figures are based on twelve months of data from 130,000 members covered by four different HMOs in Albuquerque, New Mexico (Mesa Mental Health, 1996).

Clinicians with privileges at medical-surgical hospitals are also sought for their ability to handle consultations in emergency rooms, intensive care units, and on general medical floors.

GROUP PRACTICE OR CLINIC CHARACTERISTICS

In the past, insurers saw little difference in the value of clinicians who worked in a group practice as opposed to solo practice. That is no longer true. As managed care insurers grapple with the logistics of forming comprehensive provider panels, the management of QI programs, and the standardization of patient access to care, group practices have become valued—in fact, often preferred. Especially valued are groups with three attributes:

- Incorporated as a single business
- Clinical integration among the clinicians
- Multidisciplinary functioning

Business Incorporation

To be incorporated as a single business, either for-profit or nonprofit, means that the group's owners have formed legally a professional corporation or other business entity that has the ability to sign contracts binding all members of the group. In this structure, all functioning group clinicians are employees, even those who may be owners. Ownership and employment, however, are totally separate functions. A group may be owned by one or more individuals, who usually are also employed by the group, or may be owned by a larger business (for example, a hospital system). State laws demand that the group have offi-cers, including a president, vice president, secretary, and treasurer. Typically, the president and the secretary are authorized to sign contracts and other finan-cial or legal agreements that bind the entire group. Clinicians should be alert to the fact that state laws vary greatly with regard to who can own a professional group providing healthcare services. In some states anyone can, whereas in other states ownership may not be by another corporation or may not cross pro-fessions. For example, in Texas, clinicians from different disciplines (psychia-trists and social workers, for example) may not share joint ownership of a healthcare business (a legal remnant from the days of fighting prepaid groups plans). Despite these restrictions, many groups have found creative ways to develop multidisciplinary or corporation ownership. The typical method is for the prohibited parties to form a joint holding company that, in turn, owns the group practice.

Ease of network formation and the ability to accept creative financial arrange-ments are the prime reasons that incorporated practices are preferred. Incorpo-rated groups can bring a spectrum of clinicians into a network with one subcontract (referred to as a single-signature contract). The simplicity and logis-tical ease of this arrangement make single business groups popular. Groups that are one business can also share financial risk with an MCO in ways that are impossible for expense-sharing groups in which each clinician is an indepen-dent business. The details and variations of sharing financial risk are discussed in Chapter Eight.

Clinical Integration

Clinics or integrated groups are very attractive to MCOs and MBHOs. The attrac-tiveness relates primarily to the ease of access for patients, the ability to have consistently uniform clinical documentation, and greater treatment standard-ization. The integration of clinicians is also a major asset in the deployment of QI programs such as outcomes measures and treatment protocols. Groups and clinics are preferred when they have

1. A centralized intake system, with protocols for risk assessment
2. Centralized appointment scheduling, which helps in assuring initial access to care within the required standards
3. Standardized clinical procedures, which are used across clinicians and disciplines; for example, a standardized initial evaluation report
4. One chart per patient, regardless of which clinician(s) are treating the patient
5. Basic QI activities, as required by NCQA, already under way

Clinical integration, along with business incorporation, also brings about economies of scale that permit the group to be more capable of affording and implementing new technologies such as sophisticated computer systems that can talk directly to MBHO computers. The ability of groups to upload raw outcomes data and to adopt a computerized patient record system are also distinct positives. Access and willingness to use the latest technologies are attributes that managed care payers seek—and in some cases demand—from group practices.

Multidisciplinary Integration

For many of the reasons just discussed regarding clinical integration, MBHOs prefer groups or clinics with integrated, multiple, mental health disciplines. Highly desired groups have seamless clinical functioning among psychologists, master's-level clinicians and nurses, and psychiatrists. Offering psychotherapy, medications, and psychological testing all under the same roof with one chart, one bill to the patient, coordinated claims to the MBHO, and one central telephone number are attributes that place a group practice or clinic in a highly desirable position for work with managed care insurers.

In total, whether for individual clinicians or groups, teamwork between clinicians and MBHO is the order of the day and is rewarded with substantial patient flow to those clinicians who fit the team characteristics I have described. Clinicians who can create or join behavioral healthcare delivery systems meeting these characteristics will be in the best condition to maintain economic and practice stability in the years ahead. Training clinicians for industrialized healthcare is a challenge of higher education today.

MBHOs have attributes they seek in clinicians. Similarly, clinicians seek certain qualities and practices in an MCO or MBHO. This is the topic of the next chapter. I will also offer tips on managed care practices that should alert clinicians to avoid certain managed care plans and MBHOs.

CHAPTER FIVE

Assessing Managed Care Plans
A Clinician's Perspective

Now that you know the attributes and clinical behaviors that MCOs and MBHOs look for in assessing your suitability for their provider panel, ask yourself what *you* want from *them*. What should you know before signing up to work for a managed care insurer? These are the topics of this chapter.

It is not generally wise to sign up with any and every MBHO in your geographical region. Being on multiple networks does not guarantee a steady flow of patients, or professional satisfaction, or a good income. In fact, being on many provider panels may actually drive you to distraction because of the constant completion of similar, but different, paperwork and billing mechanisms. Overall, therefore, your goal should be to work with a small group of payers who

1. Refer enough patients to you, or your referral base generates enough new patients, to balance the hassles of being in the payers' network

2. Pay the highest fees on a timely basis

3. Allow you the most autonomy, especially in clinical decisions

4. Have clinical or quality improvement forms and activities that are not a major clinician stressor

Even for those who may be employed in a clinic run by an MBHO, the last two points are very important. Although employment removes the business hassles of managing office staff and a billing system, and it automatically provides health insurance, retirement plans, and other work benefits, the management of clinical and quality activities within the MBHO is of major concern. For example, in an employed position, how is productivity measured and mandated? And with what quality activities will you have to comply? Additionally, most staff clinics have utilization management procedures that are the same, or nearly the same, as for network providers. Even though these are business and logistical issues, they will seriously affect the manner in which you provide care on a daily basis and how satisfied you are with your practice. Knowing the MBHO's practices is critical in any decision to accept a staff clinician position. The majority of what follows applies to employed clinicians as well as to subcontracted practitioners.

Whether employed or subcontracted, the process of evaluating what you want from an MBHO and finding out if a particular MBHO meets your needs is very important. Basically, the process can be broken down into three activities or stages:

- What you must know about the MBHO
- What procedures and assurances you will want at the time of contracting
- What procedures and assurances you will require in an ongoing relationship with a managed care plan

Now let's deal with each separately.

WHAT YOU MUST KNOW

It is important for you to ask a number of questions and review several documents before you can compare what is important to you in working with an MBHO with how the working relationship would actually be. This process is crucial.

In a polite and tactful manner (pushy clinicians are usually turned down immediately for panel participation unless the MBHO is desperate), you must ask the provider relations and credentialing staff several questions and request several documents if they are not already provided. The MBHO representative should be happy to supply you with the requested items and answers. If not, ask the supervisor of the provider relations staff for another staff member with whom you can talk. If they are not forthcoming, you should proceed with the particular health plan under extreme caution, if at all.

Documents to Be Reviewed

You must cordially ask for several important documents early in your discourse with any managed care payer. If you are simply mailed a solicitation to join a network (this is common), telephone their provider relations department or division and ask for whatever has not been included in the mailed packet. If the response is that you personally are odd or demanding because you asked, fax a copy of the pages in this section to show that your request is not outrageous. Remember, I own and help run an MBHO that contracts with several hundred clinicians and has run staff model clinics. Your request is not unheard-of.

The valuable documents to be reviewed are listed in Exhibit 5.1. After carefully reviewing these documents, whatever questions remain from the list that follows should be asked verbally. (The next two chapters will help you review the contract and the credentialing application. In most cases a legal review of the contract is not necessary.)

Questions to Be Answered

From the written material or discussions with a provider relations staff member, you should be able to answer basic questions that are important in assessing clinician-MBHO suitability, including the following:

1. Does the contract restrict your ability to contract with or provide services to any other MBHO or in other settings? For example, can you hold a part-time job with another practice or agency and see members of the XYZ Health Plan there?

2. Do any contract clauses prevent you from openly discussing with patients treatments that might not be covered by the particular MBHO's benefit package? A provision of this nature is known as a gag clause and is outlawed in many states.

3. How are initial and continued treatment authorizations handled, including the turnaround time from clinician submission until word is received back by the clinician?

4. What are the general length-of-treatment parameters that the MBHO will expect from you?

5. Does the MBHO have adequate access to behavioral care for its members? Nationally, 3 to 6 percent of all health plan members access behavioral treatment in any one year (called the penetration rate). Does the XYZ Health Plan and their MBHO fall in that range?

6. Does the MBHO have an adequate or excessive number of providers or specialist providers matching your specialty in their clinical network to serve the number of lives they cover in your area? Consider the average length of treatment from question 4 and the penetration rate in estimating whether there are enough or too many providers.

7. Are you responsible for assuring that new patients arrive with a referral slip from a PCP, EAP, or other required gatekeeper? If you are responsible for this, will you be paid for an initial treatment session when the patient arrives without it?

Exhibit 5.1. MBHO Documents to Be Reviewed.

1. Subcontract for Clinical Services
   Must include any referenced addenda, exhibits, or other attachments, especially the payment rates and structures (these are usually attachments).

2. Credentialing Application
   Usually requires the clinician to attach documents such as a curriculum vitae, proof of malpractice insurance, copy of diploma, peer and supervisor references, any malpractice suits that have involved you, and sometimes proof of recent continuing education activities.

3. Provider Handbook
   Should describe the initial and ongoing utilization processes and how to contact the various departments within the MBHO. *Note:* Many of the documents listed next may be in the Provider Handbook.

4. Continuing Treatment Request Form
   Should look something like the sample shown in Chapter Three.

5. List of Current Providers
   List of credentialed providers in your region or metropolitan area with telephone numbers and addresses, and most likely with any specialty services they offer (for example, children, geriatrics, neuropsychological testing).

6. Basic UM Statistics
   For your region or metropolitan area, simple, overall measures such as average number of psychotherapy and medication visits per outpatient case (these may be broken down by common diagnoses or provider disciplines), average length of inpatient and partial hospital treatments, and percentage of all enrollees who access outpatient and inpatient behavioral care. In some cases the MBHO will not have these readily available in written form, and you may need to accept them verbally.

7. Applicable QI Forms or Procedures
   Copies of the Office Site Visit assessment tool, Clinical Chart Audit tool, and forms with instructions for any required outcomes tracking.

8. Provider Satisfaction Survey Results
   A summary of the MBHO's latest survey of their providers.

9. Benefit Package Summaries
   A synopsis of the various benefit plans that are offered through the MBHO. For example, what are the limits on the maximum number of outpatient visits and inpatient days annually? Is the coverage only for acute care conditions or disorders amenable to brief treatment?

10. The Utilization Management Criteria Used
    Now that many states require that these be made available to providers and members, it is a good idea to look them over for any criteria that might create a conflict between you and your patients with the MBHO regarding what constitutes a rationale for treatment or medical necessity.

8. Are you required to communicate treatment data with PCPs? Doing so is usually good care and good business, but you need to know whether or not you must use a certain form or format. Most HMO plans write clauses into the insured's policy (often called the member certificate) and the provider's contract with the MBHO stating that all patient PCPs must be kept informed of basic treatment data about their patients. A short letter, treatment plan form, or phone call every few sessions is usually adequate to meet this requirement.

9. How often and when does the MBHO request treatment records from providers in making utilization decisions? Most HMO insurance policies contain a clause in which the member agrees that information about care by any provider paid by the insurer may be shared with the health plan, including its agents such as the MBHO. This clause technically overrides the need, at the time of treatment, for a specific release of information to be executed to the MBHO before it can release such patient information as copies of a clinical chart. However, it is always good practice to inform patients at the beginning of care about the possibility that all treatment records will be requested by their MBHO for review, especially in deciding whether further treatment should be preauthorized. Also good practice is to obtain a signed release of information at any time you are asked by the MBHO to release patient records.

10. What fees will you be paid for each type of service?

11. How are you to submit claims for payment? How quickly are claims paid?

12. Does the plan use psychiatrists for psychotherapy or only for medication services?

13. Does the MBHO prefer to work with group practices or solo practitioners?

14. Can you achieve a preferred provider status that will reduce your utilization management and other paperwork?

15. Can you be credentialed as a specialist in any clinical area? What advantages or disadvantages are there to this?

16. Do clinicians ever have to send copies of their progress notes to the MBHO for review?

17. Are you required to accept new patients for emergent and urgent appointments? To what access standards will you be held in accepting emergent, urgent, and routine new patients?

18. How long will it take to complete the credentialing process? Completion is necessary except in very exceptional cases before you can begin seeing patients for the particular health plan.

19. How often do you have to go through the recredentialing process? Every two years is most common.

20. Will you need to increase your malpractice coverage to work with this payer? For outpatient services by nonphysicians, $1 million per incident and $1 million aggregate are common, whereas for psychiatrists or clinicians doing facility-based care, $1 million per incident and $3 million aggregate are typical.

21. In what quality improvement activities will you be required to participate? What resources and time will these require?

22. What opportunities are there for you to join committees and work groups sponsored by the MBHO? Examples of such are group task forces creating treatment protocols and quality oversight committees.

23. Under what conditions may you or the MBHO terminate your work with them. A provision for sixty to ninety days advance notice without an identified cause or reason is common.

WHAT YOU WANT WHEN CONTRACTING

Once you have answers to these questions, you are ready to assess whether the MCO or MBHO meets enough of your needs to pursue contracting with them or accepting a staff clinician position. While the sheer economics of building or retaining enough patient referrals to support your desired salary will always be a major consideration, particularly in regions with an excess of practitioners, it is not wise to work for every available MBHO. As stated at the beginning of this chapter, following the rules for a multitude of payers can drive you to distraction. No MBHO will pay you for basic paperwork time or standard quality activities such as putting up with site visits or mandated participation in clinical measurement programs such as outcomes protocols. You want to limit your time that is not spent with patients as much as possible except for the non-patient activities you enjoy.

The following are common goals that clinicians must weigh once they have done due diligence, that is, gathered the information already described, regarding an MBHO.

Minimal Restrictions

Whether in the contract, credentialing process, or operating procedures, you do not want to be limited in the types of patients who can be referred to you, unless you set the limits yourself. Neither do you want your activities impeded by gag clauses or exclusivity requirements that do not allow you to receive clinical work from other sources. It must be noted that the exclusivity requirement is often present in staff positions where you are employed specifically to serve the population of one or more payers. As a network provider you also want, whenever possible, your contract to remain in force if you join or leave a group practice or move offices to another geographical region.

Maximum Clinical Autonomy

One of the major complaints that clinicians have against managed care plans is the loss of individual provider-patient autonomy in clinical decision making.

Whereas managed care implies and definitely will involve monitoring the care provided with limits and preauthorizations, MBHOs vary greatly in how restrictive they are.

This is where the written material is useful, but your due diligence must go further. From the existing provider list, call others in your discipline and ask about daily professional interactions. Ask about the procedures regarding receiving new patients, initial authorizations, and continued treatment requests. You will prefer plans that authorize more than one or two sessions to begin with and that are flexible in accepting multiple treatment approaches. For example, do they allow switches from individual to family therapy, or even to group therapy? Can one case be treated with brief psychodynamic psychotherapy, whereas another gets a cognitive behavioral approach? For psychiatrists, a major point is whether the MBHO authorizes medical doctors to conduct psychotherapy. If they do, are there special conditions?

Confidentiality for Patients

Managed care plans, especially HMOs, retain the ability in any provider contract to look at the treatment records of patients for whom they are covering service costs. The utilization management and quality improvement departments are typically the only departments having reason to review patients' clinical charts.

Because you, as a clinician, want to maintain your patients' right to confidentiality, you should find out how frequently the XYZ MBHO asks to see patient records. And, in cases of debatable utilization management services, will they accept a summary regarding care rather than insisting on copies of progress notes and other chart documents? Assessing confidentiality issues is another reason for calling existing panel providers for a read on the MBHO's practices.

A Full Continuum of Services for Patients

You will have patients who need services beyond your areas of expertise. For these patients you want and need easy access to facilities and other specialists. Assessing what specialists and hospitals are available to your patients, and how easy the referral process is, are important in determining whether you will be able to adequately treat patients who are members of the particular health plan.

Minimal Paperwork

Enough said.

Adequate Patient Referrals

The last thing you want as a network provider is to go through all of the work to assess a healthcare plan, fill out the forms, and wait to be credentialed, only to discover that you will see one patient a year who is covered by that plan. Analyzing the number of covered lives the payer has in your area, along with the number of providers similar to yourself whom they already use, will help you determine whether it is worth seeking to be in the particular network. Remember the penetration rate figures from question 5. For clinicians living in states with an any willing provider law, this is especially important. In these states, MBHOs take on all clinicians who ask to sign a contract and meet the credentialing standards, but many credentialed providers see very few patients after signing on. Instead, the MBHO steers new patients to a chosen group of providers and does not use the breadth of the provider panel.

A Speedy, Reasonable Credentialing Process

Credentialing applications and the process of verifying all of your licenses, degrees, and references—plus background checks—are complicated and time consuming. (See Chapter Seven for a more detailed discussion.) You want a reasonable application that is no more complex than the sample used in Chapter Seven. You also want to be able to complete the process of becoming fully accepted on the provider panel as quickly as possible. Credentialing that routinely takes longer than four months is excessively delayed. You will also want the possibility of being given temporary privileges to see patients who cannot go to another provider and who have emergent or urgent needs. Ask about these situations.

Ease and Speed in Financial Transactions

As a network provider, you certainly want to be able to submit charges for services rendered to the MBHO through the same process you use to submit charges to other payers. Given that almost all clinicians use computerized billing programs, you want whatever peculiarities there might be of any MBHO to be minimal and to be ones that can easily be accommodated by your billing program. In general, you want to submit all claims on a standard HCFA 1500 using nationally accepted CPT codes (see Chapter Three for a description of these). My own group practice terminated our contract with a nationally prominent MBHO when they insisted on having claims submitted on their own optically scannable forms. The hassle of completing these forms exceeded our gain from seeing patients covered by their plan.

Additionally, you want to be paid in a timely manner. Some MBHOs are notorious for being very slow in mailing out checks. Ask around. Whenever the typical turnaround time from submission of a clean claim to a check being mailed goes beyond forty-five to sixty days, the process is excessively delayed.

Low Patient Copayments

Health plans will lead you to believe that it is easy to collect 100 percent of all patient copayments due at the time of service. Wrong. Providers who very actively pursue copayments collect over 90 percent, but the amount of the copayment is a major factor. The collection rate rises sharply when patients can receive care for reasonably low copays. For an hour of treatment, copays in the range of $10 to $25 are what you want. Copays of $30 or more become much more difficult to collect.

Reasonable Quality Improvement Participation

Increasingly, MBHOs are being pushed by employers and national standards to measure clinical processes and outcomes (see Chapter Nine). The burden this places on you and your office staff must be considered. Annual site visits and quality checks on your clinical charts are routine, along with some basic assistance from you with clinical measures (a questionnaire or two that you or your patients fill out regarding patient functioning and satisfaction, for example). Extensive forms and procedures or frequent on-site activities by MBHO staff are a burden.

Additionally, from whatever quality activities you or your patients participate in, you want to be given timely and digestible feedback. Assisting in the collection of quality data that seem to disappear into a black hole is certainly not how you wish to spend your time and energy. If well done, feedback can be interesting and helpful to you in improving your clinical practice.

WHAT YOU WANT IN A WORKING RELATIONSHIP

After you begin work with an MBHO, certain ongoing business and clinical features are desirable. These sought-after characteristics should be considered at the time of initial contracting, even though they only come into play after the working relationship is established and functioning. I discuss five common ongoing desires in the sections to follow.

Continuity of Care for Former Patients

You want to be able to have patients you treated previously and who now need another episode of care reenter treatment with you. Most MBHOs prefer that patients remain with the same clinician across treatment episodes if the clinician can meet the patient's needs in an efficient manner. However, MBHOs often attempt to steer patients into a particular subgroup of the provider panel, and they may use reentering care (four to six months without services from you is often used to define a new treatment episode) or a new diagnosis as a reason to insist that patients go to another clinician or group. In assessing how possible it is for returning patients to remain with you, I have discovered that what a provider relations staff member states and what actually occurs frequently differ. This is another area for inquiry from existing members of the payer's provider panel.

The Ability to Become a Preferred Provider

Many MBHOs offer some form of a preferred provider status to clinicians and groups who have demonstrated efficient and high-quality care to members of the health plan. Generally, you want to be granted this status if it is available because the two common benefits for clinicians are receiving increased new-patient referrals and becoming exempt from some parts of the utilization management process. Here again, focusing on providing service to a limited number of MBHOs may be productive in order to attain this special status.

An Easy Recredentialing Process

Following NCQA's behavioral standards (National Committee for Quality Assurance, 1997), all providers, whether employed by or subcontracted to the XYZ Plan, must have their credentialing status updated at least every two years. What you want is a process that only asks for what has changed with your professional life since the original credentialing process. You want a recredentialing system that asks only for updated information, not that you essentially start over with a new application. Seeing the recredentialing form is the best way to check on this important logistical matter.

A Willingness to Credential Your Associates

If you are in a group practice, you will usually want the option to have your associates become contracted and credentialed by the same MBHOs with which you are associated. This is especially important when you need clinical coverage by a colleague for vacation time and when your individual practice is so full that you wish to refer patients to your associates. Both your provider relations contact and the history of colleagues in your community can aid you in determining how likely this desire is to be fulfilled.

Options to Participate in MBHO Activities

Last, you may wish to become a member of the XYZ Plan's work groups, especially since most MBHOs reimburse you for these activities. NCQA standards and many employers demand that major health plan committees and task forces must involve clinicians representing different aspects of the provider panel (psychiatrists versus psychotherapists or urban versus suburban and rural providers). Common groups to include clinicians from the provider network are the MBHO's quality improvement oversight committee and groups that are developing clinical guidelines. If participation in these activities interests you, talk to your provider relations contact to find out where in the MBHO's activities you might fit and to whom you should speak.

Given that many clinician desires and areas for due diligence revolve around the structure of the contract with the MBHO, an in-depth discussion of this document is warranted. In the next chapter, I dissect a provider subcontract; this will prepare you to understand what you will be asked to sign.

CHAPTER SIX

Understanding the Provider Subcontract

In the previous three chapters I have made frequent references to the fact that clinicians treating members of a managed care organization (MCO) or an associated managed behavioral healthcare organization (MBHO) must execute a contract with the MCO or MBHO. Although clinicians employed in a clinic run by an MBHO may not have a contract other than the company personnel manual, many of the provisions in provider contracts remain important to understand. In this chapter I will go through in some detail the provisions of a standard contract that network providers sign with MBHOs.

Contracts that subcontract a clinician or group practice to work with an MBHO vary greatly in their use of flowery legalize, as well as their specificity and overall length. The sample contract used for this discussion is a working document written in fairly plain English that has been revised and reviewed by several healthcare lawyers. It is one of the more full and extensive provider contracts available. For the purposes of discussion, I will review the provisions and the related advice points sequentially, as they occur in the contract.

PROVISIONS OF THE AGREEMENT

In contract language, *recitals* are all the provisions of the agreement after the introduction of the parties involved, up to the signature section. Any exhibits or attachments referenced in the recitals come after the signature page. In the sample contract (see Exhibit 6.1), the recitals are A, B, and then C, which has twenty-two subprovisions that are the real meat of the agreement. A, B, and the introduction to C are very typical business contract paragraphs establishing exactly who the parties are and why they wish to contract with each other.

Recitals (A–C)

Paragraph A describes the contractor, MMH, as a corporation providing "mental health, alcohol, and substance abuse health care services" that contracts with employers, HMOs, and other healthcare insurers to provide behavioral health-care services to the members of various health plans. Along with paragraph B,

Exhibit 6.1. Mesa Mental Health Professionals, P.C., Healthcare Services Agreement.

MESA MENTAL HEALTH PROFESSIONALS, P.C.
HEALTH CARE SERVICES AGREEMENT

This HEALTH CARE SERVICES AGREEMENT ("Agreement") is made and entered into this _____ day of _____ , 199__, by and between MESA MENTAL HEALTH, a New Mexico corporation ("MMH"), whose address is 6723 Academy Road NE, Albuquerque, New Mexico 87109, and _____ ("Provider"), whose address is _____.

RECITALS:

   A. MMH is a professional corporation which is engaged, in its capacity as a health care provider, in providing inpatient, outpatient, employee assistance and other mental health and alcohol and substance abuse health care services to the public ("Provider Capacity"), and in connection therewith, enters into contracts with employers, groups, health maintenance organizations, health insurers, health plan entities, and other entities and the administrators ("Administrators") thereof (collectively, "Organizations"), whereby MMH agrees to provide certain inpatient, outpatient, employee assistance and other mental health and alcohol and substance abuse health care services to members ("Members") of such Organizations under the terms of various health care plans, including health maintenance organization, preferred provider, and indemnity-type plans of, with, or relating to such Organizations (collectively, the "Plans").

   B. MMH also is now acting or may in the future act in the capacity as agent for various Organizations in the administration of the Plans of, with, or relating to such Organizations and/or as agent for the Administrators of any such Plans in offering Plan Covered Services to Plan Members ("Administrative Agency Capacity").

   C. MMH desires to contract with Provider to provide certain inpatient, outpatient, employee assistance and other mental health and alcohol and substance abuse health care services (the "Covered Services") to Plan Members, and Provider desires to provide Covered Services to Plan Members either as a subcontractor to MMH in its Provider Capacity or as a contractor with MMH in its Administrative Agency Capacity pursuant to the terms and provisions of this Agreement.

this description defines MMH as an MBHO that is not a department within a larger MCO but is a separate business that subcontracts with more than one MCO to provide behavioral services and then, in turn, subcontracts with providers for the provision of treatment services. If MMH were an MCO directly contracting with providers, these paragraphs would be somewhat simpler.

Paragraph C defines MMH's wishes to contract with providers for "certain" mental health and substance abuse services that are deemed to be "covered services." Given that administrative and clinical decision powers have been delegated to MMH by the MCOs with whom they contract, *covered services* refers to the actual benefits designed by each of the managed care plans for which MMH has been delegated by an MCO to administer. Note the use of the word *certain* proceeding the list of behavioral services. It is there to indicate that MMH, the contractor, will determine in the daily execution of the contract exactly which services the provider is being engaged to provide. In other words, the provider is not necessarily contracted to provide all services in the list. The credentialing process discussed in the next chapter is used to determine which services the contractor believes the clinician is qualified to perform.

Definitions—C(1)

This section lists the definitions used for the purposes of the contract (see Exhibit 6.2). All of these should be familiar except *administrator* and *membership certificate*. *Administrator* refers to a *third-party administrator* (TPA)—a business hired by an insurer, often a large employer that has set up a self-insured healthcare plan for its own employees, to administer the insurance plan (conduct utilization management and pay provider claims, for example) but not accept financial risk. Given that a TPA administering a full medical health plan may wish to contract with an MBHO such as MMH, this definition is included.

A membership certificate is the contract between the insured individual (also called a subscriber) and the insurer to provide prepaid healthcare insurance to him or her and to any dependents (collectively called members). In indemnity insurance language the membership certificate is usually called the policy.

You should note the fact that the definition of *provider* includes both individual clinicians and facilities such as hospitals. Although not contained in this contract, many provider contracts also include business-incorporated group practices in this definition.

Provider Services—C(2)

Recital 2a (see Exhibit 6.3) refers to an optional exhibit listing the insurance plans and their benefit structures, which may apply to what are referred to in the contract as covered services. In many contracts this exhibit is listed as to be found in the Provider Handbook, which is distributed to clinicians by the provider relations staff.

Exhibit 6.2. Subprovision 1: Definitions.

NOW, THEREFORE, FOR AND IN CONSIDERATION of the agreements, covenants, warranties, and representations of the parties contained in this Agreement, MMH and Provider agree as follows:

1. DEFINITIONS As used in this Agreement, the words and terms hereinafter described in this Paragraph 1 shall have the following meaning:

   (a) Administrators: Third-party administrators who provide administrative services in connection with insurance or alternatives to insurance and/or who manage or handle funds, premiums, fees, or other forms of consideration in connection therewith.

   (b) Clean Claim: A claim for reimbursement for Covered Services containing all of the information required by MMH for processing of claims.

   (c) Copay: Member's financial responsibility for Covered Services according to his or her Membership Certificate, subject to those limitations of the applicable benefit description set forth therein or in the Plan.

   (d) Covered Services: Those health care services that are benefits of membership as described and limited in the applicable Membership Certificate, as the same may be amended from time to time. Services are Covered Services only if they are performed, arranged, and authorized in accordance with the terms, limitations, and exclusions set forth in the applicable Membership Certificate.

   (e) Credentials Approval: The process pursuant to which MMH reviews the professional qualifications and ability of a Provider to provide Covered Services to Plan Members.

   (f) Maximum Allowable Fees: The highest allowable charge recognized by MMH for reimbursement to Provider for Covered Services.

   (g) Plans: Any health care plan, including insured or self-funded health maintenance organization, preferred provider, or indemnity-type plans of any Organization under the provisions of the Employee Retirement Income Security Act of 1984 ("ERISA") or state law, in connection with which MMH provides Covered Services in its Provider Capacity or acts as agent in its Administrative Agency Capacity.

   (h) Membership Certificate: Any contract between the Plan and a Member or between the Plan and an Organization for the benefit of a Member, whereby the Plan agrees to pay for all or part of Covered Services rendered to Members in accordance with the terms of such contract.

   (i) Medical Emergency:

      (1) The sudden onset of a medical condition causing acute symptoms of sufficient severity that in the absence of immediate medical attention, such condition could result in a serious impairment of a Member's health, bodily functions, or a serious dysfunction of any bodily organ or part; or

      (2) A situation in which there is reason to believe that the Member presents a serious threat of physical harm to himself or to others.

Exhibit 6.2. Subprovision 1: Definitions, *continued*.

(j) Medical Records: Any compilation of recorded data and information related to a Member-patient's symptoms, treatment, care, plan, prognosis, and progress, or any of the foregoing.

(k) Member: Any person entitled to any Covered Services in accordance with the terms of a Membership Certificate.

(l) Normal Business Hours: Established and identified hours during which Provider will be available to provide Covered Services to Plan Members.

(m) Provider: A health care professional, institutional health care provider, or any other person or entity that has entered into a written agreement with MMH to provide any Covered Services to Members.

© Mesa Mental Health, Albuquerque, NM. Used by permission.

Another provision for special note is 2c, which sets specific access standards for the first outpatient appointment to which the provider agrees to be held. Good clinical care dictates these standards as well as NCQA requirements. Similarly, 2d is important. It requires the provider (including hospitals) to notify the contractor whenever a newly referred member does not show up for an initial treatment appointment. The delay after the scheduled appointment is to allow for the notice to be made by mail.

Many contracts specify that patients referred as urgent or emergent who do not show up for treatment require a telephone or facsimile communication back to the MBHO. Tracking patients who do not arrive for their care is important to MBHOs for continuity of care reasons and for legal liability. Legally, once a referral is made the member becomes the responsibility of the MBHO, which must ensure that patients presenting with significant clinical risk are monitored. This monitoring is an effort to ensure that the referred member is seen for evaluation or treatment. You must be aware that, even though it is not stated in this contract, once a member makes an appointment with you, then you have a similar responsibility and legal liability.

Section 2e is important in that it requires the provider to have a twenty-four-hour, on-call mechanism for patients to receive urgent or emergent care. You should know that simply having an answering machine informing callers to contact the nearest emergency room or mental health center is not considered adequate unless you can show that the recommended facility has specifically agreed to care for your patients. Many contracts ask for a description of your after-hours availability and specify that those who cover for you must have expressly agreed to do so. Generally, a system of colleagues for on-call coverage 365 days per year is required.

Of special importance is paragraph 2g. It is one of the provisions described in Chapter Five that you must make sure is present in any contract for nonemployed

Exhibit 6.3. Subprovision 2: Provider's Services.

2. PROVIDER'S SERVICES

During the term of this Agreement, Provider agrees to provide the following services:

(a) Those Covered Services authorized by MMH to Members referred to Provider by MMH in accordance with the level of benefits authorized pursuant to the Plan and as may be described in Exhibit "A" attached hereto.

(b) In providing Covered Services, Provider agrees that Provider will not discriminate against any Member on account of age, sex, race, religion, color, national origin, handicap, sexual orientation, or payor source.

(c) Provider agrees to offer, and if accepted by the Member, to provide referred Members with an initial appointment as follows:

(1) Routine cases—within seven (7) business days from the date of referral;

(2) Urgent cases—within forty-eight (48) hours from time of referral; and

(3) Emergency cases—within twenty-four (24) hours from time of referral.

MMH shall conduct initial screening of cases to determine the extent of urgency, and such determination shall be binding upon Provider to the extent of Provider's obligation set forth above to schedule and conduct initial appointments, but not otherwise. Provider agrees to insert documentation in the Member's Medical Records to reflect any refusal on the part of the Member of an appointment offered by Provider within the above-described time frames, together with the reasons for such refusal, if disclosed by the Member to Provider or otherwise known by Provider.

(d) In providing Covered Services, Provider agrees to notify MMH concerning those Member-patients who fail to appear for scheduled appointments, as follows:

(1) Routine cases: within seven (7) working days after non-appearance;

(2) Urgent cases: within twenty-four (24) hours after non-appearance; and

(3) Emergency cases: within the same day after non-appearance.

(e) Provider agrees to provide Covered Services to members referred by MMH to Provider during normal business hours and on an on-call basis twenty-four (24) hours per day, seven (7) days a week during the term of this Agreement.

(f) Provider agrees to cooperate fully and in good faith with MMH in the conduct of any grievance proceeding or procedure initiated by MMH, or by a Member or a Plan.

(g) Nothing contained herein shall be construed to restrict Provider or MMH from entering into other agreements or subcontracts to provide Covered Services to Plans or Organizations.

(h) Provider agrees to notify MMH immediately in the event that Provider is at any time unable to comply with the requirements described in Subparagraphs (c) and (e) above of this Paragraph 2.

(i) Provider agrees to maintain all required licensure certifications, permits, registrations, and applicable approvals and authorizations for every Covered Service provided pursuant to applicable laws, rules, and regulations and as may be further required by MMH from time to time during the term of this Agreement. Provider at all times under this Agreement shall provide only those Covered Services which Provider is so authorized to provide.

clinicians. This provision explicitly states that nothing in the contract impairs your ability to contract with or work for other MBHOs, MCOs, or healthcare entities. Always make certain that the contracts you sign have this provision.

Prior Authorization—C(3)

This is a standard managed care section requiring you to have an initial authorization from the MBHO, except in cases of emergency, before beginning any care with members for whom reimbursement is expected from the MBHO (see Exhibit 6.4). You should refer back to the fairly rigid definition of *emergency* in C(1). Additionally, you should know that beginning treatment with out-of-pocket payment from the member and then later requesting authorization for treatment coverage by the MBHO may well result in a denial of coverage or a request that the patient be transferred to another clinician if the MBHO believes that another provider may be better suited to treat the particular patient. At the very least, postponed requests for authorization will result in the MBHO perceiving you as a noncooperative provider. If you have existing patients in your care who change to a health plan with which you contract or are already in your care at the time you sign the MBHO's contract, contact the MBHO immediately for direction.

Compensation—C(4)

Paragraph 4a refers to the exhibit containing the "Payment Schedule." Obviously, you are interested in the fee schedule, and you should study it to make sure that it includes all services (usually listed by CPT code) you are likely to provide (see Exhibit 6.5). Note that the fee schedule lists fees that are the maximum allow-

Exhibit 6.4. Subprovision 3: Prior Authorization.

3. PRIOR AUTHORIZATION

Except in the case of Medical Emergencies, Provider shall obtain prior authorization of MMH before:
(a) Admitting any Member for inpatient services, partial hospital services, intensive outpatient services or any sub-acute services at participating facilities or any other facilities;
(b) Administering any psychological testing to or for any Member; or
(c) Performing any outpatient or other services other than those authorized in advance by MMH.

In the absence of such prior authorization by MMH, Provider shall not have any right to be paid by any person or entity for any services rendered by Provider. Provider agrees to notify MMH concerning Provider's performance of any Covered Services and of any facility admission due to a Medical Emergency prior to the end of the next business day thereafter.

© Mesa Mental Health, Albuquerque, NM. Used by permission.

Exhibit 6.5. Subprovision 4: Compensation.

4. COMPENSATION FOR PROVIDER'S SERVICES

    (a) Provider shall be compensated on the basis shown in the payment schedule set forth in Exhibit "B" attached hereto and incorporated herein (the "Payment Schedule"), less applicable Copay, for those Covered Services authorized by MMH and rendered by Provider. Provider agrees to accept such payment based upon the Payment Schedule as full payment for all Covered Services rendered pursuant to this Agreement. Such payment is inclusive of New Mexico gross receipts tax, with the result that, upon payment to Provider of such payment based upon the Payment Schedule, no additional amount shall be due to Provider in respect of the New Mexico gross receipts tax. Such payment shall be made to Provider within sixty (60) days after receipt by MMH of Provider's Clean Claim for Covered Services rendered by Provider. In the payment of any sums due and payable to Provider pursuant to this Agreement, Provider understands and agrees that MMH is acting as agent for the Plans. With respect to any matters in which any of the Plans or their principals is obligated to make payment to Provider, Provider agrees not to seek payment of any such amount from MMH. Notwithstanding anything contained herein to the contrary, the sole responsibility and obligation of MMH pursuant to this Agreement is to administer the Plans. MMH represents to Provider that as agent for the Plans, MMH has full power and authority to bind each Plan in accordance with the provisions hereof. Upon Provider's written request, MMH agrees to furnish to Provider evidence of its authority to act on behalf of any Plan.

    (b) Notwithstanding anything contained in this Agreement to the contrary, the payment based upon the Payment Schedule described in Exhibit "B" attached hereto shall be the Maximum Allowable Fees payable to Provider for all Covered Services performed. The Payment Schedule shall remain in effect unless and until MMH notifies Provider in writing of any changes thereto. Provider shall be bound by any such changes to the Payment Schedule, subject to Provider's right to terminate this Agreement without cause upon sixty (60) days' prior written notice, pursuant to the provisions of Paragraph 10 (d) below.

    (c) Provider agrees not to bill Members for Covered Services except for the applicable Copay for Covered Services, and except only for such Copay, payment to Provider based upon the Payment Schedule shall constitute payment in full for all Covered Services rendered to Members hereunder.

    (d) Under no circumstances shall Provider (including, without limitation, non-payment by MMH, denials by MMH Utilization Review, insolvency of MMH or of the applicable Plan or Organization, or breach or termination of this Agreement by MMH) seek compensation from, have any recourse against, or impose any charge upon any Member; provided, however, that Provider may bill and collect any applicable Copay from Members for authorized Covered Services, and may bill and collect for services which are not Covered Services. The provisions of this Subparagraph (d) shall survive termination of this Agreement, without regard to the cause of termination, and shall be construed to be for the benefit of Plan Members.

Exhibit 6.5. Subprovision 4: Compensation, *continued.*

(e) Each Plan provides for coordination of benefits for Members having other group health coverage, including Medicare. Provider agrees to promptly inform MMH in writing of any other health coverage maintained by a referred Member. Provider agrees to bill or assist MMH in billing the other coverage provider for such other coverage according to the standard coordination of benefits procedures established by the Plan. The provisions of Paragraph (c) above of this Paragraph 4 notwithstanding, Provider shall be entitled to bill and be paid Provider's usual and customary charges if combined benefits of the Plan and those of the other coverage provider equal or exceed Provider's usual and customary charges. Provider consents to the release of medical information by the applicable Plan or Organization to other coverage providers as may be reasonable or necessary to accomplish coordination of benefits.

(f) Provider shall be solely responsible for billing and collecting any amounts for Provider's services which represent the applicable Copay for Covered Services, and for services which are not Covered Services, and MMH shall have no obligation to bill or collect any such amounts on behalf of Provider.

(g) Notwithstanding anything contained in this Agreement to the contrary, MMH will have no obligation to make any payment to Provider for any Covered Services rendered by Provider for which a Clean Claim billing in respect thereof is not submitted to MMH within ninety (90) days of rendition of services. Provider agrees that all claims for payment for Covered Services, other than for applicable Copay, shall be made directly to MMH or to any Plan as directed in writing by MMH on forms and in the manner required by MMH, and shall include such information, including referral information, as may be necessary to verify the amount of any applicable Copay charges.

© Mesa Mental Health, Albuquerque, NM. Used by permission.

able. The allowed amounts include the copayment from the patient, which you must collect.

For example, if the allowed rate for a psychotherapist is $65 for a forty-five-to fifty-minute session of psychotherapy (CPT code 90806) and the patient is required to pay a $20 copay, then the MBHO will reimburse you 50 percent for each authorized 90806 performed; you must collect the $20. Remember that 100 percent copay collection is nearly impossible, especially when the copays are steep (greater than $25 for forty-five to fifty minutes of psychotherapy). Although it is possible under the benefit structure and the insured's member certificate to discontinue care to patients who do not make their copayments, denial of ongoing care can only be done ethically, and in most states legally, if the patient does not have a significant risk of harm to self or others. If the patient has a distinct need for ongoing care, you are responsible for facilitating the transfer of care to another provider.

One of the advantages in this sample contract is its provision that MMH will pay provider-submitted clean claims within sixty days.

Provisions 4c and 4d specify that the provider may only collect the copayment due under the benefit structure from the patient and at no time, even in the event of no insurance payment, may charge the patient more. This is a typical managed care rule designed to protect consumers.

Coordination of benefits is the topic of paragraph 4e. Some patients have more than one healthcare insurer. In that case, one insurance is always primary and the other secondary. Which is primary and which is secondary must be determined by telephoning the insurers if the patient is not absolutely certain. In all cases, government-sponsored insurers (Medicaid and Medicare) are secondary. The secondary insurance can be billed for any copayment due under the primary payer's benefit structure. Therefore, 4e is designed to compel subcontracted clinicians to provide information to both insurers as needed to process the claims for payment correctly. It also allows the provider to collect a larger fee than is listed in the MMH payment schedule if the combined benefits of the two insurers will allow this.

Medical Records—C(5)

This section establishes that the clinical records kept by any provider are the property and responsibility of the provider but that the records must be available for review by the MBHO or any authorized governmental authorities (see Exhibit 6.6). With these rather large exceptions, the provider is then mandated to protect the confidentiality of patient records. Paragraph 5b stipulates that the provider will obtain a release of information from each patient, allowing MMH to review or audit treatment records for utilization, quality, legal risk, or patient grievance purposes. This stipulation about obtaining a release from the patient, in reality, is only necessary and legally important if the patient did not sign a release allowing the MBHO access to his or her records at the time of enrollment in the insurance plan. If such a release was signed at enrollment, this second release is unnecessary but is good to do for consumer involvement. If the patient refuses to allow the release of records, all insurance benefits for the treatment episode may be terminated.

Although obtaining a release is mandated, most clinicians do not obtain it. Why? Because they are already bogged down with treatment cases and managed care paperwork. Also, they know that in the process of signing up for insurance with an MCO, the subscriber has almost always agreed in the member certificate to a clause stating that the MCO or any of its delegated entities (an MBHO, for example) has the right to review the member's treatment records at any time for any reasonable purpose. Most patients, however, do not realize that when they go for treatment their treatment records will be open to the payer.

Exhibit 6.6. Subprovision 5: Medical Records

5. MEDICAL RECORDS

(a) Provider agrees to maintain Medical Records for each Member referred to Provider for Covered Services for such period, in such form, and containing such information as may be required pursuant to Titles XVIII and XIX of the Social Security Act, and the rules and regulations applicable thereto, and as may be required by any other applicable federal and state laws, rules, and regulations.

(b) Provider agrees to maintain the confidentiality of Medical Records and other information pertaining to Members consistent with all applicable federal and state laws, rules, and regulations governing confidentiality, release of information, and security of information. Provider agrees to obtain and provide to MMH the consent of each Member to whom Provider shall render Covered Services, for MMH and the applicable Plan or Organization to review Provider's Medical Records relating to the Member, as may be necessary or desirable to enable MMH, and such Plan or Organization to conduct quality assurance, risk management and peer review programs, and grievance procedures and utilization control mechanisms.

(c) Provider agrees to maintain Medical Records of Members and provide information to MMH, the applicable Plan and Organization, and any state or federal agency having jurisdiction as may be necessary for compliance by MMH or the Plan with applicable federal and state laws, rules, and regulations, for a minimum of four (4) years or for such longer period as may be required by any such applicable federal or state laws, rules, and regulations.

(d) Provider hereby assumes all liability and risk associated with maintaining the confidentiality and security of Medical Records and other information relating to Members and the release or disclosure thereof, and agrees to indemnify and hold MMH harmless from and against any and all claims, loss, liability, and expense, including, without limitation, reasonable attorney fees in any way relating to or arising out of any failure to maintain such Medical Records and other information and in any way relating to or arising out of any improper or unauthorized disclosure thereof.

(e) The provisions of this Paragraph 5 of this Agreement shall survive the termination of this Agreement.

(f) Provider agrees to comply with the New Mexico Medicaid Fraud Act, New Mexico Stat Ann. 30–44–1 et.seq. (1978) and other applicable laws, rules, and regulations governing the maintenance of Medical Records.

(g) Until the expiration of four (4) years after the rendition of Covered Services to any Member pursuant to this Agreement, Provider agrees to make available, upon written request from the Secretary of Health and Human Services of the United States or the Comptroller General or any of their duly authorized representatives, the contracts, books, documents, and records of Provider that are necessary to verify the nature and extent of the cost of providing Covered Services to Plan Members.

Exhibit 6.6. Subprovision 5: Medical Records, *continued.*

(h) In the event that Provider is requested to disclose any books, documents, or records relevant to this Agreement by any governmental authority having jurisdiction for the purpose of an audit or investigation, Provider shall immediately notify MMH of the nature and scope of such request and shall make available to MMH upon its request, all such books, documents, or records for inspection or copying.

(i) Provider agrees to indemnify and hold MMH harmless for the amount of any reimbursement denied or disallowed, plus any interest, penalties, and legal costs relating thereto, in the event that any amount of reimbursement is denied or disallowed by the Plan or any governmental agency having jurisdiction as a result of any failure of Provider to comply with any of Provider's obligations set forth in this Paragraph 5.

© Mesa Mental Health, Albuquerque, NM. Used by permission.

Therefore, it is helpful in the name of honesty to inform patients about who can review their records and to obtain a release of information to the MBHO.

Note that, regardless of which professional ethics any of us as clinicians have sworn to uphold, whoever pays the bill in today's society may look at what is in the chart. This presents many ethical dilemmas for us (see Chapter Twelve). To underdocument in the chart risks (1) the loss of important information that may be needed by the patient for future care, (2) your not being paid for services when medical necessity is not clearly documented, and (3) your being removed from the payer's network for noncompliance with record standards. (See Chapter Nine for a discussion of how and why MCOs are now routinely auditing patient charts in providers' offices. To document fully, however, risks potentially harmful data being released to a wide array of individuals who are not directly involved in the clinical treatment of the patient.

There is no way, with the rules we must follow today, to have a fully confidential treatment chart. Even when only the patient pays for services, the treatment record by most state laws can be reviewed by the patient or any guardian, and may be required to be released in certain legal situations. Clinical care today presents many conflicting forces and ethics. We face a landscape filled with land mines that were never there before healthcare insurance became widespread.

Also of note in section 5 are the provisions that the provider will maintain the records for a minimum of four years, shall follow all applicable state and federal regulations, and shall protect the MBHO from being liable for any damages or monetary consequences related to provider mismanagement of clinical treatment records. This last item (see 5i) is especially important to the MBHO, given that governmental insurers very often audit providers' treatment charts to look for fraud. Note that there is no clause giving the provider or patient any clear recourse if the MBHO mismanages the "confidential" data. Many states have addressed this with strict insurance regulations surrounding confidentiality, but still the only recourse for providers and patients most often is to complain to the MBHO to seek amends or to file a civil lawsuit.

Credentialing, Utilization, and Quality Assurance—C(6)

This section (see Exhibit 6.7) extends the requirements of cooperation and availability as set for treatment records to a broad array of venues, including site reviews of the provider's facilities and you as the provider having to administer questionnaires to patients on behalf of the MBHO (usually satisfaction or clinical outcomes measures). A special note is warranted in relation to the provision requiring that you open your treatment records to review by clinical peers selected by the MBHO. Such reviews are occurring more frequently as MBHOs are required to be legally responsible for the care provided by their providers (refer back to Chapter Two and the case of *Boyd* v. *Albert Einstein Medical Center*). Being a sole practitioner no longer guarantees that other clinicians will not see your office charts. In fact, cooperating with peer reviews of this nature may well be a determining factor in whether the MBHO continues to contract with you.

Office site visits became mandatory in 1997 for MCOs to do if they wish to obtain accreditation from the National Committee for Quality Assurance (NCQA). Inspectors making such visits usually look for things such as handicap assessability, security of treatment records, basic office safety, and security of any medications kept in the office.

You should also note that the contract calls for you to provide care within the prevailing standards in your community and the customary rules of ethics from applicable professional associations. The rules of ethics regarding confidentiality from your professional association and what is expected from the other provisions of this contract may well conflict. I know of no case law or accepted operational standard that provides guidance here. However, the reality is that most MBHOs and MCOs refuse to pay or to continue contracting with a practitioner who will not allow clinical records to be reviewed.

Provider as Independent Contractor—C(7)

Much of this section (see Exhibit 6.8) is designed to establish for tax, liability, and labor laws that you as a network, nonemployed provider are entirely separate from the MBHO. Note the statement that MMH does not have the right to exercise any control over the provider's clinical judgment or methods. This statement is ubiquitous in provider contracts and is designed to prevent the MBHO from being liable for bad outcomes in treatment such as the case of *Wilson* v. *Blue Cross of Southern California,* which is discussed in Chapter Two. This clause puts the total responsibility for care back on you as a clinician.

Exhibit 6.7. Subprovision 6: Credentialing, Utilization, and Quality Assurance.

6. CREDENTIALING, UTILIZATION, AND QUALITY ASSURANCE

Provider agrees to cooperate fully with MMH and any applicable Plan and Organization, together with any other MMH-approved entity in establishing, maintaining, conducting, and performing utilization review, quality assurance, risk management, grievance proceedings and procedures, and peer review programs and mechanisms, to include, without limitation, on-site reviews of facilities and records, and procuring and providing Member-patient questionnaires relating to Covered Services provided under this Agreement. In addition, Provider agrees to comply with and be bound by those credentialing policies and criteria as may be adopted and amended by MMH from time to time. Provider further agrees that all Covered Services rendered to Members shall be performed in accordance with prevailing standards of care in the community and customary rules of ethics and conduct of applicable professional associations and organizations, and as may be required pursuant to applicable governmental laws, rules, and regulations.

© Mesa Mental Health, Albuquerque, NM. Used by permission.

What is left unsaid here is that the MBHO will certainly tell you what services and methods of care they will or will not pay for; that is not assumed to be exercising control over your judgment. Financial decisions are a major controlling factor, and MBHOs are open to liability for using their mighty sword of "we won't pay for that." And you must keep in mind that you cannot blindly abide by MBHO decisions because, as in the case of *Wilson* v. *Blue Cross of Southern California,* providers can be sued for malpractice because they did not follow their own judgment, irrespective of financial considerations.

Insurance—C(8)

There is little of surprise here except that many providers have not thought about making sure their office has a general liability policy protecting against things such as a patient being hurt in an accident in the office. Additionally, many providers have taken out malpractice policies with lower coverage limits than those required here. High limits are quickly becoming the national standard. Then there is the "dream on" clause asking the provider to add MMH to their insurance so if something goes wrong, the insurance company will be required to provide MMH with legal representation and coverage for any legally awarded damages. Most insurers will not do this, and even if they will, it's not in your interest to push for it. Many contracts have dropped this request.

Indemnification—C(9)

This wordy and lengthy section is very much the standard contract language of all business contracts. For example, if the MBHO, as in the case of MMH, is a subcontractor to a larger MCO, then this very same set of provisions will be in

Exhibit 6.8. Subprovisions 7–9: Independence, Insurance, Indemnification.

7. PROVIDER AS INDEPENDENT CONTRACTOR

Provider, in the rendition of Covered Services to Members hereunder, shall at all times be acting as an independent contractor practicing psychiatry, psychology, counseling, or related professional mental health care services and not as an employee or agent of MMH. Neither MMH nor any representative of MMH has the right to exercise any control or direction over the exercise of Provider's judgment or the selection of the methods to be employed by Provider in the rendition of Covered Services hereunder, all such matters being subject to Provider's sole determination consistent with principles of sound medical practice and ethics. Nothing contained herein shall be construed or interpreted as creating a joint venture or partnership between MMH and Provider. Provider shall have the right at all times to practice at other health care facilities or locations, wherever located. Neither Provider nor anyone employed or engaged by Provider shall have any claim under this Agreement or otherwise against MMH for vacation pay, sick leave, retirement benefits, social security benefits, workers compensation insurance, disability benefits, unemployment insurance benefits, or other employee benefits of any kind or nature whatsoever. Nothing contained in this Agreement shall be construed as imposing any obligation upon MMH to refer Members, any particular volume of Members, or any proportionate share of Members in relation to other contracted or subcontracted providers practicing in the same or similar specialty as Provider, to Provider for the performance of Covered Services, all such matters being subject to the sole and uncontrolled discretion and determination of MMH.

8. INSURANCE

During the term of this Agreement, Provider agrees to procure and maintain in full force and effect both professional liability insurance and general liability insurance, each with coverage limits of not less than one million dollars ($1,000,000) per occurrence and three million dollars ($3,000,000) in the aggregate per annum for personal injury and two hundred fifty thousand dollars ($250,000) for property damage. In addition to and not in limitation of the foregoing, such professional liability insurance shall have such coverage limits and contain such insuring agreements and other provisions as may be required for Provider to be at all times during the term of this Agreement a qualified health care provider under the New Mexico Medical Malpractice Act. All insurance required hereunder shall be procured from reputable insurance companies authorized to sell such insurance in the state of New Mexico. Provider agrees, within ten (10) days after the date of this Agreement, and thereafter on each anniversary date, if any, hereof, to furnish to MMH appropriate evidence of the continued existence of such insurance and the payment of premiums required thereunder for the ensuing year. To the extent obtainable, Provider shall cause MMH to be named as an additional insured under all such policies of insurance. Such insurance policies shall contain a provision to the effect that the insurance coverage provided thereby shall not be amended or canceled without the insurer first giving thirty (30) days' prior written notice to MMH of any proposed amendment or cancellation. In addition, within ten (10) days after the date of this Agreement and on each anniversary, if any, thereafter, Provider agrees to provide MMH with a copy of each such insurance policy or a certificate or certificates of insurance complying with the foregoing provisions of this Paragraph 8.

Exhibit 6.8. Subprovisions 7–9: Independence, Insurance, Indemnification, *continued.*

9. INDEMNIFICATION

    (a) Of MMH by Provider

        Provider agrees to indemnify and hold MMH and its physicians, employees, and agents harmless from and against any and all claims, loss, liability, and expense, including, without limitation, reasonable attorney fees, in any way relating to or arising out of Provider's rendition of Covered Services or other medical services to Members, or arising out of or in any way related to any failure by Provider to comply with Provider's obligations contained in this Agreement. The foregoing indemnification undertaking on the part of Provider to MMH shall include, without limitation, reasonable attorney fees and expenses incurred by MMH or its physicians, employees, or agents in the defense of any such claim and also any attorney fees and expenses incurred by MMH in the enforcement of the obligation of Provider to provide such indemnity to MMH. Provider's indemnity obligations shall survive termination of this Agreement and extend to and continue for the benefit of MMH and its physicians, employees, and agents, to include those who, subsequent to the occurrence of an indemnifiable event hereunder, thereafter ceased to be a physician, employee, or agent of MMH.

    (b) Of Provider by MMH

        MMH agrees to idemnify and hold Provider and its physicians, employees, and agents harmless from and against any and all claims, loss, liability, and expense, including, without limitation, reasonable attorney fees, in any way relating to or arising out of any failure by MMH to comply with MMH's obligations contained in this Agreement. The foregoing indemnification undertaking on the part of Provider to MMH shall include, without limitation, reasonable attorney fees and expenses incurred by Provider or its physicians, employees, or agents in the defense of any such claim and also any attorney fees and expenses incurred by Provider in the enforcement of the obligation of Provider to provide such indemnity to Provider. MMH's indemnity obligations shall survive termination of this Agreement and extend to and continue for the benefit of Provider and its physicians, employees, and agents, to include those who, subsequent to the occurrence of an indemnifiable event hereunder, thereafter ceased to be a physician, employee, or agent of Provider.

    (c) Limitation on Indemnification

        To the extent, if at all, that 56–7–1 NMSA 1978 (1986 Repl.) is applicable to any agreement to indemnify contained in this Agreement, and any such agreement to indemnify is interpreted to indemnify against liability, claims, damages, losses, or expenses including attorney fees, arising out of bodily injury to persons or damage to property caused by, or resulting from, in whole or in part, the negligence, act, or omission of the indemnitee or the agents or employees of the indemnitee, or any legal entity for whose negligence, acts, or omissions of any of them may be liable, any such agreement to indemnify contained in this Agreement shall not extend to liability, claims, damages, losses, expenses, including attorney fees, arising out of (i) the preparation or approval of maps, drawings, opinions, reports, surveys, change orders, designs, or specifications by the indemnitee, or the agents or employees of the indemnitt; or (ii) the giving or failure to give directions or instructions by the indemnitee, or the agents or employees of the indemnitee, where the giving or failure to give directions or instructions is the primary cause of bodily injury to persons or damage to property.

the MCO-MBHO contract. These provisions establish that if one party in this contract is sued for any reason, that party will not turn around and seek to involve the other party or to attempt placement of responsibility or blame with the other party.

Sections C(10)–C(18)

These provisions (see Exhibit 6.9) are also standard business items. You should always note in any contract you sign what the terms of termination are. For example, this contract renews automatically each year (called an evergreen clause), and either party can terminate the agreement without having to give cause with sixty days advance, written notice. And as is common, some activities that began during the contract continue in force after termination; here, maintaining treatment records for patients seen during the contract and allowing the MBHO access to them continue after termination.

In C(17) the contractor is protecting its proprietary products from release to the public or other healthcare providers. Examples of items that are often considered proprietary are quality tools or reports (such as satisfaction and clinical outcomes assessment forms and reports) and any knowledge you might gain about the inner workings of the MBHO if you serve on an MBHO work group or committee.

Coverage Determinations—C(19)

Here the MBHO is asserting that it is the sole determiner of what constitutes a covered service, who is an active insured member, and who is not (see Exhibit 6.10). This is a standard healthcare provider provision that means if you disagree with an MBHO decision, you may appeal to the MBHO but cannot seek a second opinion from anyone else other than your state's Department of Insurance.

Advertising—C(20)

This provision sounds more worrisome than reality suggests it is. What the MBHO is really asking is that you agree to be included in their listings of providers in their network. Although the provision is vague enough to allow the MBHO to put your name in a direct advertising brochure or on a billboard, that is very unlikely unless you have extremely high stature in your community or healthcare in general.

Medicare—C(21)

This section is not very common yet but will be increasingly common as more and more Medicare beneficiaries sign up with managed care plans that administer their Medicare insurance. Special contract provisions like this are also likely to be in contracts that include services for Medicaid beneficiaries. Given that unique rules come with all government-sponsored insurance plans, this

Exhibit 6.9. Subprovisions 10–18: Terminations and Other Items.

10. TERM AND TERMINATION
   (a) The term of this Agreement shall be for a period of one year, subject to auto-
       matic renewal from year to year thereafter unless terminated as provided
       herein.
   (b) MMH shall have the right to terminate this Agreement immediately and with-
       out advance notice in the event that MMH or the applicable Plan or Organiza-
       tion determine in good faith that the services provided by Provider to Plan
       Members do not meet prevailing standards of care in the community, or are
       endangering the well-being or health of any Member, or if Provider fails to
       cooperate, participate in, comply with, or satisfy the requirements of any
       quality assurance, credentialing risk management and peer review programs,
       or grievance proceedings and procedures and utilization control mechanisms
       adopted by MMH or the applicable Plan or Organization, or if Provider fails
       to comply with the requirements of Paragraph 5 or of Paragraph 2(f) hereof.
   (c) MMH and Provider shall each have the right to terminate this Agreement at any
       time upon sixty (60) days' prior written notice to the other party, without cause.
   (d) Notwithstanding any termination of this Agreement (other than for any of the
       reasons described in Subparagraph (c) above of this Paragraph 10), Provider
       agrees to continue to provide Covered Services to Members who have been
       referred to Provider by MMH and who continue to be under the care of
       Provider at the time of termination, until arrangements are made by MMH for
       the transfer of such Members to a third party health care provider for continu-
       ation of their care. MMH agrees to reimburse Provider for such continuation
       of provision of Covered Services at the Reimbursement Rates attached hereto
       as Exhibit "A."
   (e) This Agreement will terminate immediately and automatically upon any
       termination, cancellation, lapse, or material change in Provider's professional
       or general liability insurance coverage required to be maintained pursuant to
       this Agreement.
   (f) This Agreement shall terminate immediately and automatically upon any
       revocation, suspension, limitation, or expiration of Provider's license, permit,
       or authorization or credentialing to provide Covered Services, and upon the
       conviction of Provider of a crime which adversely reflects upon Provider's
       ability to practice Provider's profession or upon Provider's moral character.
   (g) This Agreement shall terminate immediately and automatically in the event
       that Provider engages in fraud or deception in
       connection with this Agreement or in connection with the rendition of
       Covered Services to Members, or knowingly permits such fraud or deception
       to be perpetrated by another.
   (h) Notwithstanding any termination of this Agreement, Provider agrees to retain
       and provide MMH with access to Medical Records and information as required
       pursuant to Paragraph 5 of this Agreement.
   (i) Either party hereto shall have the right to terminate this Agreement immedi-
       ately upon written notice to the other party in the event that the other party

Exhibit 6.9. Subprovisions 10–18: Terminations and Other Items, *continued.*

breaches any material term, covenant, or condition of this Agreement and fails to cure such breach within ten (10) days after written notice by the non-defaulting party of such breach. If the defaulting party commences cure of such breach in good faith and within ten (10) days after delivery of such default notice and gives written notice to the non-defaulting party of the action which is being taken to effect such cure, then this Agreement shall not be terminated as a result of such breach unless the defaulting party thereafter fails to pursue such cure diligently and in good faith to completion within a reasonable period of time but in no event more than thirty (30) days after giving notice of cure to the non-defaulting party.

11. ATTORNEY FEES, NONWAIVER, AND MEDIATION

(a) In the event that MMH or Provider resorts to legal action to enforce any of the terms or provisions of this Agreement, the prevailing party in such action shall be entitled to recover the expenses incurred therein, including, without limitation, court costs and reasonable attorney fees.

(b) No delay or omission by MMH or by Provider to exercise any right, power, or remedy shall impair such right, power, or remedy or be construed to be a waiver by MMH or by Provider of any breach or default or an acquiescence therein. A waiver by MMH or by Provider of any breach or default hereunder shall not constitute a waiver of any subsequent breach or default.

(c) In the event of a controversy or claim arising out of or related to this Agreement, MMH and Provider agree to initially attempt to amicably resolve any such controversy or claim by themselves or by submission of such claim to non-binding mediation before a mutually agreeable mediator within sixty (60) days after the date such controversy or claim first arises. In the event that the parties are unable to resolve the controversy or claim after having both exercised reasonable efforts to resolve the same either informally or by mediation during the initial sixty (60) day period after the date such controversy or claim arises, either MMH or Provider may institute an action in a court of competent jurisdiction for declaratory relief concerning the rights and obligations of the parties pursuant to this Agreement, or the non-defaulting party hereto may institute an action in a court of competent jurisdiction for damages on account of any breach of this Agreement by the other party, or for equitable relief in appropriate circumstances, the parties' remedies being cumulative.

12. FRAUD AND ABUSE

The parties enter into this Agreement the intent of conducting their relationship in full compliance with applicable state, local, and federal law, including Medicare and Medicaid anti-fraud and abuse provisions. Notwithstanding any unanticipated effect of any of the provisions hereof, neither party will engage in any conduct that would constitute a violation of the Medicare and Medicaid anti-fraud and abuse laws, rules, and regulations.

Exhibit 6.9. Subprovisions 10–18: Terminations and Other Items, *continued.*

13. NOTICES

Any notice required or permitted to be given pursuant to the terms hereof shall be in writing and shall be effective two (2) days after deposit in the United States mails with postage prepaid, and addressed to MMH or to Provider, as may be applicable, at their addresses set forth at the beginning of this Agreement.

14. ENTIRE AGREEMENT

This Agreement constitutes the entire agreement of the parties hereto with respect to the subject matter hereof. To be effective, any modification or amendment of this Agreement must be in writing and signed by the party to be charged thereby. Notwithstanding the foregoing, MMH may amend this Agreement unilaterally in order to comply with applicable federal and state laws, rules, or regulations, and Provider hereby appoints MMH as Provider's attorney-in-fact to execute such amendments hereto as MMH in its sole discretion may deem necessary to cause this Agreement to comply with any such laws, rules, or regulations. Unless Provider agrees otherwise, no such amendment will be effective until the passage of thirty (30) days after the date that such amendment is provided in written form to Provider. Any provision of law or regulation that invalidates or otherwise is inconsistent with the terms of this Agreement or that would cause one or both of the parties to be in violation of applicable law shall be deemed to have superseded the inconsistent terms of this Agreement, provided that the parties agree to exercise their best efforts to accommodate the terms and intent of this Agreement to the greatest extent possible consistent with the requirements of such law, rule, or regulation. In addition to and not in limitation of the foregoing, MMH may propose to amend this Agreement from time to time upon thirty (30) days' prior written notice to Provider. If such proposed amendment is not acceptable to Provider, the then-current provision of the Agreement shall continue to apply hereunder, provided that Provider gives MMH written notice of Provider's election to reject such amendment within such thirty (30) day notice period. Failure of Provider to provide such written notice within such time period shall constitute Provider's consent and agreement to such amendment.

15. BINDING EFFECT

This Agreement shall be binding upon and inure to the benefit of the parties hereto and their respective heirs, legal representatives, successors, and assigns.

16. SEVERABILITY

In case any one or more of the provisions contained in this Agreement shall for any reason be held to be invalid, illegal, or unenforceable in any respect, such invalidity, illegality, or unenforceability shall not affect any other provision hereof, and this Agreement shall be construed as if such invalid, illegal, or unenforceable provision had never been contained herein. In addition, the parties agree to endeavor in good faith to execute a written amendment to this Agreement adding a valid, substitute provision which accomplishes the parties' intent as nearly as possible in originally including the invalid, illegal, or unenforceable provision in this Agreement.

Exhibit 6.9. Subprovisions 10–18: Terminations and Other Items, *continued.*

17. PROPRIETARY INFORMATION AND PRODUCTS

Provider agrees that Provider and Provider's employees and agents shall at all times hold in the strictest confidence and will not, without any prior written consent of MMH, disclose to any third party or use any proprietary, secret, or confidential MMH information or products. All MMH proprietary information and products shall be identified by MMH and provided to Provider in written form. The MMH proprietary information and products shall at all times be and remain the exclusive property of MMH. Upon termination of this Agreement, Provider shall cease any and all use of MMH proprietary information and products and shall return the same to MMH immediately and without retention of any copies thereof. Provider agrees that during the term hereof and thereafter to keep all MMH proprietary information and products confidential and not to disclose any such proprietary information or products to any third party or entity, to the extent not generally known to the public. Provider acknowledges and agrees that in the event of any breach of Provider's obligations contained in this Paragraph 17, that MMH will not have an adequate remedy at law and shall be entitled to immediate injunctive relief in addition to any other remedies which may be available. Provider agrees that the restrictions imposed upon Provider pursuant to the terms of this Paragraph 17 are fair and reasonable and are reasonably required for MMH's protection. Nothing contained herein shall be interpreted as preventing the disclosure of proprietary information and products to the extent that such disclosure is required by law.

18. ASSIGNMENT AND SUBCONTRACTING PROHIBITION

This Agreement is an agreement for professional and specialized services and shall not be assigned or subcontracted by Provider to any person or entity in any manner. MMH shall have the right to assign this Agreement to any entity who shall hereafter succeed to its rights to act in its Provider Capacity or in its Administrative Agency Capacity with respect to Organizations and the Plans of, with, or relating to such Organizations.

section requires that the provider meet the special rules and assist the MBHO in meeting them. The specific requirement in the first paragraph of this section that the provider must have elected to accept assignment with Medicare refers to the provider having agreed not to charge Medicare recipients for any portion of the charges for covered services that Medicare does not pay (responsibility for the payment of services rendered has then been "assigned" only to Medicare, except for any copayment for which the patient is responsible). In short, this means that the provider has agreed with Medicare to the same provisions as in 4c and d of this sample contract. Implied, but not explicitly stated in this provision, is that to be a contracted provider with MMH, you must be willing to accept Medicare referrals if MMH accepts a contract to treat Medicare recipients.

Additional Plans—C(22)

This is a paragraph contained in many contracts. It basically binds you to accepting new referrals from any managed care plan that might contract with MMH (such as Medicare). The clause has spread widely as a means of locking providers into serving governmental insurers (Medicaid, Medicare, and the military's TriCare plan) that the MBHO might contract with in the future. This provision requires you to accept patients, now and in the future, from the MBHO, irrespective of the payer source or payment schedule. Although this is extremely controlling of providers, remember that you can bail out of working with MMH with only sixty days advance notice.

The next order of business, after having agreed to a contract with an MBHO, is to fill out their credentialing application. The process of credentialing is the topic for the following chapter.

Exhibit 6.10. Subprovisions 19–22: Insurance Benefits Decisions and Working with Other Insurers.

19. COVERAGE DETERMINATIONS

Provider acknowledges that determinations of Covered Services, Members and Co-pays may vary by Plan and within a Plan. Accordingly, the right of Provider to be compensated for rendition of Covered Services shall be conditioned upon the determination by MMH that the person receiving services from Provider is a Member and that the services rendered by Provider are in fact Covered Services. Provider agrees to be bound by MMH's determination of the foregoing, without regard to whether or not the determination is made prior to, during, or after the rendition of services by Provider.

20. ADVERTISING

Provider agrees that MMH may use Provider's name, address, telephone number, and a list of Provider's services in a roster of participating health care providers of MMH or of any Plan with which MMH has contracted or shall contract with. Such rosters are intended for the use of existing and prospective Plan Members and subscriber groups, as well as other existing or prospective Plan participating health care providers. In addition, Provider agrees that MMH may use Provider's name generally for advertising and marketing purposes.

21. MEDICARE

The terms and provisions of this Agreement shall be applicable to those Medicare beneficiaries with whom MMH has contracted or may hereafter contract with. Provider agrees to accept Medicare assignment for Members and to comply with all laws, rules, and regulations applicable to rendition of services to Medicare beneficiaries. Provider shall be compensated for services rendered to Medicare beneficiaries who are Members of any of the Plans, as follows:

(a) In those cases where MMH provides primary coverage for the Medicare beneficiary, as determined by federal Medicare rules and regulations and the rules and regulations of the New Mexico Department of Insurance regarding Medicare insurance supplements and coordination of benefits provisions, Provider will be compensated as described in Paragraph 4 of this Agreement. Provider and MMH agree to share information and to assist each other in determining Members' eligibility as Medicare beneficiaries.

(b) In cases where MMH provides secondary coverage for the Medicare beneficiary, as determined by federal Medicare rules and regulations and the rules and regulations of the New Mexico Department of Insurance regarding Medicare insurance supplements and coordination of benefits provisions, Provider will be compensated only for the difference between the Medicare allowable charge under assignment of benefits provisions and the actual reimbursement received by Provider from Medicare as shown on the Medicare Explanation of Medical Benefits ("EOMB"), minus any required deductible or co-payment and any applicable risk withhold. Payment of the Medicare allowable difference, minus any applicable Member deductible or co-payment and

Exhibit 6.10. Subprovisions 19–22: Insurance Benefits Decisions and Working with Other Insurers, *continued.*

> any applicable risk withhold, shall constitute payment in full to Provider. If the Medicare payment for services provided to a Medicare beneficiary constitutes payment in full for the service, no additional charge shall be made by Provider to any person or party, including the Member-Medicare beneficiary for such services provided.
>
> (c) Provider hereby elects to [accept] [reject] Medicare assignment for Members enrolled in the MMH Medicare Supplement Benefit Plan. (Provider's Medicare number is _____ .)

22. ADDITIONAL PLANS

MMH shall have the right to contract with additional plans to act as their agent in arranging for the provision of medical, hospital, and other health care services and Provider agrees to provide Covered Services to Members thereof as may be requested by MMH.

IN WITNESS WHEREOF, MMH and Provider have executed this Agreement as of the date and year first above written.

MESA MENTAL HEALTH,
a New Mexico corporation

By: _____

Vice President Marketing and Network Services

_____
(Print Provider Name)

By: _____
(Signature)

_____
(Title)

CHAPTER SEVEN

The Credentialing Process

After agreeing to a contract with an MBHO, the next step is to complete the process of becoming a credentialed provider with the MBHO. Being a credentialed provider means that the MBHO has certified that you are competent to practice independently with the health plan in the specialty areas for which you are credentialed by the MBHO's credentialing committee and board of directors or trustees. The process is very similar to that used in hospitals where mental health staff have to submit their credentials and are given privileges by the hospital to practice in the facility. The word *credentialed* is very similar in meaning to the phrase *to be privileged* as it is used by hospitals, except that credentialing is broader and includes outpatient care. Credentialing is done in exactly the same manner for subcontracted and MBHO-employed clinicians.

Remember from Chapter Three that the credentialing department or division of an MCO or MBHO is housed within the quality improvement arm of the organization. Credentialing is the major means available to an MCO or MBHO to ensure that the providers in their network meet and maintain certain standards such as honestly representing their background and proving that they have training in specialty areas in which privileges are requested. While this may seem unnecessary to many, I can assure you from personal experience that it is most important. As a member of a credentialing committee, I have experienced firsthand the discovery of a provider who had never completed his degree, even though he proudly displayed a diploma over his desk. I was there for the revelation that a prominent local provider had successfully hid from other, less-scrupulous MBHOs his history of malpractice actions related to sexual misconduct with patients. Only a thorough credentialing process will detect items like this.

For the purposes of illustration, I will use parts of an actual credentialing application from two regional MBHOs—INTERACT of Columbus, Ohio, and Alliance Behavioral Care from the University of Cincinnati.

The process begins with your completion of a paper or electronic credentialing form known as the credentialing application. Applications are usually obtained from someone in the provider relations department or division. To date, attempts to standardize credentialing applications across MCOs and MBHOs have failed, despite the common recognition that almost every application asks for the same information. Therefore, for at least a few years to come, you will have to complete a unique application for each MBHO.

Once completed, the application is sent to the MBHO's credentialing department or division. Typically, it takes two to six months to become fully credentialed. As you will see in the coming discussion, the process is quite involved.

THE APPLICATION FORM AND CREDENTIALING PROCESS

The sample application form parts shown in Exhibits 7.1 through 7.4 are typical credentialing form material.

The Credentialing Application

The application (see Exhibit 7.1) begins by informing you of the various documents that you must submit with the application. You will note that the list contains several documents that apply only to physicians (for example, drug enforcement administration number and proof of board certification). Psychiatrists, as physicians, always have the most documentation to supply; applications often ask for their information without making it clear that nonphysicians do not need to supply some of these items. The category Continuing Medical Education does apply to everyone, and you should send certificates for the continuing education programs that you have completed in the specified time period.

The first two pages of the application gather basic practice and personal information. Of note in the Practice Information section are the beginning questions about specialty and subspecialty. If you are a clinical social worker who specializes in treating individuals with substance abuse problems, you would list your specialty as Clinical Social Work and your subspecialty as Substance Abuse (or Chemical Dependency).

Exhibit 7.1. Credentials Verification.

ALLIANCE CREDENTIALS VERIFICATION ORGANIZATION
Provider Application

Please attach copies of the following documents: (without copies application *will be returned to you):*

- ❏ Copy of *all* Current State Medical Licenses, Wallet Size Card
- ❏ Copy of ECFMG Certificate (if applicable)
- ❏ Copy of Medical School Diploma(s)
- ❏ Copy of Residency and Fellowship Certificates, if applicable
- ❏ Copy of DEA Certificate
- ❏ Copy of Professional Liability Certificate
- ❏ Copy of Proof of Board Certification, if applicable, or Letter of Board Eligibility/Qualified
- ❏ Copy of Continuing Medical Education, past 24 months
- ❏ Curriculum Vitae
- ❏ Current Photograph-1 *copy*

ESTIMATED START DATE _____

PERSONAL INFORMATION

_____
Last Name   First   M.I.   Maiden (if applicable)

_____
Home Address   City   State   Zip   Telephone

_____
SSN #   DOB   Birthplace   Citizenship

❏ Male ❏ Female Marital Status: ❏ M ❏ S Spouse's Name (optional): _____

US Citizen? ❏ Yes ❏ No If no, Indicate status of your Visa at the present time: _____

Foreign Languages Spoken, Fluently: _____

PRACTICE INFORMATION

Practice Specialty: _____ Subspecialty: _____

Degree: ____ Contact person regarding this form: _____ Phone #:_____

E-mail/Internet Address: _____

Primary Office Address:

_____
Group Practice Name   Tax ID#   Office Manager

_____
Street Address   City

_____
State   Zip   Phone #   Fax #   County

Exhibit 7.1. Credentials Verification, *continued.*

Secondary Office Address:

Group Practice Name	Tax ID#	Office Manager
Street Address		City
State Zip Phone #	Fax #	County

Third Office Address:

Group Practice Name	Tax ID#	Office Manager
Street Address		City
State Zip Phone #	Fax #	County

Academic Office:

Academic Office Address		Tax ID#
City State Zip Phone #		Fax #
Department/Division Room #/Building		M.L. #

Office Hours (Specific to each location, Mon.–Sat. and after hours): *Attachment is acceptable*

First Office: _____

Second Office: _____

Third Office: _____

Preferred Correspondence Address: Primary   Secondary   Third   Academic   Home

Age limit for patients you treat? _____ How many patients do you see per hour (ave)? _____

Do you accept new patients? ❑ Yes ❑ No

Do you accept: ❑ HMO pts.   ❑ Medicare   ❑ Medicaid

Do you have 24 hour coverage? ❑ Yes ❑ No   Night/Beeper, Answering Service #: _____

List physicians in your coverage group: _____

_____

BILLING INFORMATION

Primary Billing Name	Street Address
City State Zip County Phone #	Fax #
Secondary Billing Name, if applicable	Street Address
City State Zip	County

Patient Account Manager: _____ Office Manager: _____

For claims submission, does your office use HCFA 1500 forms? ❑ Yes ❑ No

Do you have the capability for electronic claims submission? ❑ Yes ❑ No

Of note are the questions about your on-call back-up coverage. Even though the form asks for names of physicians in your coverage group, if you have no physicians in your coverage group list those clinicians who cover for you. The MBHO is always interested in knowing if your back-up coverage system includes clinicians already in the MBHO's provider network.

Verification of Your Training and Background

Beginning with Educational Information, the application asks for data that must be confirmed by external sources. These items will be checked through primary source verification, that is, by contacting the original source to affirm that the information you have supplied is true and accurate. Each agency, graduate program, professional reference, internship, and hospital that you have listed will be contacted separately by mail. Waiting for all of these facilities to respond can often delay your application. In some cases you may be asked to contact the programs or supervisors by telephone to urge them to expedite their reply.

All applicable state licensing boards and federal agencies (especially the Federal Drug Enforcement Agency for psychiatrists) will be contacted to verify your license and standing. Your malpractice carrier will be contacted. Very important is the check with the National Practitioner Data Bank, which contains reports on malpractice claims. Until recently, malpractice insurers only reported malpractice suits filed and settlements made for physicians, but now psychotherapists and psychologists are also routinely reported to this national, government-sponsored center in Virginia.

Professional society memberships, publications, and continuing education are most often not primary source verified; the MBHO depends on the photocopied data you supply.

Your professional history and hospital affiliations are checked diligently. The Hospital Affiliations section only applies to psychiatrists, psychotherapists, and psychologists who are on the staff at one or more hospitals. If you are on a hospital staff, you must have gone through a similar credentialing process, although for hospitals it is often called privileging. The Appointment Category item usually has only three possible answers: Allied Healthcare Provider (for nonphysicians), Active (for physicians who rotate on-call for the hospital after hours), or Courtesy, which is for physicians who occasionally treat patients in the hospital.

Verification is very time consuming, especially if your universities, hospitals, or references are slow to respond. You now can see why credentialing often takes up to six months.

Credentialing is also expensive. Most state licensing boards and universities charge fees, as does the National Practitioner Data Bank, for reporting about you. Between staff time and fees charged, most MBHOs spend over $200 to credential a single clinician. Given the expense and time, many MBHOs use

Exhibit 7.2. Credentialing Application: Verified and Nonverified Information.

EDUCATIONAL INFORMATION
Attach copies of medical diploma(s) or ECFMG, residency, or other training certificates.
Undergraduate Education

College or University	Degree	Graduation Date
Street Address	City	State Zip

Medical, Psychology, Social Work, or Other

College or University	Degree	Graduation Date
Street Address	City	State Zip

If a foreign Medical Graduate, list ECFMG# _____ Date Issued _____

Post-Graduate Education-*Internship, residency, fellowship, preceptorship teaching appointments or equivalent positions.*

Internship

School or Hospital	Name of Supervisor
Specialty/Department	Inclusive Date (Month/Year)
Street Address	City State Zip

Residency

School or Hospital	Name of Supervisor
Specialty/Department	Inclusive Date (Month/Year)
Street Address	City State Zip

School or Hospital	Name of Supervisor
Specialty/Department	Inclusive Date (Month/Year)
Street Address	City State Zip

Fellowship

School or Hospital	Name of Supervisor
Specialty/Department	Inclusive Date (Month/Year)
Street Address	City State Zip

LICENSURE AND OTHER REGISTRATIONS
List all active licenses and licenses held in the last five years. A copy of all current licenses must accompany this application along with a copy of your DEA certificate.

OH Licensure #:_____ Type*:_____ Original Issue Date:_____ Exp. Date:_____

KY Licensure #:_____ Type*:_____ Original Issue Date:_____ Exp. Date:_____

Exhibit 7.2. Credentialing Application: Verified and Nonverified Information, *continued*

State:_____ License #:_____ Type*:_____ Original Issue Date:_____ Exp. Date:_____

State:_____ License #:_____ Type*:_____ Original Issue Date:_____ Exp. Date:_____

State:_____ License #:_____ Type*:_____ Original Issue Date:_____ Exp. Date:_____

State:_____ License #:_____ Type*:_____ Original Issue Date:_____ Exp. Date:_____

DEA #:_____ Issue Date:_____ Exp. Date:_____

Medicare Provider #:_____ Medicaid Provider #:_____ State:_____

Type (i.e. MD, Psychology, Social Work, Other)

SPECIALTY BOARD CERTIFICATION

Are you certified by a specialty board? ❑ Yes ❑ No If yes, specialty: _____

Date Certified: _____ Expiration Date: _____

Have you ever been recertified? ❑ Yes ❑ No   If yes, date: _____

Are you certified by more than one specialty board? ❑ Yes ❑ No If yes, specialty: _____

Date Certified: _____ Expiration Date: _____

Have you ever been recertified? ❑ Yes ❑ No   If yes, date: _____

Have you applied for examination by a board? ❑ Yes ❑ No If yes, which board: _____

Are you scheduled to sit for examination by any board? ❑ Yes ❑ No If yes, date: _____

If you have been accepted into any board process, give year when acceptance
will terminate: _____

PROFESSIONAL LIABILITY INSURANCE
Please attach copies of certificate(s).

Present Carrier Name and Complete Address			Policy #
Amt. of Coverage	Effective Date	Expiration Date	Any Restrictions
Past Carrier Name and Complete Address			Policy #
Amt. of Coverage	Effective Date	Expiration Date	Any Restrictions

PROFESSIONAL SOCIETY MEMBERSHIPS AND/OR FELLOWSHIPS
List all professional fellowships, memberships, and societies, past and present.
List additional information on a separate sheet.

Name of Organization			Inclusive Dates	
Complete Street Address		City	State	Zip
Name of Organization			Inclusive Dates	
Complete Street Address		City	State	Zip

Exhibit 7.2. Credentialing Application: Verified and Nonverified Information, *continued*

ACADEMIC APPOINTMENTS

List all teaching & university appointments held. List additional information on a separate sheet.

Institution Name and Complete Address	Position	Dates
Institution Name and Complete Address	Position	Dates
Institution Name and Complete Address	Position	Dates

PUBLICATIONS   *Please furnish a list of scientific papers or essays you have written.*

CONTINUING MEDICAL EDUCATION

Physicians must provide proof that they have met the continuing medical education requirement set by the recognition award of the AMA, AOA, or other continuing medical education required by state law, if greater. Please attach a list of continuing medical education activities you have participated in during the past 24 months.

NOTE: For physicians not licensed in Ohio, attach a certificate of AMA Physician's Recognition Award. A computer generated printout from a specialty society may be submitted.

PROFESSIONAL HISTORY

List in chronological order all places of practice since completing training.
*Complete addresses and dates are required. **Explain gaps larger than six months.***
*List additional information on a separate sheet. **A curriculum vitae is not acceptable unless all information requested here is provided.***

Name of Group/Organization	Complete Address	Date	Contact Person
Name of Group/Organization	Complete Address	Date	Contact Person
Name of Group/Organization	Complete Address	Date	Contact Person
Name of Group/Organization	Complete Address	Date	Contact Person

HOSPITAL AFFILIATIONS

Please provide all hospital affiliations, including past affiliations, employers and locum tenens. Do not include internships, residencies or fellowships. List additional information on a separate sheet.

Institution Name and Complete Address		Inclusive Dates
Appointment Category	Specialty	Any Restrictions?
Institution Name and Complete Address		Inclusive Dates
Appointment Category	Specialty	Any Restrictions?
Institution Name and Complete Address		Inclusive Dates
Appointment Category	Specialty	Any Restrictions?

Exhibit 7.2. Credentialing Application: Verified and Nonverified Information, *continued.*

Institution Name and Complete Address		Inclusive Dates
Appointment Category	Specialty	Any Restrictions?
Institution Name and Complete Address		Inclusive Dates
Appointment Category	Specialty	Any Restrictions?
Institution Name and Complete Address		Inclusive Dates
Appointment Category	Specialty	Any Restrictions?

Have you ever voluntarily relinquished your privileges? ❑ Yes ❑ No
If yes, provide an explanation.

PROFESSIONAL REFERENCES
*Please list the names of at least **three** references with whom you have worked closely and who have personal knowledge of your clinical abilities, ethical character, health status, and ability to work well with others. (Psychologists and Psychotherapists must have an evaluation within their specialty).* **One reference must be the individual with the most recent organizational responsibility for your performance, and, if you graduated within the last three years, one reference must be your Residency Program Director.** *If all three are not local, please provide two additional references who are local practitioners, if possible.*

Name Title	Phone #	Fax #
Complete Address		
Name Title	Phone #	Fax #
Complete Address		
Name Title	Phone #	Fax #
Complete Address		
Name Title	Phone #	Fax #
Complete Address		
Name Title	Phone #	Fax #
Complete Address		

Exhibit 7.2. Credentialing Application: Verified and Nonverified Information, *continued*.

PLEASE NOTE:

If there are any lapses of time between professional activities or post-graduate training, a full and detailed explanation must be provided on a separate sheet of paper which is signed personally by you and which is attached to this application form. You may attach a Curriculum Vitae or other listing, provided it clearly outlines activities in chronological order.

I understand that I have the burden of providing adequate information to demonstrate my qualifications. I understand that any misstatement or inaccuracies in or omissions from this application constitute grounds for denial of this application. If any material changes occur affecting my professional status, it is my obligation to notify the Credentials Verification Organization. All information submitted by me in this application is true and complete to the best of my knowledge.

_____   _____

Applicant Signature   Date

_____

Printed Name
_____

subcontracted credentialing vendor organizations (CVOs), which have their own NCQA accreditation process, to do all primary verification and compile your application data into a formal credentialing file.

The long list of yes or no questions at the end of the application is a feature of all credentialing applications. This is often called the Attestation Page; it is where the provider attests to various legal and health facts that might impair his or her ability to serve as a network provider. The list (see Exhibit 7.3—a sample from INTERACT of Columbus, Ohio) solicits information about any past or pending sanctions on your ability to practice. Note that it includes questions about revocation of your state license to practice, your medical history (especially as it relates to substance abuse), your legal history, and your malpractice history. Having to mark yes to one of these items does not necessarily mean that you will not be credentialed. But you will need to supply detailed data to the MBHO's credentialing committee concerning any item marked yes.

At the end of all credentialing applications you are asked to sign a release (see Exhibit 7.4) in which you authorize the MBHO to contact all of the sources necessary to confirm your training and background. As you can see, this is an extensive release that gives the MBHO the power to access data from almost any source involved in your professional history. Also included are statements in which you agree to follow the stated rules of the MBHO and you accept all responsibility for the proof of the statements you have made in the credentialing application. Only sign this if you have given a true accounting of your background (the facts will be checked) and if you are willing to have your professional history fully investigated.

Once verified, your application must be approved by two administrative bodies within the MBHO. First, your verified application will go to the credentials committee for approval. Then it must be sent on to the board of directors or trustees of the organization. Only after both groups have approved you as a provider may you begin routinely seeing patients referred by the MBHO. Waiting for these two administrative bodies alone to act on your application can add one to two months to the total time.

Temporary Credentialing

MBHOs usually have a means of giving temporary privileges after checking the basics of your application, for example by having a copy of your university diplomas, a copy of your state license, and the face sheet from your malpractice insurance. Even though this mechanism may be in place, it is used only in the most dire of situations in order to have a patient seen. The reason for the reluctance is that accrediting organizations such as NCQA and JCAHO frown on this practice; when conducting site visits to MBHOs, they reduce their scores if temporary privileges were granted frequently.

Exhibit 7.3. Credentialing Application Attestation.

PLEASE RESPOND TO EACH OF THE FOLLOWING QUESTIONS:

A. Has your medical or professional license ever been revoked, suspended, or limited? ❏ Yes ❏ No

B. Is there action pending? ❏ Yes ❏ No

C. Have you ever voluntarily surrendered your license? ❏ Yes ❏ No

D. (Physicians) Has your narcotics license every been revoked, suspended, or limited? ❏ Yes ❏ No

E. Are you now, or have you been, treated for alcohol or substance abuse? ❏ Yes ❏ No

F. Do you suffer from any physical or mental condition which impairs your ability to practice in your area of specialty, e.g., Medicine, Psychology, Social Work and/or Counseling? ❏ Yes ❏ No

G. Have you ever been denied hospital privileges? ❏ Yes ❏ No

H. If you were granted privileges, were they ever limited, suspended, or renewal denied? ❏ Yes ❏ No

I. Have you ever resigned from the staff of any hospital or medical organization because of problems regarding privileges or credentials? ❏ Yes ❏ No

J. Have you ever been denied professional liability insurance, or has your insurance ever been canceled or refused renewal? ❏ Yes ❏ No

K. Have you ever been the subject of disciplinary proceedings by a professional association or organization? (i.e., state licensing board; county, state, or national society; hospital medical or clinical staff)? ❏ Yes ❏ No

L. Have you ever been a defendant in any lawsuit? ❏ Yes ❏ No

M. Have you ever been convicted of or pleaded guilty to a crime? ❏ Yes ❏ No

If you have answered "yes" to any of the above questions, please explain on a separate sheet.

Source: © Interact Behavioral Healthcare Services, Inc., Columbus, OH. Used by permission.

Annual Updates

As stated in the credentialing application, you are required each year to send the MBHO a copy of your malpractice insurance and state license renewals. In addition, if there is any change in your status at any time—for example, the filing of an ethics complaint against you with a state licensing board—you are to notify the MBHO's credentialing department. Unless you have a history of such complaints, it is unlikely that such a report will result in your removal from the MBHO's network.

Exhibit 7.4. Alliance Credentials Verification Organization, Applicant's Consent and Release.

In applying for credentialing or re-credentialing as a provider of a Health Alliance affiliated organization, Hereinafter "Alliance"; including Alliance Partners, The Christ Hospital, The Jewish Hospital, St. Luke Hospitals, University Hospital, all officers, agents, employees, and other representatives of Alliance, all committees of Alliance, including the Credentials and Quality Improvement Committee, and all members of such committees and all providers of Alliance, any of whom have responsibility for obtaining or evaluating the applicants or provider's credentials or acting upon his/her applications to/or conduct in Alliance), I expressly accept these conditions during the processing and consideration of my application regardless of whether or not I am granted participating provider status; and, if I am granted participating provider status, throughout my tenure as a participating provider of the Alliance.

1. I hereby release the Alliance, its agents and employees, and any third parties (including but not limited to all individuals, government agencies, organizations, associations, partnerships, corporations, limited liability companies or other entities, whether hospitals, insurers, or health care facilities, from whom information has been requested by the Alliance or its agents or who have requested such information from the Alliance or its agents) from any and all civil liability which may arise from any acts or omissions, communications, reports, recommendations or disclosures about me or my practice of medicine including information gathering or data collection, investigations, reviews, monitoring or evaluation relating to my professional qualifications, credentials, clinical competence, clinical performance, character, mental or emotional stability, health status, physical condition, ethics, behavior or any other matter that might directly or indirectly effect my competence, patient care or the orderly operation of the Alliance or any hospital or health care facility associated with the Alliance, including otherwise privileged or confidential information.

2. I hereby authorize the Alliance, its agents, employees, and any managed care organization for whom the Alliance provides credentialing services to consult with physicians on the staffs of any hospital or health care facility or the administrators or persons charged with management responsibilities of such hospital or health care facility with which I am or have been associated with in the past and with others who may have information bearing on my professional qualifications, credentials, clinical competency, clinical performance, character, mental and emotional stability, health status, physical condition, ethics, behavior or any other matter that might directly or indirectly have an effect on competence, patient care or the orderly operation of the Alliance or any hospital or health care facility associated with the Alliance. I also authorize the Alliance, its agents and employees to inspect any and all records and/or documents that may be material to such questions. I hereby release all physicians, hospital, health care facilities, third parties, individuals, institutions, organizations and therein representatives, agents and employees from civil liability from their provision of oral or written information, records or documents to the Alliance, its agents or employees in response to any inquiry emanating from the Alliance, its agents or employees related to my professional qualification, credentials, clinical competence,

Exhibit 7.4. Alliance Credentials Verification Organization, Applicant's Consent and Release, *continued.*

clinical performance, character, mental and emotional stability, health status, physical condition, ethics, behavior or any other matter that might directly or indirectly have an effect on competence, patient care or the orderly operation of the Alliance or any hospital or health care facility associated with the Alliance, including otherwise confidential or privileged information.

3. I understand and agree that I have the burden of producing adequate information for proper evaluation of my professional qualifications, credentials, clinical competence, clinical performance, character, mental and emotional stability, health status, physical condition, ethics, behavior or any other matter that might directly or indirectly have an effect on competence, patient care or the orderly operation of the Alliance or any hospital or health care facility associated with the Alliance and for resolving any reasonable doubts about such professional qualifications and the aspects thereof stated herein.

4. I have received and read a copy of the by-laws or rules and regulations in force at the time of my application and I hereby agree to be bound by the terms thereof in all matters relating to consideration of my application and my potential practice as an Alliance provider.

5. I hereby accept full responsibility for knowing and abiding by the by-laws, rules and regulations of each Alliance associated hospital and/or health care facility within which I may practice or provide medical care.

6. I hereby represent that I have not requested participating provider status for any procedure for which I am not duly qualified, eligible or certified. Furthermore, I realize that certification by a recognized medical board does not necessarily qualify me to perform certain procedures. I recognize that additional documentation and/or proof of my qualifications to perform certain procedures may be required by the Alliance.

7. I acknowledge that any misstatements, inaccuracies or omissions from this application, whether made by myself or on my behalf by my representative, agent or employee, constitute cause for denial of participating provider status or cause for summary dismissal from participating provider status upon notice of said misstatement, inaccuracy or omission.

8. I am willing to appear for personal interviews with regard to my application.

9. I hereby represent that I have voluntarily entered into this Consent and Release Agreement; and, that I have no questions regarding the content herein.

_____   _____
Applicant Signature   Date

_____
Printed Name
_____
© Alliance Behavioral Care, Inc., Cincinnati, OH. Used by permission.

RECREDENTIALING

At intervals no longer than every two years, MBHOs will ask to recredential you. For providers with whom the MBHO believes there has not been a sound match, this is usually the time recredentialing is not requested, and notification of a contract termination is sent. Even though only a small percentage of providers are not recredentialed, you must be aware that all MBHOs profile their providers on such things as number of patient complaints, average length of treatment, and compliance with MBHO policies. These factors are strongly considered at the time of recredentialing.

The recredentialing process is basically a shortened form of the original process. You will be asked to update your original application material, and primary verification will again be conducted for items that could have changed, such as your malpractice history, your status with your state licensing board, and so on. Once all verification is done, your recredentialing application must again be approved by the MBHO's credentialing committee and the board of directors or trustees.

If you and the MBHO are timely in gathering and processing the updated information, there should be no lapse in your ability to continue work with patients covered by the MBHO.

As a newly contracted and credentialed clinician you will be very interested in the financial arrangements related to managed care—especially how you will be paid. The financial aspects of managed care are the focus of the next chapter.

CHAPTER EIGHT

The Finances of Managed Care

Discounted *fee-for-service, case rates, capitation,* and *copayments* are terms that have been mentioned in previous chapters. The purpose of this chapter is to explain these financial terms and their impact on your professional functioning. In contracting and credentialing yourself with an MBHO, you will certainly want to understand how you are going to be paid.

There are two components to the financial equation: (1) what the patient must pay at the time of service (the copayment, also called a copay) and (2) what the MBHO pays you (this is where things get complicated). We will begin with the simplest: what you collect from the patient.

WHAT THE PATIENT PAYS

One feature of managed care that clinicians and members generally like is the fixed, straightforward, patient copayment system used by most plans. Copayments are always collected by you or your reception staff either immediately preceding a treatment session (or hospital admission) or immediately following the service. That is not to imply that you will collect 100 percent of all copays due. There will always be patients who find the copays beyond their means or who try to manipulate the system so they won't have to pay. For example, a young college student adamantly insisted to a receptionist after his first session in my office that all copays for his care had already been electronically transferred from his college trust fund to the Mesa Mental Health checking account. This seemed especially odd, given that he had no idea how many treatment sessions he would need. The quick and assertive receptionist replied, "Well, until Western Union calls with a news flash, that'll be $20 now and every time you come." He claimed he had no money with him and left with a $20 balance that was never paid.

A collection rate on copays of 90 to 95 percent is about the best you can expect. Of course, MBHOs insist that you should be collecting 100 percent because each member's certificate (the insurance policy) firmly states that copayments must be paid at the time of service.

With nonpaying patients you must use your own judgment and ethics. For patients whose mental condition is not urgent or who do not present as high risk for harm to self or others, MBHOs will back you if you withhold care for lack of payment. A common clinician policy is to make no further appointments for individuals without urgent needs who have a financial balance equal to or greater than two or three copays.

VARIATIONS ACROSS PLANS

Exactly what copay is due from a particular patient varies with the patient's insurer, as well as with the particular plan in the insurer's product line under which the person is covered. In selling healthcare insurance, a single MCO typically has three to twenty different benefit structures available to employers and other groups. These subplans can have flashy names like the "Freedom Plan" or just plain boring names like the "JA Plan," for example. You must be careful because each of these plans may require members to copay a different amount. And the covered benefits may vary with the plan; coverage for substance abuse treatment varies, for example.

The rule regarding copays is, *The lower the monthly premium paid by the employer or insured, the steeper the copays due, especially for specialty care such as mental health.*

Each MBHO with whom you work should provide you with a listing or chart of copays due by plan, as they have been sold to employers or other groups. Most copay breakdowns are simple—something like the following:

- $20 for all outpatient services of forty-five to sixty minutes in length
- $12.50 for twenty- to forty-minute services
- $10 for ten- to twenty-minute services
- $12.50 for sixty- to ninety-minute group therapy services
- $200 per inpatient or outpatient hospital admission

A bit more complicated are insurers who sell plans having copays based on a percentage of a maximum allowable charge. For example, All-American HMO's Patriot Plan might have a copay for forty-five to sixty minutes of psychotherapy, which is 30 percent of All-American's "maximum allowable rate" ($80) for an hour of psychotherapy, resulting in a copayment due of $24. Percentage copayments in mental health range from 20 to 50 percent of a maximum allowable. Obviously, 50 percent copays are harder to collect.

A few plans have tiered rates. In this system a common arrangement is to have no copayment for the first few outpatient treatment sessions (often up through session five), a low copay for the next set of sessions (often sessions six to ten), and a much larger amount for the conclusion of the maximum benefit (often sessions eleven through twenty). Tiered copays require you and the patient to track what session number each treatment visit represents. Obviously, tiered copays are cumbersome for office staff and patients.

Most Medicaid managed care programs for poorer Americans have no copayments of any kind.

Recall from Chapter Six that your contract with the MBHO prohibits you from charging the patient more than the applicable copay when the service is among those the MBHO has authorized you to provide. In addition, almost no insurers (managed care or traditional indemnity) will allow you to bill the patient for treatment-related telephone calls or paperwork time, even if the paperwork is completing forms for the MBHO. Because treatment-related telephone calls are not a covered service, you can bill reasonable charges for these to the patient, such as for after-hours crisis calls. But billing the patient for paperwork time other than for clearly necessary clinical reports is not considered professionally appropriate by MBHOs or most clinicians.

In my own company, for example, a patient called our customer service line to complain that her psychologist (a network provider for us) had charged her $120 to complete the one-page continued treatment request form required to seek authorization for sessions beyond the initial six. You can be sure that this clinician received a stern reprimand from our provider relations staff.

WHAT THE MBHO PAYS

For clinical services provided, the largest portion of your income will come from insurer-paid dollars. There are three very different methods of paying you: discounted fee-for-service, case rates, and capitation. I will discuss these in order of complexity, beginning with the simplest: discounted fee-for-service.

Discounted Fee-for-Service

The components to this term are *discounted* and *fee-for-service* (FFS). *Discounted* refers to the fact that managed care payment rates are almost always lower than what practitioners charge when they can obtain the full fee that is usual and customary in their community. Hence, the reference to MBHO payments as being discounted.

See Table 8.1 for regional examples of this. You will note the considerable variation in community standards by region of the country for what clinicians charge as their full rate (often called the usual and customary rate) and what rates actually get paid by insurers. Even the remaining indemnity insurers now have fixed maximum rates that they will pay. Always remember that the amount actually paid to you, as a clinician, by an MBHO is the fee schedule amount *minus* the patient copayment due. Hence, if you are a psychotherapist with a managed care subcontract that says you will be reimbursed at the rate of $60 per fifty-minute session of authorized psychotherapy and the patient you just saw has a $20 copay, then the MBHO will pay you $40.

Fee-for-service means that you are paid separately for each service provided, for example, fifty minutes for an individual psychotherapy session (current practitioner terminology [CPT] code = 90806) or a twenty-minute medication management session (CPT code = 90862). The MBHO's utilization management department will have authorized, for each patient, which services (by CPT code) you can bill for, the maximum number of services that will be paid for, and the time frame during which the authorization is valid. It is very important to pay attention to the dates of authorization. Services provided outside these dates will certainly be rejected for payment by the MBHO's computerized claims system.

To receive payment for authorized services (or a denial of payment for nonauthorized services), a claim must be submitted to the MBHO's claims department. All government insurers insist that claims be submitted using the HCFA 1500 form, and almost every private insurer has adopted this same form. A copy of the form may be downloaded free of charge from the Health Care Finance Authority's web site at www.hcfa.gov. Many medical office supply houses also have them in preprinted form. Rapidly, however, insurers are refusing to process paper HCFA 1500s; rather, they insist upon their submission through electronic data interchange (EDI) from your computer to their computer via modem. Medicare now only accepts EDI claims.

Case Rates

Payment via a case rate system means that you receive one lump sum for the treatment of each patient. For example, an MBHO may determine that the average outpatient psychotherapy patient uses six sessions (possibly excluding a few diagnostic groups such as patients with psychoses, eating disorders, or primary personality disorders). Based on this analysis they might stop authorizing care via a discounted FFS basis and turn to a case rate system. Under the case rate system you are paid one lump sum for the psychotherapeutic treatment of patients to whom the case rate system applies (usually groups of diagnoses). In

Table 8.1. Fees: Usual and Customary Versus Managed Care (HMO) by Type of Provider and Region.

Service	East Coast		Mid-West		West	
	U & C	HMO	U & C	HMO	U & C	HMO
Psychiatrists						
Individual Psychotherapy 45–60 min.	$130–$160	$70–$100	$110–$150	$60–$85	$125–$150	$70–$100
Group Therapy 60–90 min.	$50–$80	$30–$50	$50–$70	$25–$40	$35–$45	Not Used
Medical Evaluation 45–60 min.	$150–$200	$90–$120	$150–$200	$85–$110	$130–180	$80–$110
Medical Check 15–20 min.	$60–$80	$40–$65	$50–$80	$40–$60	$40–$70	$30–$55
Psychologists						
Individual Psychotherapy 45–60 min.	$110–$140	$70–$100	$100–$130	$65–$90	$95–$130	$55–$90
Group Therapy 60–90 min.	$40–$60	$25–$40	$40–$60	$25–$40	$35–$50	$25–$40
Psychological Testing per Hour	$120–$160	$90–$120	$100–$150	$80–$110	$100–$150	$75–$100
Psychotherapists						
Individual Psychotherapy 45–60 min.	$90–$120	$65–$90	$55–$80	$40–$70	$60–$85	$45–$65
Group Therapy 60–90 min.	$35–$65	$30–$40	$30–$50	$25–$35	$30–$60	$25–$35

this scenario, the patient and you decide together how much care is needed; your insurance reimbursement is fixed, but the length of treatment is not.

For example, a patient needing psychotherapy for a depressive disorder with moderate alcohol abuse could be referred to you, as a psychologist, with a lump sum payment of $420. The $420 figure comes from the assumed average of seven sessions multiplied by what the MBHO pays psychologists for an hour of psychotherapy (in this example, $75 with a $15 copay = $60). In a typical case rate system you are not financially rewarded or discouraged from referring this patient to a psychiatrist for medication. Note that the case rate amount is based on the primary diagnosis (a depressive disorder) and not on the secondary disorder (alcohol abuse). Most case rate systems assume that most patients will have some secondary diagnosis, so there is no extra payment for such. The case rate is often determined by what primary condition you assess the patient to have following the first treatment or evaluation session (usually billed as a diagnostic evaluation service; CPT code = 90801). Commonly, all mood and anxiety disorders have the same case rate payment, whereas diagnoses such as a substance dependence or an eating disorder have a different, and usually higher, case rate payment. Much as with discounted FFS payments, case rates vary depending on the licensure level of the clinician and the region of the country.

Regardless of whether the patient attends one or thirty sessions, the payment from the insurer remains the same. This places you, as a provider, at financial risk for the amount of care given. It is an example of how more and more financial risk is now being moved from insurers to providers.

An important question is, What is the copayment structure under the case rate system? Does the patient pay a copay for every session or just up through the assumed average on which the case rate is based? Complex state insurance regulations often dictate the answer. The complexities and variations across states in how copayments can be set up with case rates have helped slow the spread of case rates as a mechanism for outpatient care.

Case rates, however, are common for inpatient care, where copayment structures are much simpler; often, no copay is required or is a set amount not involving the length of the hospital stay.

For many years the federal government has been paying hospital room and procedure charges through Medicare on a case rate system. Medicare case rates are used for both general medical and specialty care, including psychiatry. The rates are based on the patient's primary diagnosis, using a system called Diagnostic Related Groups (DRGs). Each diagnosis per patient that is the focus of care results in a fixed sum being paid to the hospital.

Professional fees to clinicians under Medicare are increasingly being paid through a similar system called the Resource Value Based Scale (RVBS), where each procedure or set of procedures is assigned a set payment. For psychiatric cases, for example, the doctor treating an inpatient diagnosed with Major Depression would receive a fixed amount that is designated as the total payment for a typical hospitalized patient having major depression. The fee for the doctor does not change whether the patient stays in the hospital one day or twenty days.

Although case rates are easy from the financial accounting perspective and relieve you of the case-by-case hassle of requesting from the MBHO more sessions or facility days, there are several potential problems. First, there is the reversal of incentives from FFS payment mechanisms. Under an FFS system the clinician is motivated by the financial arrangement to provide more care, and possibly to overtreat, whereas a case rate system financially rewards lesser care, and possibly undertreatment. This major issue is discussed more fully in Chapter Eleven.

Three logistical problems with case rates are (1) fairness of the case rate system, (2) what services are covered, and (3) utilization reporting to the MBHO. Fairness is of the most concern to clinicians. The question here is, If the case rate is based on some historical (or hypothesized) utilization average across a large population of MBHO patients, do your patients on the average reflect that population? If yes, there is fairness in the payment system. If no, you could be grossly under or overpaid in treating a large number of case-rated patients. In most cases it will be difficult for you to establish, for any MBHO, that patients referred to you absolutely do not reflect the population used to develop the case rate. However, there is hope on the horizon; some MBHOs are beginning to install pretreatment assessment procedures to monitor the impairment levels of patients such that payment can be adjusted based on the severity of the presenting illness. Changing utilization authorizations or payment amounts based on the degree of patient impairment is called risk adjustment.

A common risk adjustment mechanism is to base payment on the degree of impairment the patient reports at the time of the first appointment. For example, if a patient is administered a diagnostic screening instrument immediately prior to the first appointment and scores above certain cut-off values on the assessment (for example, reports a high degree of impairment in daily occupational functioning or presence of suicidal ideation), then your reimbursement for this patient's care might be adjusted upward to compensate for being a more complex patient.

Another logistical issue is what services over what time span are covered under the case rate. If you are a psychologist conducting psychotherapy and you believe that psychological testing is needed, is administering psychological tests a part of the case rate or a separate MBHO authorization and payment? And at what point does treatment end, such that reengaging in care results in a new payment authorization? In response to this latter point, many MBHOs set returning to care after a four- or six-month period without care from you as beginning a new treatment episode, which begins a new authorization and payment cycle. My advice here is twofold:

1. Get the details clear before accepting a case rate payment method.

2. If you specialize in the treatment of especially difficult cases, check very carefully into the payment schedule. A case rate arrangement may be a financial mistake for you.

If you request from the MBHO an individualized case rate for your patients, be prepared with hard data and a written proposal to show why most patients will need the amount of treatment you suggest as necessary.

The last item regarding case rates—utilization reporting—is a sore point for clinicians. In order for the MBHO to track the appropriateness and financial performance of the case rate system, you will usually be required to submit HCFA 1500 forms for all services, just as though you were being paid by FFS. The hassle and cost of providing these data when they have no effect on payment is aggravating. The alternative at this point rests with MBHOs doing more on-site inspection of clinical records. As they review charts for quality reasons, they can also measure utilization (average number of sessions per case, for example) from a sampling of your patient records rather than from submitted HCFA 1500 forms. The question then becomes how comfortable are you with insurance company employees in your office reading your clinical records? Most clinicians are going to say, "not comfortable at all."

Capitation

The third type of payment mechanism is capitation. Although capitation exposes you, as a clinician, to the most financial risk, it also allows you the greatest autonomy in deciding how clinical care will be delivered.

Financially, capitation is a method by which you are paid a fixed amount per health plan member, usually each month, to provide whatever care each member requires that is within the plan's benefit structure. The fixed, monthly payment amount is not based on who needs treatment but on the entire membership of the MBHO within a defined geographical region, most often defined by zip codes, counties, or even whole states. To see a full sample capitation contract between an MCO and a small MBHO, refer to Appendix C.

The specifics of bidding, contracting, and implementing capitation arrangements are complex and well beyond the scope of this text. If you want detailed capitation contracting information, you should consult *The Complete Capitation Handbook* (Zieman, 1995), *The Psychiatrist's Guide to Capitation and Risk-Based Contracting* (American Psychiatric Association, 1997), and *The Comprehensive Managed Care Tool Kit* (Daniels, Zieman, and Dickman, 1996). In this section, I will discuss the basics of capitation contracting.

The first capitation arrangement began in 1910 when Drs. Yokum and Curran made an agreement with logging employers in Tacoma, Washington (see Chapter Two). The contract had all of the basics that are contained in contracts used today except strict provisions to meet national quality standards. The basic provisions of capitation are that the capitated behavioral group is contracted to do the following:

1. *Provide all medically necessary care to the population of covered members within the geographic region defined in the contract.* The population may be members of a commercial health plan, recipients of a government program, or employees of a large employer and their dependents.

2. *Accept a fixed per member per month (PMPM) amount and any health-plan-mandated copayments by members accessing treatment as full monthly payment for all care needs of the entire defined population.* Note that this provision clearly places the capitated entity at financial risk. Whether the monthly costs of providing care to the population exceed or remain below the revenues generated by the PMPM and copayments, the capitated group receives the same monthly PMPM. Some contracts, however, do include *risk bands* that define points at which, if the cost of care provision is very low, the PMPM paid is less and, if costs rise to a fixed point well above the amount assumed in negotiating the contract, the PMPM is increased.

3. *Provide administrative and management services to implement the necessary care to members.* These services are specified in the contract. Commonly included are

- A centralized patient intake system.

- Utilization management (UM) functions, including the authorization and denial of services to providers following the insurance benefit package(s) applicable to members of the defined population.

- Formation of the provider network necessary to serve the population. Often, this includes negotiating discounted rates and contracts with emergency rooms, psychiatric inpatient units, and of the outpatient clinicians. Credentialing providers for the network is also frequently included.

- Access by members to a customer service department for complaints and questions.

- A system for adjudicating and paying claims submitted by network providers for services rendered to members of the population.

- Quality improvement (QI) activities, including the development of behavioral treatment pathways, meeting NCQA behavioral standards, and implementing outcomes tracking programs.

The capitated behavioral group or delivery system is usually allowed to make a modest profit (usually 3 to 7 percent) from the contract. However, the highly competitive nature of contract bidding, in addition to the extreme downward pressure on healthcare costs today, have resulted in many capitation arrangements under which capitating behavioral groups have lost money. You must be careful and skillful when negotiating capitation contracts. Given that over 90 percent of my own company's revenues are from capitation contracts, I can assure you that capitation contracting is not for the anxious or for those with weak financial backgrounds.

Capitation is also not appropriate for solo practitioners or even small group practices. Capitated agreements and the execution of the care delivery system required can only be mastered by large, business-integrated group practices or integrated delivery systems (IDS). Integrated delivery systems are often the combined efforts of a hospital and its associated clinicians (called a physician-hospital organization [PHO]) or an incorporated clinical entity such as an independent practice association (IPA) in which clinicians have formally allied to serve as a single-source provider group. Whether it is a group practice or an IDS, once an organization contracts to care for more than fifty to one hundred thousand insured lives, it becomes a mini-MBHO. Examples of group practices and IDS groups that have become small MBHOs are profiled in Chapter Fourteen.

Obtaining and maintaining capitation contracts generally requires the following steps:

1. Forming a behavioral business entity capable of providing the treatment needs of the populations available for contracting: commercial MCOs, governmental groups (especially Medicaid and Medicare), or large, self-insuring employers.

2. Developing the basic management structures needed by capitation contracts, such as a sophisticated healthcare computer system, written utilization management policies and procedures, and a full quality improvement program.

3. Marketing to MCOs, governmental sources, and large employers.

4. Responding to requests for proposals (RFPs) from MCOs, government programs, or large employers desiring to capitate their insured populations. Responding to RFPs requires writing a detailed written proposal describing how you can and will meet the contractual requirements. Proposals may run from one hundred pages up to the massive seven-volume medical and behavioral proposal that I helped write for a state Medicaid contract. Each proposal must include your proposed PMPM rates.

5. If selected as the winning proposal, negotiating the PMPM amount along with the treatment or administrative details.

6. Accepting a contract after the negotiation process or walking away if the terms cannot be negotiated to achieve your necessary profitability or contingency margin and other needs.

7. Preparing for the start of the contract period. Most important are transition issues. How will members currently in treatment make the transition to providers in your network who may be different from their existing clinicians?

8. Implementing the contract for its specified period, usually from two to three years for initial contracts, sometimes for up to five years for subsequent contract extensions.

9. Communicating with the contractor during the contract period to work out daily issues.

With regard to PMPM rates, the amounts vary greatly depending on the treatment services included. For example, are both inpatient and outpatient mental health included? Are substance abuse services included? The amounts also vary with the management services purchased (intake, UM, QI). If the full range of the items listed is included, the agreement is often referred to as full capitation. Also affecting price are the size of the copayments due from patients, the care utilization patterns of the contracted population, the size of the contract population, and the region of the country to which the contract applies. Rates in the western United States are almost universally far below the rates east of the Mississippi River. This seems to be primarily due to the fact that mental health professionals have traditionally been paid at higher rates in the East, and many areas still have a large number of psychotherapy services being provided by psychiatrists. In the West, particularly along the Pacific Coast and around Minneapolis (both areas of very early HMO dominance), psychotherapy is not frequently done by psychiatrists. Given their higher salaries, many MBHOs restrict psychiatrists to medication evaluation and management services only.

Regarding contracted population size, contracts for populations below ten to fifteen thousand members are generally to be avoided. Small contracts present increased financial risk. The population may not represent a normal curve in their mental health utilization, so a handful of very ill individuals needing services could make the contract a financial nightmare. Small contracts must be priced at a higher rate and are best accepted by groups already managing large capitation contracts.

Turning to the clinical implications of capitation financing, I stated at the beginning of this discussion that capitation increases clinical autonomy. This refers to the fact that capitation contracts generally include both the provision of clinical care and utilization management. For the group implementing the contract there is a distinct incentive to redesign the delivery of treatment services in a creative and cost-efficient manner. Prevention, special clinical programs, and crisis services are also highly rewarded in capitated systems. Clinicians involved in implementing capitation contracts often report that they specifically enjoy the autonomy to develop new clinical delivery methods.

Because capitation contracting for behavioral services is rapidly increasing across the country, clinicians must be well prepared to consider capitation possibilities now and in the future. Large clinical groups must certainly look toward capitation as a means of maintaining or increasing their market share.

Having discussed the financial variations within managed behavioral healthcare, it is now time to turn our attention fully to a topic that has been frequently mentioned throughout the text—quality improvement. As we have seen, QI is an area of major emphasis today and will only become more dominant in future years.

CHAPTER NINE

The Emphasis upon Quality Improvement

"Give us your report card," is the demand. Healthcare is a targeted industry; it is being challenged to demonstrate its outcomes, costs, efficiency, and ability to change. Newspapers in states and metropolitan areas are publishing the mortality rates of their hospitals. Licensing boards are providing open access to providers' files containing information about who has malpractice claims and how many there are. Health plans scramble to be certified by a quality accrediting body so that their billboards and other marketing materials can proclaim that the plan has received a seal of approval. Nearly every clinic or hospital in the country has a patient satisfaction survey. Practitioners from the most densely populated cities to the most rural towns are having their patient charts reviewed by insurance payers. The magazine *Consumer Reports* frequently reports on healthcare quality.

Data are being demanded. The public, especially employers, want to know what they are buying with their healthcare dollars—dollars that make up over 14 percent of the U.S. gross national product. Gone are the days when practitioners can point to their diplomas or smiling patients leaving their doors and say, "Of course, I provide the finest quality of care." The call is for well-defined, publicly available processes and data to support claims of quality care. Society now demands a report card that is meaningful to consumers.

What began in manufacturing during the 1960s and continued through the 1980s with studies and revolutionary ideas by quality gurus such as Deming,

Juran, and Crosby (Deming, 1986; Juran, 1988; Crosby, 1983) has spread to medicine and all the healing arts. Developing and selling the tools to measure and report quality data has become a business in its own right. Variability in providers' practices and outcomes is under heavy scrutiny. Specific treatment protocols telling practitioners how to diagnose and treat common conditions now proliferate. Clinicians scream that the *art* of their profession has been snatched away.

As noted in Chapter One, the measurement and assurance of quality is the next frontier for managed care. Although it is taking place under a microscope, so to speak, the implementation of quality processes is an opportunity for managed care to shine in a way that indemnity insurance never could. With no direct connection between payer and clinician, the indemnity arrangement simply provided no method for either the payer or the consumer to systematically monitor the quality of the care received.

Managed care, however, includes signed contracts between employers and government payers with MCOs and MCHOs—contracts that clearly spell out quality parameters that must be met. And providers sign contracts with MCOs and MBHOs (see Chapter Seven) that mandate provider participation in the collection of data for quality improvement processes. Beyond contractual mandates, consumers, clinicians, employers, and MCOs are learning the power of ongoing data to provide accountability and a path to improved processes and programs. Although healthcare is only in its infancy with regard to measuring and improving its processes, this is a start. This beginning can move healthcare from a murky profession in the public's eyes to a data-driven profession that shows openly what it does, how it does it, and what the costs are.

Even clinicians are beginning to accept their role in being data providers and centers of change based on the data. For example, I was recently in Roswell, New Mexico, to meet with some of the providers for Mesa Mental Health. While there, I had lunch with a psychiatrist who is now treating the grandchildren of some of his first patients. When I arrived early to complete the office site visit that is required of all network providers for Mesa, the good doctor simply remarked, "You're the third managed care outfit to come and inspect us." He patiently completed the morning's paperwork while I went around with his office manager, checklist in hand, noting that, yes, he had sample medications well secured; yes, his patient charts were kept in order and were legible; yes, he had sound policies to protect patient confidentiality; and yes, his office was handicapped-accessible. In his pick-up truck on the way to grab a burrito, he told me he looked forward to the report he would get in six to twelve months showing his follow-up medical records chart review and a list of any complaints that had come in about him.

Before the sopaipillas arrived to polish off the meal, though, he went on the offensive. Why did Mesa insist on only credentialing a psychiatrist to see children if the psychiatrist had completed a child fellowship? He objected. He'd been treating children for forty years, and when he completed training there were no child fellowships. I took his ideas under advisement. After a study into the matter by our credentialing committee, we changed our policy. Child privileges would be offered if we could have references from colleagues (such as pediatricians) who were aware of his work with children. I think this made the good doctor happy, and it facilitated access for child patients in Roswell to a fine psychiatrist. This policy change, however, came under careful scrutiny for how it affected Mesa's quality standards and ultimately our report card.

Quality measurement and improvement processes are here, even if only in an early, evolutionary form. But what is measured, reported, and used in quality improvement, quality management, and quality assurance (they are synonymous terms) programs? We begin with a discussion of an MBHO's quality plan and its processes followed by discussions on quality standards and quality accreditation.

THE QUALITY PLAN AND THE QUALITY PROCESS

Every MBHO has a quality department with dedicated staff and an extensive document that summarizes the organization's quality activities and goals. This blueprint for the organization is typically revised annually and is supplemented by an annual evaluation of the organization's progress in quality, as well as recommendations for the coming year.

The organization will also have a quality committee that oversees all quality activities. The quality committee typically reports directly to the president or CEO of the company and has approval of major items such as the annual quality plan with the board of directors or trustees.

The main components of the quality plan can be seen in Figure 9.1. In addition to the programs shown on the umbrella, prevention programs are also frequently included. We will examine each separately.

Quality Improvement Teams

In order to develop and implement the major projects of the quality plan, teams of appropriate individuals are assembled to address each project. Known as QI teams, these groups design, measure, and implement the larger or more complex quality programs. QI teams are usually chartered for specific projects to be completed within a specified time period. The more routine or smaller projects are usually handled by one or more staff members in the quality department.

Common QI team projects are the implementation of a clinical outcomes tracking mechanism (discussed later in this section) or the designing of a new set of processes to pay claims to providers faster and more accurately.

Quality Management Program

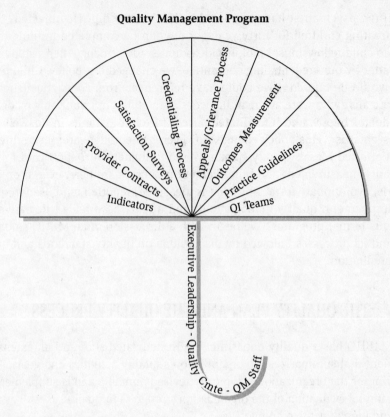

Figure 9.1. Quality Management Program.

Source: Carol Furgal for Mesa Mental Health, Albuquerque, NM. Copyright © 1997, Used by permission.

Indicators

An *indicator* is a data point that is collected over a period of time to measure a process or outcome. Every MBHO has dozens of indicators. The indicators are usually grouped by the department within the MBHO to which they apply and are collected. They may also be classified, as in Tables 9.1 and 9.2, by the service area to which they apply, for example access to care, satisfaction with care, or productivity of the MBHO's operations. The data related to each indicator are collected and reported to the quality committee on a regular basis such as quarterly, biannually, or annually. Based on the data, changes in the MBHO's functioning may be recommended, or a QI team may be chartered to investigate and modify current practices.

In the sample indicator summaries shown in Tables 9.1 and 9.2, the "measurement domain" refers to the broad type of indicator each represents (access to service for members, satisfaction with care, quality of care, and so forth),

Table 9.1. Customer Service Indicators.

Measurement Domain*	Indicator	Numerator	Denominator	MMH Standard	Display Method
1. Access-Care	Answered Phone Time	Total time all callers waited	Total # of calls	25 seconds (NCQA 30 sec)	Bar graph; Run graph Quarterly
2. Access-Care	Phone Abandonment	Number callers abandoning	Total # of calls	≤ 5 percent (NCQA ≤ 5 percent)	Bar graph; Run graph Quarterly
3. Access-Service	Issues—calls requiring research and response	Total issues by Types	Total # of calls by type	Not Applicable (No NCQA Std.)	Combination Bar and Run graph quarterly
4. Access-Service	Resolutions within 48 hours to issues identified in indicator 3	percent of total issues	Total # of calls	Resolution within 48 hrs (No NCQA Std.)	Indicator 3, 4 combined one graph
5. Quality-Service	Service observation surveys (a) observed unsatisfactory	# observed unsatisfactory	Total observed	≤ 95 percent Satisfactory ≤ 95 percent	Bar graph; Run chart quarterly
	(b) percent rated by pt. as unsatisfactory	# reported by pts as unsatisfactory	returned	Satisfactory (No NCQA Std.)	

*Measurement Domains: Access (care or service), Satisfaction, Quality (care or service), Cost, Productivity

Table 9.2. Clinical Service Indicators.

Measurement Domain	Indicator	Numerator	Denominator	MMH Standard	Display Method
Satisfaction	Patient Satisfaction w/Care (items 6, 10, & 15 on Sat Survey)	# of responses rating satisfied or higher for each question	Total number of patients responding to each question	90% rate as satisfied or higher	Histogram, quarterly with data displayed by year compared with national OMP database
Quality of Care	Patient Change Post-treatment (Basis-32 & SF-36)	BASIS-32 & HSQ overall scores; # of satisfied or higher on questions 14 & 20 on Sat Survey	Total number of patients responding to BASIS-32, HSQ, & questions 14 & 20 on Sat Survey	95% score better 3 months after beginning care; 90% rate as satisfied or higher	Histogram, quarterly with data displayed by year compared with national OMP database
Quality of Care	Hospital Readmission Rate	# of patients readmitted within 90 days	Total number of inpatient admits	5% or less inpatients readmitted within 90 days	Annually as a percentage
Quality of Care	Outpatient F/U post-inpatient	# of patients d/c'd with out-patient appt w/in 10 bus. days	Total number of inpatients discharged	95% have appointment within 10 business days	Annually as a percentage
Quality of Care	Rate of Reported Suicide	Completed injury reports from clinicians	Total number of patients seen	Rate/1000 ≤ national OMP database	Annually as a percentage
Quality of Care	Chart Completeness	# charts w/initial eval. & progress note for all tx services	Total number of charts reviewed	95% of charts fully complete	Histogram, quarterly trend data from previous years

Measurement Domain	Indicator	Numerator	Denominator	MMH Standard	Display Method
Satisfaction	Patient Satisfaction w/ Timeliness of Outpt. Appt.	# of satisfied or higher responses	Total number of Satisfaction Surveys returned	90% satisfied or higher	Histogram, quarterly compared with national OMP database
Quality of Care	Practice Guideline Follow Through ADHD	# of cases guideline used	# of new patients entering care in Albuquerque	No standard	Histogram of total guidelines use & % of treatment population
	Substance Abuse	# of cases guideline used	# of new patients entering care in Albuquerque	No standard	Histogram of total guidelines use & % of treatment population
	Depression	# of cases guideline used	# of new patients entering care in PCP offices using guidelines	No standard	Histogram of total guidelines use & % of treatment population

whereas the reporting mode is specified by the two columns labeled "numerator" and "denominator." In each case the data are used to calculate a percentage meeting the standard set for the indicator. "Display method" refers to how the data will be shown to the quality committee or the MCO.

Indicators tend to be of two broad types: (1) those used internally by the MBHO to monitor its own functioning and (2) those that are reported to the full MCO and are likely to be used in compiling a consumer-meaningful report card for public distribution.

Of special note here is the resource intensity of a full quality program. In any MBHO a significant portion of the annual budget is devoted to quality activities. To monitor each of the dozens of indicators tracked and to respond to the data with QI teams and modified procedures is a weighty task. For example, in Table 9.1, indicator 5 uses observations and surveys. MBHO staff listen in on a fixed number of customer service department calls per month and rate the customer service staff member's performance in handling the call; a written survey about the call is then sent to the caller. The resources used for this one indicator are extensive.

Several quality indicators involve practitioner assistance in data collection or, at least, improvement activities based on the data collected. The most common ones to directly involve clinicians are adverse incidents (suicides and homicides), patient satisfaction with care, clinical outcomes (see the discussion later in this chapter), use of clinical guidelines, and data collection surrounding prevention programs.

Practice Guidelines

Guidelines are suggested procedures and decisions to diagnose or treat a particular disorder or common patient presentation. Three synonymous terms— *protocols, algorithms,* and *pathways*—refer more specifically to step-by-step procedures for diagnosing and treating patients, and often to data to be collected to measure the use of effectiveness of the prescribed procedures.

Most MCOs and healthcare clinics are adopting practice guidelines and frequently practice protocols for how clinicians are to handle common or high-risk cases. The purposes behind guidelines are twofold: (1) to reduce the variability in practice patterns among clinicians, thereby assuring patients of standardized, high-quality care, and (2) to allow clinicians to focus less energy on the treatment of basic conditions while directing their science and art to the more difficult and challenging cases. By having standardized protocols, MBHOs can also allow individuals with less training to perform certain duties. For example, nurse practitioners can manage antidepressant medications in follow-up visits, or nonclinicians can perform routine, new-patient telephone triages at the initial intake stage. Although many clinicians object to algorithms permitting others to do the work once reserved for licensed clinicians, others are relieved not to be performing routine duties. I think of my neuropsychologist friend who told me about the protocols used to train his psychometric technician, and his sigh of relief as he said, "I don't ever want to give another Wechsler [Intelligence Scale] myself."

Guidelines and protocols are developed by a team of seasoned clinicians who study the available literature and best practices. A guideline is usually a description of best practices and when to consider using them. A protocol or algorithm is typically much more specific and often comes with a flow chart (see Figure 9.2). Protocols may be very focused or quite broad. Figure 9.2, for example, shows only one part of a larger pathway designed for both mental health and primary care by a QI team that included psychologists, psychiatrists, family physicians, quality specialists, and the medical director of a health plan. The algorithm to follow assumes that a diagnosis of simple major depression has been made and that the patient is not one who triggers an immediate referral to the mental health department.

Guidelines and protocols may be developed by a group practice or MBHO or may be purchased from professional associations and private companies. As a general rule, those available from associations and private firms are more likely to be broad guidelines than specific algorithms.

Provider Contracts

This topic was discussed in Chapter Six, where it was pointed out that subcontracts with providers now include a specific clause that binds clinicians to assisting in the collection of quality data. What should also be there is a clause binding the MBHO to feed back the data in a usable form to network providers. Progressive MBHOs do this and generally provide data that are very helpful to clinical providers.

Outcomes Measurement

Until recently, it was not at all common for clinicians to measure clinical indices with their patients before, during, and after treatment. This was left to formal research studies done by academicians and graduate students. But now, clinical outcomes tracking is becoming commonplace in staff model clinics and will certainly become routine in the future for small and large group practices, if not for solo practitioners. Outcomes measurement, however, is not the rigorous empirical science of academic studies and is not intended to replace strict scientific research. Outcomes programs are designed to provide ongoing (over years) clinical data that are used as a quality feedback mechanism to constantly improve clinical care.

Exhibit 9.1 shows an example of a full-feature outcomes protocol that has been used across the country since 1995. Note that this program measures behavioral symptoms, daily functioning for both activities of daily living and

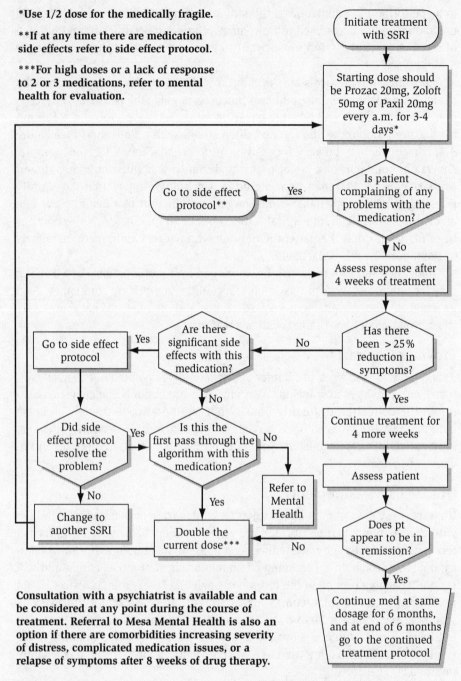

*Use 1/2 dose for the medically fragile.

**If at any time there are medication side effects refer to side effect protocol.

***For high doses or a lack of response to 2 or 3 medications, refer to mental health for evaluation.

Initiate treatment with SSRI

Starting dose should be Prozac 20mg, Zoloft 50mg or Paxil 20mg every a.m. for 3-4 days*

Is patient complaining of any problems with the medication?

Yes → Go to side effect protocol**

No

Assess response after 4 weeks of treatment

Has there been >25% reduction in symptoms?

No → Are there significant side effects with this medication?

Yes → Go to side effect protocol

Did side effect protocol resolve the problem?

Yes → Is this the first pass through the algorithm with this medication?

No → Refer to Mental Health

No → Change to another SSRI

Yes → Double the current dose***

No → Double the current dose***

Yes → Continue treatment for 4 more weeks

Assess patient

Does pt appear to be in remission?

Yes → Continue med at same dosage for 6 months, and at end of 6 months go to the continued treatment protocol

Consultation with a psychiatrist is available and can be considered at any point during the course of treatment. Referral to Mesa Mental Health is also an option if there are comorbidities increasing severity of distress, complicated medication issues, or a relapse of symptoms after 8 weeks of drug therapy.

Figure 9.2. Treatment of Major Depression or Major Depression with Dysthymia (Not for Dysthymia Alone) (Ages 18–65).

Copyright © 1996 by Mesa Mental Health. Used by permission.

physical health, general physical health, and patient satisfaction. To complement these measures a patient chart audit is completed to gather treatment information such as diagnoses, number and type of treatments used, and any adverse events (suicide or homicide) that might have occurred.

Of special importance in any outcomes project is the use of reliable and valid instruments that are used by others so that the outcomes data are comparable with others. Data from multiple sites are also highly desirable; they make it possible to compare groups. Reporting that your patients improved X amount over six months is not nearly as meaningful as knowing that your patients improved X compared to themselves and Y compared to similar patient populations across the country.

To be an effective QI project, results from outcomes measures must be used to improve processes and treatment. This means doing timely analyses of the data and supplying the data to individuals and groups who can and will use it. As an example of using the data for care improvement, data from the program shown in Figure 9.2 have been used to develop a profile of outpatients who are at high risk for deterioration resulting in hospitalization. Based on this knowledge, my group began a more intensive initial evaluation and therapy program for patients who match this profile.

As was noted in the discussion of indicators, an active quality assurance program requires significant resources. Nowhere is this more true than in an ongoing outcomes measurement program.

The tools for outcomes measurement and reporting have become big business. Several for-profit and nonprofit groups sell sound outcomes programs. Also, many of the larger MBHOs and PHOs have developed their own. Most of those developed by MBHOs and PHOs for their own use remain proprietary and unavailable to the broader mental health community. This is partly because they believe that their own outcomes system gives them a marketing edge that would be lost if others used their methodology. Some people, including myself, believe that sharing common tools and comparable data enhances an MBHO. It is what you do with the data that counts, not the method of collecting the data.

My group and our main competitor in Albuquerque—Lovelace Health Services (see Chapter Thirteen)—both use the outcomes system shown in Exhibit 9.1 and feel very comfortable with our arrangement.

Satisfaction

The measurement of patient satisfaction was once the mainstay of many quality plans. Today, it remains important but is inadequate alone. Measuring the satisfaction of patients is now usually built into the larger system of outcomes measurement, as in the example.

There is more to satisfaction measurement, however, than just finding out whether patients believe their treatment helped them and whether they liked

Exhibit 9.1. Outcomes Management Project.

OUTCOMES MANAGEMENT PROJECT
Quality Improvement Center
The Center for Quality Innovations and Research   University of Cincinnati College of Medicine
Naakesh Dewan, M.D., Executive Director;
Gayle L. Zieman, Ph.D., Director for Research and Development

Methodology

1. Pre-Treatment Assessment (in the waiting room before first appointment)
   A. Consent Form
   B. Beginning Services Survey
      • Patient satisfaction with access to care & expectations from treatment
      • Demographics
   C. Behavior and Symptom Identification Scale (BASIS-32)
      • Daily Living Function
      • Relation to Self/Others
      • Depression/Anxiety
      • Impulsive/Addictive Behavior
      • Psychosis
   D. Health Status Profile w/ Depression Screener (also referred to as the SF-39)
      • Health Perception
      • Physical Functioning
      • Limitations Attributed to Physical Health and to Emotional Problems
      • Social Functioning
      • Depression
      • Bodily Pain
      • Energy/Fatigue
   E. Progress Evaluation Scale (optional for inclusion in the assessment battery)
      • Family Interaction & Functioning
      • Occupational Functioning
      • Getting Along with Others
      • Feelings and Moods
      • Use of Free Time
      • Attitude Toward Self
2. Follow Up at 3 & 6 months after began care (mailed to patient and mailed back)
   A. Behavior and Symptom Identification Scale (BASIS-32)
   B. Health Status Profile
   C. Progress Evaluation Scale (optional)
   D. Satisfaction Survey
      • Overall Satisfaction
      • Satisfaction with Psychotherapy and Therapist
      • Satisfaction with Medication and Physician
      • Satisfaction with Office Functioning
3. Follow Up at 6 months (from patient chart)
   A. Treatment Events Checklist
      • Diagnoses and Current Status of Treatment
      • Treatments Provided (includes medications)
      • Adverse Events (since began treatment)

the reception staff. Satisfaction must also be measured with providers, PCPs, and members who never accessed care. MBHOs routinely survey their network of providers for satisfaction with things such as the utilization management procedures and timeliness of being paid. PCPs are surveyed for degree of comfort in referring patients to the MBHO and for whether they received adequate communication regarding their patients who began behavioral care.

The measurement of health plan members who never accessed care is fairly new. It has been stimulated by a National Committee for Quality Assurance (NCQA) requirement that all health plan members be asked their perceptions of their insurer. The basic question here is whether or not members failed to enter treatment because of some dissatisfaction with the care system.

Appeals and Grievances

As was briefly noted in Chapter Three, appeals and grievances are the formal methods by which members and providers can register serious complaints and seek a review of what has displeased them. Most appeals and grievances are filed around utilization management decisions. An appeal is the first formal request and is usually handled at the committee level. If the party filing the complaint continues to disagree with the decision at the appeal level, then they may "grieve" the issue and file a written request for a grievance. A grievance is much more serious. In many states these must be reported to the Department of Insurance for the state. A grievance hearing usually involves high-level management staff from the MBHO and any MCO that owns or contracts to them. Additionally, the "grieved" individual or family is usually allowed to have legal counsel present at a grievance hearing.

Appeals and grievances are of importance to the quality department in that they represent serious cases of dissatisfaction with the MBHO and potential legal exposure. The quality staff and the quality committee usually track the number of appeals and grievances closely. For MBHOs that are part of or contracted to a larger MCO, the number of each is reported religiously to the MCO.

Prevention Programs

Although capitated entities such as MBHOs are in the long run rewarded financially by useful prevention programs, such programs have not had high priority or been very prevalent. Medically, MCOs have generally focused on childhood immunizations and prenatal care. Some drug abuse, parenting, and mental health screening in primary care programs have been used by MBHOs, but preventive programs in behavioral health have been minimal.

The picture is changing now that MBHOs are upholding the quality standards for behavioral health set forth by the NCQA (National Committee for Quality Assurance, 1997) and other groups. The NCQA standards clearly specify that MBHOs must have active prevention programs and that these programs must focus on commonly diagnosed conditions or disorders that involve high utilization of services by health plan members. Now groups like my own are studying their indicators and outcomes data to develop prevention programs that will serve their contracted populations. This standard has even changed my own schedule; educational classes that I once did as needed for schools, I and a colleague now do regularly in the evenings.

The basic prevention standard, along with all of the main NCQA standards for MBHOs, are found in Appendix C at the end of this text.

National standards and quality accreditation are certainly taking center stage with MCOs, MBHOs, and the purchasers of healthcare insurance. I will discuss these next.

NATIONAL STANDARDS

The attempt to arrive at nationally accepted and used standards for MBHO functions, both administratively and clinically, remains an area of major evolution. Several agencies and collaboratives have attempted to promulgate criteria to standardize functions across healthcare systems and to create a single report card for conveying the results. To date, there is no one set of standards.

In this section I will review the better-known standards that are available:

- Health Plan and Employers Data and Information Set
- National Committee for Quality Assurance standards
- Performance Measures for Managed Behavioral Healthcare Programs
- The Mental Health Statistics Improvement Program
- Foundation for Accountability standards

Health Plan and Employers Data and Information Set (HEDIS 3.0)

In 1993 the NCQA released the first version of HEDIS. Specifically designed for MCOs, HEDIS provides standards and a report card in the following areas: quality of care, access and patient satisfaction, membership and utilization, finance, and descriptive information on health plan management.

The most recent version of HEDIS, version 3.0 (National Committee for Quality Assurance, 1996), contains 104 indicators for health plans to measure—71 in a distinct reporting set and 33 in a test set. Behavioral health measures in the set include

- Time to follow-up care after hospitalization.
- Availability of mental health or chemical dependency providers.

- Inpatient discharges per one thousand health plan members.
- Average length of stay for hospitalizations.
- Percentage of members receiving inpatient, day or night care, and outpatient care.
- Hospital readmission rates for specific mental health disorders.

In 1996 a special version of HEDIS was released for Medicaid. Developed in conjunction with the Health Care Financing Administration (HCFA) and the American Public Welfare Association, the standards are designed to develop a report card system for Medicaid agencies and state administering authorities, as well as managed care insurers.

HEDIS is the most widely accepted and used set of standards in the country. Almost all health plans now report HEDIS data. Ask for it.

National Committee for Quality Assurance (NCQA) standards

In addition to HEDIS, NCQA has developed a set of MCO standards that go well beyond the HEDIS criteria and are used in assessing health plans for accreditation. The NCQA Behavioral Standards (National Committee for Quality Assurance, 1997) are an addition to the general MCO standards. For a review of the entire set of standards applying to MBHOs, see Appendix C.

Performance Measures for Managed Behavioral Healthcare Programs (PERMS 1.0)

PERMS is a set of behavioral health standards and report card items developed by AMBHA (American Managed Behavioral Healthcare Association, 1995), a trade association representing many of the largest managed behavioral carve-out firms in the country (see Chapter Thirteen for more detail). PERMS has twenty-three items for measurement and reporting. The items include readmission rates to inpatient care after an inpatient discharge, utilization data such as the number of inpatient days per one thousand members each plan used, and the average number of outpatient treatment sessions per episode of care. Many items from PERMS were adopted wholly, or in slightly modified form, into HEDIS 3.0.

The Mental Health Statistics Improvement Program (MHSIP)

The MHSIP standards were developed by the National Institute of Mental Health within the U.S. Department of Health and Human Services (National Institute of Mental Health, 1989). The standards are a culmination of efforts over several decades to standardize services and reporting mechanisms among publicly funded programs for the mentally ill, especially the severely and persistently mentally ill. MHSIP is different from the other standards in that it consists of more than criteria. It is a set of projects and operational guidelines for agencies and organizations that includes performance criteria and measurement tools. For example, it comes with its own patient satisfaction survey. MHSIP has measurement criteria in the following areas:

- Patient-client data
- Event data (treatment events)
- Human resources data
- Financial data

The MHSIP operational guidelines and measurement criteria are used by many federally funded and state-funded programs. Some states have incorporated the standards into managed care Medicaid contracts.

Foundation for Accountability Standards (FACCT)

FACCT, as an organization, is relatively new compared to the others producing standards. FACCT is an outgrowth of the Jackson Hole Group on healthcare, spearheaded by Dr. Paul Ellwood (see Chapter One).

In devising standards FACCT has focused on outcomes measures for specific diseases. The FACCT modules provide outcomes measurement tools and reporting criteria to accompany the recommended data points. In behavioral health, for example, FACCT has produced a methodology for the assessment of Major Depressive Disorder (Foundation for Accountability, 1996). The measurement tools include several commonly used public-domain instruments. The protocol assesses patient satisfaction, clinical outcome, and comorbid conditions in order to provide risk adjustment for simple versus complex conditions, as well as to determine physical health and impairment in daily life due to depression. It is too early to tell how extensively the FACCT system will be adopted nationally.

Before closing the discussion of standards, I should note that several large employers and employer cooperatives have formed their own MCO and, in some cases, MBHO standards, which they insist all insurers meet in order to contract with the company to cover employees for healthcare. As an example, Digital Equipment Corporation has issued their third edition of standards, which contains a seventeen-page section just for behavioral health (Digital Equipment Corporation, 1997). Other large companies with such standards include the Ford Motor Company, the Honeywell Corporation, International Business Machines, and Xerox.

ACCREDITATION

Three national organizations accredit managed care organizations: the Joint Commission on Accreditation of Healthcare Organizations (JCAHO), the National Committee for Quality Assurance (NCQA), and the Utilization Review

Accreditation Commission (URAC). All three organizations offer training in their standards and make a site visit with a team of professional reviewers to determine whether an organization meets their standards for provisional, partial, or full accreditation. Full accreditation with JCAHO and NCQA is for three years before another site visit is required; the period is two years with URAC.

JCAHO has been accrediting facilities and treatment programs for over thirty years. In the area of managed care, the Joint Commission accredits MBHOs, provider networks, integrated delivery systems, and preferred provider organizations. New is a program labeled ORYX, which accredits performance and quality measurement systems such as outcomes programs.

NCQA, as previously mentioned, accredits both managed care health plans and managed behavioral healthcare organizations. At this time NCQA is the clear leader in the accreditation of managed care programs.

Last, URAC accredits organizations that conduct utilization management or have a provider network. Accreditations can be obtained by MCOs, MBHOs, provider networks, workers' compensation organizations, and physician-hospital organizations.

In the next chapter I will discuss the giant force in managed behavioral healthcare: government. From Medicaid and Medicare to the military's TriCare, government healthcare programs are the behemoths that steer healthcare policy.

CHAPTER TEN

Managed Care in the Public Sector

The federal government is the largest insurance entity in the country. More than one-third of all Americans—over 90 million people—are insured for healthcare by federal tax dollars.

The two mammoth federal programs are Medicare and Medicaid. There is good reason for the healthcare adage—as Medicare and Medicaid go, so goes the rest of healthcare. Medicare insures citizens over age sixty-five and people of any age with certain disabilities. Medicaid is a jointly funded federal-state health insurance program for low-income and other needy people, as well as individuals eligible for federal income support. Both programs began in the mid-1960s and have grown dramatically, as shown in the following list of government statistics (Health Care and Finance Authority, 1997):

- Enrollment growth (in millions of recipients), 1967 to 1998 (estimated): Medicaid from 10 to 38.1; Medicare from 19.5 to 39.1

- Cost increases (in billions), 1980 to 1996: Medicaid, from $24.0 to $160.1; Medicare from $33.9 to $193.9

- National healthcare costs paid by government, 1965 to 1996: 25.0 percent to 45.8 percent

In this chapter I discuss the rapid movement by both the Medicaid and Medicare programs into managed care, especially plans of an HMO type. Indemnity payment systems are quickly fading in the public and private sectors of the American economy.

In addition to the two huge programs administered by the Health Care and Finance Authority (HCFA), there are two other federal health insurance programs: the Federal Employees Health Benefits Program (FEHBP) and TriCare.

Created by Congress in 1959, the FEHBP provides healthcare insurance to over nine million federal workers, dependents, and retirees. FEHBP recipients are allowed to choose from a variety of local and national insurers contracted to the program (Butler and Moffit, 1995). In line with private companies, the FEHBP has rapidly turned to managed care insurers, so much so that more than 20 percent of all recipients are enrolled in an HMO-type plan, while large percentages are enrolled in point of service (POS) and preferred provider organization (PPO) plans.

TriCare is the insurance program for the U.S. Department of Defense (DoD). Its forerunner by several decades, the Civilian Health and Medical Program of the Uniformed Services (CHAMPUS) was a traditional indemnity plan. After several managed care demonstration projects, DoD formed TriCare through a network of subcontracted private MCOs that serve DoD's twelve domestic service regions. With the final transition of regions into the TriCare program in 1997, my friend, a senior policy analyst in the Office of the Assistant Secretary of Defense, Health Affairs, remarked, "If you're in uniform, you're getting managed care. That's almost nine million active duty and retired personnel plus their dependents" (Paris, M., personal communication, April 9, 1997). Under TriCare, all active duty personnel and their dependents must enroll in the HMO option, which uses military medical facilities as preferred providers and a civilian network as needed. Retirees may also choose from POS and PPO options. In TriCare, mental health services are carved out with a single MBHO managing behavioral care needs and finances for each of the domestic regions.

In addition to the four large federal programs, all states have general state tax funds that are designated for health insurance. These funds typically cover state employees and dependents, special needy groups targeted by the state (the uninsured, for example), and enhancements to Medicaid (for example, substance abuse benefits; substance abuse is not covered under the federal plan).

All of these programs establish the thesis of this chapter, that is, the business of healthcare within the public sector is swiftly becoming indistinguishable from business with private, commercial insurers. To further your understanding of the Medicaid and Medicare programs and their transition to managed care, I will discuss each program separately.

MEDICAID

The Medicaid program covers the healthcare costs, most often with no recipient copayment, of over thirty-eight million Americans, or 13.8 percent of the entire U.S. population (Health Care and Finance Authority, 1997). Over 50 percent of recipients are children. The distribution of the covered population also differs significantly from state to state and city to city. For example, in New York City 18.8 percent of the population is covered by Medicaid, whereas in Denver, Medicaid recipients represent only 8.8 percent of the population.

At its inception in the mid-1960s, the Medicaid system functioned as a traditional, indemnity-type insurer. Providers were paid using a fee-for-service system, and essentially any licensed clinician could sign up to serve Medicaid clients simply by applying for a Medicaid billing number. Now, Medicaid has moved to fixed payment amounts per service (discounted fee-for-service), including hospital rates. Medicaid rates have frequently been below what private insurers pay for the same procedures. The any willing provider nature of the plan, however, has most often remained intact.

Medicaid is jointly funded by the federal government and the states; the majority of costs are born by the federal government, with states providing matching monies. The amount paid by any one state ranges from around 25 to 40 percent, depending on a complex set of calculations that include factors such as the poverty level in the state.

It is important to note that Medicaid benefit structures have always been quite different from commercial insurance. Medicaid has had a broader depth of coverage and more complexity than private healthcare insurance. There are three main benefit differences:

• Medicaid pays for many services, especially those for the chronically ill such as the seriously mentally ill (SMI: diagnostic groups such as Schizophrenia and Bipolar Disorder), which have never been covered in private insurance plans. Among these benefits are that cases are coordinated by case managers, and that care is provided in nursing homes, residential treatment centers (nonhospital programs, usually for long-term care), and psychosocial rehabilitation programs for SMI individuals.

• The providers used by Medicaid include many community health clinics, residential treatment centers, and community mental health centers. These providers are often nonprofit organizations and, in the case of community health clinics and community mental health centers, they are frequently supported by other federal and local tax-based funds.

• Medicaid requirements and payment mechanisms have often been convoluted and invasive by private standards, especially in relation to facility-based arrangements such as with hospitals and psychosocial rehabilitation centers. For example, hospital daily reimbursement levels have been based on an analysis of the costs incurred by hospitals to treat Medicaid recipients in a particular region. Medicaid for behavioral services has also had its own quality standards—the Mental Health Statistics Improvement Program (MHSIP) (see Chapter Nine)—which include financial and management requirements that go beyond what private businesses consider appropriate for external organizations to require.

Managed Care Medicaid

Managed care for Medicaid began in the mid-1980s with pioneer states such as Wisconsin, Hawaii, and New York, which started demonstration projects that enrolled Medicaid recipients into private HMO health plans. What began as a few demonstration projects with HMOs became a stampede by the mid-1990s. By late 1997, approximately 40 percent of all Medicaid recipients were enrolled into private HMO plans, which contracted with the recipient's state government to provide coverage (Rosenbaum, 1997).

The motivation for states to push for an HMO to manage their Medicaid system has come primarily from intense financial pressures. With the national bill for the Medicaid program having risen from $24 billion in 1967 to almost $170 billion thirty years later, states and the federal government have declared themselves unable to reign in costs. From an annual cost increase rate of 22.4 percent between 1988 and 1992, the shift to HMOs has often been cited as the main force behind the reduction to only a 9.5 percent cost increase rate between 1992 and 1995 (Holahan and Liska, 1997). By moving state Medicaid populations to private contracts, states have also been able to lessen the governmental bureaucracy involved in the program and probably have lessened the amount of provider fraud.

For states to move to private HMOs was very complicated until late 1997. States had to seek a two-year waiver from HCFA to try managed care. Waivers came in the form of a very limited managed care program (called a 1115 waiver) and the more extensive project (called a 1915b waiver). The massive proposal and subsequent negotiations with HCFA were significant hurdles for states wishing to change to managed care. Despite these hurdles, by mid-1997 thirty-eight states had waivers and were somewhere in the process of implementing managed care for specific recipients or local regions, or on a statewide basis.

I can personally attest to the difficulties of the waiver system and the magnitude of state contracts for managed care Medicaid. While New Mexico was waiting for approval of its 1915b waiver request in late 1996 and early 1997, I was leading the mental health team with Blue Cross and Blue Shield of New Mexico in a bid to cover seventy thousand Medicaid recipients. The state request for proposals was a several-hundred-page document that made private RFPs pale in comparison. For twelve months several of us devoted ourselves to making a bid to be one of the MCOs selected for a statewide Medicaid contract. First, we traveled the state to meet the existing providers, most often the staff of community mental health centers and residential treatment centers (I love RTCs; I started my professional career in an RTC). I enjoyed visiting with a gathering of rural providers at a church in mountainous Rio Arriba County and dropping in at the community mental health center in sand-swept Alamagordo, New Mexico. The last four months, however, were long, desk-bound weeks of writing our response to the state's hundreds of specifications and questions. Throughout the process, HCFA ordered the state to change many of the specifications— major things like whether Native Americans would or would not be included and when the start-up date would be. We scrambled as the changes came down.

Finally, we took our proposal (seven, four-inch-thick notebooks of material) and the top twenty leaders of our Medicaid team to Santa Fe for an entire afternoon of presentations to a large state procurement panel. They loved us and our fine plan for implementing services. But in the end we refused to stay in contention when price bidding moved to a level so low that we believed we could not ethically implement the proposed delivery system we had worked so hard to develop. As stated in Chapter Eight, managed care at-risk contracting is not for the meek or business-naive.

But back to the changes ushered in during 1997: the Balanced Budget Act of 1997 gave states the power to require mandatory enrollment of Medicaid recipients (except children with special needs) into HMO plans without obtaining a waiver from HCFA. This much less restrictive process is accelerating the movement of Medicaid eligibles into managed care programs.

A true statement about state Medicaid programs is that if you have seen one Medicaid plan, you know one Medicaid plan. Variation across states is tremendous. Many states have gone for extensive demonstration or regional projects (California and Colorado), while others (Tennessee, Iowa, Arizona, and New Mexico) have performed rapid, statewide conversions. Most states have gone for a carve out of behavioral services through awarding separate contracts to medical MCOs and MBHOs. A few have included (carved in) behavioral services in contracts with full MCOs (for example, Florida, New Mexico, Pennsylvania, and initially Tennessee). A few states have partially or totally chosen to leave behavioral services out of managed care conversions for now (Minnesota, Oklahoma, and Kentucky, for example).

Permutations and special twists abound. To give an idea of the different ways of doing it, we will briefly examine the contrasting managed behavioral programs in two states: Massachusetts and Arizona.

Massachusetts

In July 1992 Massachusetts became the first state to implement a statewide managed care Medicaid program for mental health. Approximately 375,000 recipients were enrolled under the specifications of the state's 1915b waiver from HCFA to carve out behavioral services. MassHealth, as the state program is known, chose a single MBHO to implement the program, with the MBHO receiving one capitation rate (per member per month) for nondisabled recipients and another for disabled individuals. Clinicians, agencies, and hospitals were paid on a discounted fee-for-service basis. The behavioral program required prior approval for all twenty-four-hour services such as hospital admissions, but outpatient visits could be up to eight per year before the MBHO began utilization management.

In the first year the number of recipients receiving outpatient care rose 10.6 percent, whereas hospital admissions dropped 7.2 percent and hospital lengths of stay fell over 12 percent (Callahan, Shepard, Beinecke, Larson, and Cavanaugh, 1995). Financially, the annual average cost per enrolled member dropped from $553 to $402. Quality and satisfaction results were quite variable. Access to care increased, but so did the percentage of dollars going to administer the program. Clinical outcomes have been variable.

Despite its pioneer beginnings, MassHealth is held out as one of the most successful state Medicaid conversions. So much so that in 1995, Massachusetts received HCFA approval to expand its program, including greater services to children and eligibility changes that brought more children into the program.

MassHealth has entered into its second phase for the provision of behavioral services. The MBHO handling behavioral services for MassHealth has changed to Value Behavioral Health (see Chapter Thirteen). And there are many new specifications, including one saying that after discharge from inpatient psychiatric care, a patient must be seen for follow-up within three days.

Arizona

Prior to 1982 Arizona was the only state not participating in the national Medicaid program. As an alternative to traditional Medicaid, Arizona in the early 1980s developed a managed care program under the Arizona Health Care Cost Containment System (AHCCS). The program was designed to serve primarily the acute medical care needs of Medicaid-eligible individuals and used private HMOs. In 1989, long-term care, such as nursing home care, was added.

The medical program in its first ten years was estimated to have reduced care costs by 11 percent (by 7 percent when administrative costs are included) and to have significantly improved access to care for members (McCall, 1997). Quality of care issues have been assessed by comparing Arizona outcomes with those of New Mexico where managed care Medicaid only began in 1997. On quality the results are mixed; some are better and some are worse than a non-managed care program.

For behavioral healthcare services, Arizona began managed care in 1990 for a portion of eligible adults and children. Administratively, the state was divided into five regions and in each region a nonprofit MBHO, often a local collaborative of providers, was awarded a contract to manage behavioral services throughout the region. In 1992 SMI adults were added to the program, followed in 1995 by the addition of substance abuse services. State substance abuse grant funds, which previously had not been included in the Medicaid system, were combined with Medicaid funds. The five regional authorities have often subcapitated to large group or agency providers for services or paid on a case rate basis.

Although many point to Arizona as a model program, it should be noted that one of the nonprofit regional MBHOs became financially insolvent. And many complain that the program has severely impaired consumers' rights to a choice of providers and has reduced the amount of care provided to unacceptable levels.

In closing this section, one special feature of the Arizona program should be noted: the blending of Medicaid dollars with state grant monies. This blending is the goal of many states. Given that Medicaid never covered some services, most notably substance abuse rehabilitation for adults, states developed many internally funded programs to cover these services. As states stabilize their managed care Medicaid programs, the next goal is to blend these state-funded programs into the Medicaid programs.

MEDICARE

The nation's largest healthcare program is Medicare. The program will have an estimated 39.1 million recipients in 1998 (33.8 million retirees age sixty-five and older and 5.3 million disabled individuals below age sixty-five). The program has also grown to consume 12 percent of the total federal budget (Health Care and Finance Authority, 1997).

Like Medicaid, Medicare followed a traditional indemnity plan model entirely for its first twenty years of operation. Medicare's benefit structures followed the traditional covered medical benefits of private insurance more closely than Medicaid's did. For example, Medicare has not covered nursing home care or psychosocial rehabilitation programs—services that can be paid for through Medicaid.

Medicare moved to a managed indemnity model during the 1980s, with caps on reimbursement rates to clinicians and hospitals. The reimbursement rate-setting system used—known as the prospective payment system—is a method derived from analyzing the costs of providing care for beneficiaries. This system is very complex and has been amended repeatedly by legislation and changes in HCFA regulations. Two of the central reimbursement methods are Diagnostic Related Groups (DRGs) and the Resource-Based Relative Value Scale (RBRVS). DRGs are Medicare's form of case rates. Hospitals and clinicians are paid a set amount for major procedures such as hospitalizations. This amount must cover all costs for the entire episode of care—a hospitalization for Major Depression, for example—regardless of the complexity of the case or length of the care. The RBRVS is a rate schedule for procedures such as those used in outpatient care. The fee schedule is based on a system of weighted values for certain procedures. For example, a psychiatrist will be reimbursed more for an initial medication evaluation if the complexity of a case is greater, not necessarily by the amount of time spent with the patient.

Although the nation has generally endorsed Medicare as a great program, financial predictions have projected that the costs will vastly outstrip the payroll tax revenues of the program (Hammonds, 1997). In other words the program may go broke in the near future, especially when the post–World War II baby boomers reach retirement age early in the next century.

This fear brought the federal government to the conclusion in the mid-1980s that managed care should be allowed for Medicare recipients. Initially, very few HMOs were interested and, given the prediction that enrolling retirees would not be prosperous, the original HMOs adding Medicare programs were known as Social HMOs. When these original Social HMOs demonstrated financial viability, many HMOs stepped up to the plate. By 1997, 13 percent of all Medicare recipients were enrolled in HMO plans (Lamphere, Neuman, Langwell, and Sherman, 1997).

Medicare HMOs function like standard HMOs except that the payment of the premium comes from the federal government for the standard benefit prescribed by HCFA.

The amount paid by the government to the HMO is less than what the government spends on the average Medicare recipient. The figure had been 95 percent of the average cost, but with the Balanced Budget Act of 1997, the figure is 90 percent from 1998 forward.

Plans can add enhanced benefits for which an extra premium may be charged to the retiree. The enhanced benefits commonly offered by HMOs to seniors are an annual physical examination, an annual eye examination, reduced prescription costs, and dental care. Even though many plans offer some enhanced benefits without an additional premium, some are expanding coverage significantly and charging an additional fee. The average additional premium for 1996, however, was only $13.42 per month (Managed Care, 1997).

Although the federal government openly declares its desire for a large percentage of beneficiaries to join HMOs, the impact of the 1997 Balanced Budget Act on the readiness of HMOs to accept more members is unknown. Additionally, HMOs have been accused of marketing to the wellest Medicare recipients. If they are asked to take a broader array of beneficiaries, their willingness is again unknown.

In the attempt by HCFA to lessen the cost of Medicare, proposals also call for reduced Medicare support for graduate medical education. Medicare has long supported teaching hospitals and residency programs by paying additional dollars for services offered in teaching hospitals. This money is likely to disappear as care is assumed by Medicare HMOs (Desmarais and Hash, 1997). The Balanced

Budget Act of 1997 also reduces funds to medical education. The exact impact these events will have on medical education is unclear, but states are scrambling to find other sources of education revenue. Based on projections in mid-1997, the state of Minnesota, for example, believed that medical training in that state alone would lose up to $90 million during calendar year 1999 (Hamburger, 1997). The same experience is expected in other states. As the delivery of health care becomes much more cost conscious, the education of physicians and nurses is likely to be cut back in some form. For a review of managed care's impact on graduate education for all mental health professionals, see Schuster, Lovell, and Trachta (1997).

The last several chapters have focused heavily on the nuts and bolts of MBHOs and working with them. In the next chapter, I show how specific MBHOs describe their missions and their offerings.

CHAPTER ELEVEN

Today's Managed Behavioral Healthcare Organizations

Throughout this text I have referred to managed behavioral healthcare organizations (MBHOs) as generic entities. Before concluding this text, I wish to give you a sense for the specific MBHOs with whom you may work now or in the future. This chapter provides individual profiles of several MBHOs, ranging from large to small and national to regional.

Please note that the data given in the profiles were wholly supplied by the companies themselves and are unverified. The national firms, for example, only allowed me access to their public relations staff. Hence, the information presented here is not necessarily a balanced view and does not include data from providers and members.

There is considerable variation in size and function among the approximately three hundred MBHOs in existence today, who collectively cover over 120 million lives (National Committee for Quality Assurance, 1997). As a general rule, though, MBHOs come in three basic types:

- National carve-out companies
- Integrated behavioral departments
- Regional carve-out companies

The national carve outs are the most visible entities; they are usually huge firms that accept contracts to manage the behavioral healthcare care needs for large national employers such as the Fortune 500 corporations. Many of them also manage sizable populations of Medicaid or Medicare recipients, and several even cover regional military populations for the U.S. Department of Defense.

Integrated behavioral departments, however, are usually a division of a large metropolitan or regional medical system. They become MBHOs when the medical system is both an insurer and a care delivery system bound together. In this arrangement the behavioral department serves as the manager and provider of care by being contracted to the branch of their firm that is an MCO. In a variation, the behavioral departments of large medical systems have a close alliance with one or more MCOs and serve as the MBHO for those MCOs.

Last, regional carve outs are fairly local groups that frequently began as integrated group practices and have matured into managing regional populations under capitation for managed care insurers, states, or, in many cases, for the national carve-out companies. In this chapter I profile two MBHOs from each type, beginning with the national carve outs.

NATIONAL CARVE-OUT COMPANIES

Most of the national carve-out companies began in the 1980s when insurers and employers recognized that they had little experience in managing behavioral services, yet the dollars going for mental health and substance abuse services were rising dramatically. Following often-humble beginnings, these companies developed to fill the need for managers of behavioral care; they covered large populations such as those of employers with staff in many states or governmental clients seeking contractors for statewide or multistate regions.

Throughout the 1980s and 1990s these firms have grown and proliferated. The 1990s, however, has been a period of strong consolidation in which many national MBHOs have merged with others. A sample of prominent national carve-out companies includes Green Spring Health Services, Human Affairs International, MCC Behavioral Care, Merit Behavioral, OPTIONS Health Care, PacifiCare, U.S. Behavioral Health, United Behavioral, and Value Behavioral Health.

Many of these companies came together to form—or are now members of—their own trade association: the American Managed Behavioral Healthcare Association (AMBHA) (see Appendix D). As discussed in Chapter Nine, the members of AMBHA developed a set of quality indicators known as PERMS, which each of the member MBHOs is to use. Taken together, the firms composing AMBHA cover the behavioral healthcare needs of over 60 million Americans. Given this, the chances that you, as a clinician, will work with one or more of them is extremely high.

Many of these companies also have employee assistance programs (EAPs) that can be purchased separately by employers for their employees or as part of an integrated packet covering the full range of work-related and personal behavioral services.

For the purposes of this chapter, we will profile two national firms: Value Behavioral Health, Inc., and OPTIONS Healthcare.

Value Behavioral Health, Inc.

Value Behavioral Health (VBH) is one of the largest specialty managed behavioral healthcare companies in the nation (see Exhibit 11.1). It contracts with approximately one thousand employer and governmental entities, including approximately 20 percent of the Fortune 500 corporations. VBH, through its many service options, covers the care for almost twenty-four million Americans. To serve this large client base from coast to coast, Value operates ten regional client service units.

VBH is very proud that in 1997 it won the prestigious Managed Behavioral Healthcare Leadership Award presented by Eli Lilly Pharmaceuticals and the

Exhibit 11.1. Value Behavioral Health, Inc.

Corporate Headquarters: 3110 Fairview Park Drive South, Falls Church, VA 22042
  Tele: (703) 205–7000

Year Founded: 1982

Chief Executive Officer: Charlton Tooke

Medical Director: Ian Shaffer, M.D.

Doing Business In: All 50 states

Number of Credentialed Providers: 40,000 clinicians/locations and over
  2,000 facilities/programs

NCQA Expected Survey Date: 1998

Services Offered: Managed Mental Health and Substance Abuse Treatment
  State Medicaid Initiatives
  Public-Private Child Welfare Initiatives
  Utilization Management Services for Insurers
  Employee Assistance Programs

Captitated Contracts:

Type of Program	Number of Contracts	Covered Lives
Commercial MH/SA Only	233	13.5 million
Commercial EAP Only	677	2.7 million
Commercial MH/SA & EAP	83	1.85 million
Medicaid or Client w/Medicaid	12	251,000
Utilization Management Only	20	5.15 million
Other	—	—
Total	1,025	23.5 million

National Managed Health Care Congress. VBH has been a leader in the development of AMBHA and its PERMS quality data set.

Services Offered. Commercially, VBH has subcontracted with twenty-two HMOs across the country to provide behavioral services to over 3.7 million Americans. As a carved-out MBHO, Value integrates services with the medical delivery system for employed members and their dependents, as well as Medicare and Medicaid enrollees. Specifically, VBH has partnered since the early 1980s with three large HMOs: Paramount Health Care, Healthnet of California, and Blue Care Network of Southeast Michigan.

Nationally, VBH is known for its partnership with local and regional provider-based groups that are responsible for developing and delivering the full continuum of care and local management services. The groups, called Clinical Groups by Value, are responsible for the entire care continuum that members within a fixed geographic region (usually defined by groupings of zip code areas) may need. The groups manage their own intake and utilization management systems and quality programs, with clinical and quality oversight provided by VBH. In 1997 VBH had twenty-six such partnerships with regional carve-out groups.

In the world of managed care Medicaid, VBH's public sector division is active in managing care in New Mexico, Texas, and Kansas. KansCare for Families is a partnership between VBH and two local entities: the Salvation Army and Youthville, Inc. The project is one of the first to implement a comprehensive system of care for children placed in out-of-home custody. The project integrates foster care, mental health treatment, and ancillary services for children and families into a managed care system. In the Commonwealth of Massachusetts, Value formed a partnership with OPTIONS in 1996 in which it was responsible for the management and care delivery for over 250,000 Medicaid enrollees and 30,000 uninsured individuals. In New Mexico and Texas, VBH is the subcontractor to an HMO that is responsible for serving Medicaid recipients statewide.

Value is very active in employee assistance programs through its workplace services division. VBH offers traditional assessment, brief counseling, and referral through clinical offices and on-site counselors within the workplace. In addition, programs in disability management, health and wellness, and legal and financial independence are available to corporations through an available menu of service options. As can be seen in Exhibit 11.1, VBH is a very large EAP contractor.

Quality Programs. Value is one of the most active MBHOs in quality initiatives. In addition to being a leader in the development of PERMS through their chief medical officer, Ian Shaffer, M.D., VBH carefully tracks member satisfaction with care, corporate or governmental client retention, and patient improvement by collecting the global assessment of functioning (GAF) ratings assigned by providers as patients progress through care. VBH also hires an independent company to conduct twelve mock referrals per month to each of VBH's clinical groups as a monitor of timeliness, courtesy, proper clinical determination of member needs, and communication with the prospective patient. In addition, VBH has put into place the infrastructure to support all of its corporate and state clients in meeting the 1997 NCQA standards.

The Future. VBH has begun offering telephonic depression screening. The dynamic new service was designed by the Harvard Medical School Telepsychiatry Project. The screening is accomplished via an interactive voice system that administers the test through a prerecorded series of questions to which callers respond by pushing numbers on their telephone. The caller is allowed to remain anonymous; immediate feedback is given on the test results and, if appropriate, referral information is provided. Value is expanding this service to its business clients nationwide.

VBH is also offering a nationwide, personalized wellness and preventive health counseling and referral service to its EAP clients. Services will include weight-loss, smoking-cessation, exercise, and dietary programs.

OPTIONS Health Care, Inc.

Founded in 1986, OPTIONS leads the industry in delivering care to the most Medicaid recipients and is a major manager of mental healthcare needs for the U.S. Department of Defense in serving active duty, retired, and Veterans Affairs beneficiaries (see Exhibit 11.2). OPTIONS holds itself to the standards of (1) immediate access to exceptional patient care and (2) the highest clinical and business ethics. Nationally, OPTIONS is very proud of its collaborative relationships with community providers (especially partnerships with community mental health centers), government agencies, and consumer groups.

OPTIONS was the first MBHO to win the Managed Behavioral Healthcare Leadership Award presented annually by Eli Lilly Pharmaceuticals and the National Managed Health Care Congress. In addition, they were the recipients of the sixth annual Excellence in Healthcare Risk Award and in 1996 were acknowledged with a Model Outcomes Program Award by the Outcomes Roundtable (sponsored by the National Alliance for the Mentally Ill and Johns Hopkins University).

To serve their nationally diverse contracts, OPTIONS maintains twenty-four local service centers for provider relations and for administrative and customer service functions.

Services Offered. OPTIONS covers more than four million lives for mental health and substance abuse services. The largest populations served are Medicaid recipients who reside in Colorado, Florida, Massachusetts, Nebraska,

Exhibit 11.2. OPTIONS Health Care, Inc.

Corporate Headquarters: 240 Corporate Boulevard, Norfolk, VA 23502
Tele: (800) 451–3581

Year Founded: 1986

Chief Executive Officer: Ronald Dozoretz, M.D.

Medical Director: Donald Fowls, M.D.

Doing Business In: 46 states plus Puerto Rico

Number of Credentialed Clinicians: 15,000 in 22,000 practice locations

NCQA Initial Survey Date: May, 1998

Services Offered: State Medicaid Initiatives
　　　　　　　　Managed Mental Health and Substance Abuse Treatment
　　　　　　　　Public-Private Child Welfare Initiatives
　　　　　　　　Employee Assistance Programs
　　　　　　　　Medicare Programs

Captitated Contracts:

Type of Program	Number of Contracts	Covered Lives
Commercial MH/SA Only	14	72,000
Commercial EAP Only	25	167,000
Commercial MH/SA & EAP	10	25,000
Medicaid Only	3	4,100,000
Utilization Management Only	1	9,000
Other (Veterans, TriCare, State & Local Governments)	10	1,817,000
Total	63	6,190,000

New Mexico, Puerto Rico, Tennessee, and Vermont. Also in the public sector, OPTIONS provides managed care management for two of the twelve domestic military regions under TriCare—the DoD's comprehensive managed care program. Commercial MCO contracts, EAPs, and state child welfare programs round out the service lines offered by OPTIONS.

Colorado Health Networks is a prominent public-private partnership for OPTIONS and those eligible for Medicaid in Colorado. Since 1995, Colorado Medicaid plan recipients have received services through business partnership programs with eight nonprofit community mental health centers. As a result of these partnerships and their combined quality improvement steering committee, Colorado recipients have experienced increased access to care, improved satisfaction, and much greater consumer involvement in directing their own care and in helping to design new programs. At the same time the state of Colorado has realized significant savings in expenditures, with an overall goal of 8 percent savings compared to before the program began. The Colorado program won the Model Outcomes Program Award in 1996 that is given by the Outcomes Roundtable.

In commercial programs, OPTIONS specializes in coordinating care with primary care providers. New programs include PCP Hotline—a direct line for PCPs to call with their questions on such topics as referrals and medications—and PCP Notification—a program that swiftly informs PCPs when one of their patients has been referred for behavioral services.

Of special note is OPTIONS' *CareFirst* program, which is designed to involve all aspects of clinical care, including treatment protocols, treatment planning, and case management. This program has increased clinicians' involvement in care management and expanded access to care for clients. The program offers clinicians the ability, through an interactive voice response system, to telephonically register that patients have begun care or to check an array of utilization information regarding patients.

Quality Programs. OPTIONS is accredited by the national Utilization Review Accreditation Commission (URAC) and supports the standards set down by NCQA and the PERMS standards developed by the American Behavioral Healthcare Association (AMBHA). In May 1998, OPTIONS underwent its first NCQA accreditation site visit.

In addition to the Model Outcomes Award, Colorado Health Networks received one of the three finalist awards in the Quality Cup Competition sponsored by the Rochester Institute of Technology and *USA Today*. The award honors teams who have made exceptional contributions to their employers' quality improvement programs.

The Future. OPTIONS is very active in seeking to expand its services to a larger number of states, federal agencies, and employers. Quality and clinical programs developed in states such as Colorado are being integrated into the care delivery system in other areas served by OPTIONS.

INTEGRATED BEHAVIORAL DEPARTMENTS

Since the 1970s many large hospital or medical systems have merged with an MCO or started their own. In this scenario the medical system becomes the exclusive care delivery system for the MCO or the large preferred provider group of the MCO. In either arrangement the medical system is almost always paid on a global capitation plan (medical and all specialty services combined) under which the anticipated cost of care for MCO members is prepaid monthly to the medical system. In turn, the medical system subcapitates to the various medical departments for specialty care.

When a managed care insurer and a medical system are linked, the department of psychiatry or behavioral medicine is usually one of the first to be subcapitated. Psychiatric services and costs are usually viewed by the larger medical system as among the most confusing and difficult to manage, so behavioral services are often quickly given their own share of the full medical costs to administer. This represents a carved-out contract (see Chapter One) in that psychiatry has its own budget and a fairly autonomous delivery system separate from the general medical system. The arrangement, however, is conducive to the sharing of expertise among behavioral health providers and medical colleagues. Frequently, behavioral clinicians are colocated in medical clinics.

For the purposes of this chapter, we will profile two integrated behavioral departments: Park Nicollet Medical Center of Minneapolis and Lovelace ParkCenter in Albuquerque.

Park Nicollet Mental Health Department

The mental health department is a division of the Park Nicollet Medical Center, which is contracted with Health Partners, one of the largest health plans in the greater Minneapolis area (see Exhibit 11.3).

Beginning in 1978, the mental health department became capitated to serve the behavioral needs of 30,000 members of the predecessor to Health Partners. Today, the department is capitated to serve nearly 337,000 commercial lives under Health Partners and approximately 10,000 Medicaid recipients. The department has its own capitation rates and negotiates its own contracts, which are separate from the larger Park Nicollet system. In addition to serving Health Partners and Prepaid Medical Assistance (Minnesota's Medicaid plan), the department is a major provider for Blue Cross and Blue Shield of Minnesota through both capitation and discounted fee-for-service arrangements.

The department has one large center and five other outpatient locations to serve the five metropolitan counties in the western region of the Twin Cities. Services on the west side of the river (St. Paul, Minnesota) are handled by Ramsey Medical Center. For the purposes of assigning members to the correct system for care, the location of their PCP is used. Park Nicollet's mental health department does not have its own inpatient facility; it contracts with one psychiatric hospital where Park Nicollet psychiatrists admit and treat patients. The departmental staff consists approximately of (in full-time equivalents) twenty-three psychiatrists, six psychologists, and fifty master's-degreed psychotherapists. To meet service needs in the more geographically distant metropolitan areas and in times of peak patient need, the department has over fifty subcontracted providers.

Health Partners has retained the MCO functions of credentialing providers, managing quality improvement functions, paying claims that come in from the subcontracted network. The department is responsible for its own intake and utilization management systems.

Exhibit 11.3. Park Nicollet Medical Center—Mental Health Department.

Corporate Headquarters: 3800 Park Nicollet Boulevard, Minneapolis, MN 55416

Year Mental Health Department Founded: 1978

Chief Executive Officer/ Medical Director: Michael Feldman, M.D.

Operations Administrator/Clinical Director: Greg Winkel, L.I.C.S.W.

Doing Business In: Minnesota

Number of Credentialed Clinicians: 81

NCQA Accredited: 1996

Services Offered: Managed Mental Health and Substance Abuse Treatment
State Medicaid Initiatives

Capitation Contracts:

Type of Program	Number of Contracts	Covered Lives
Commercial MH/SA	2	337,000
Commercial EAP Only	—	—
Commercial MH/SA & EAP	—	—
Medicaid Only	1	10,000
Utilization Management Only	—	—
Other	—	—
Total	3	347,000

Of special note is that all behavioral services to members of the Health Partners plan do not require a referral from the member's primary care physician. The commercial benefit plans administered under capitation follow the Minnesota parity law adopted in 1995, which requires an equality between medical and mental health benefits. All MCO members in Minnesota have unlimited mental health outpatient or inpatient usage, as long as the service is medically needed; copayments are set at $10 for outpatient visits, with no copayment for inpatient admissions.

Services Offered. Five of the six offices are comprehensive mental health clinics colocated with medical offices. To serve the broader Park Nicollet medical system, there is a well-developed inpatient and outpatient consultation service that is accessible either by telephone or on site. Two psychiatrists and one clinical nurse specialist are devoted to medical unit consultations.

For the mental health system, four clinicians are always on call after hours. To better handle crisis situations the department offers a daily drop-in clinic for families having child-related problems and two drop-in groups for adults.

Several special programs serve the population of health plan members needing care. These programs include groups for parents with children or adolescents showing oppositional or defiant behaviors and a special track with educational and cognitive behavioral components for adult victims of physical or sexual abuse. Cognitive behavioral groups for depression are also prominent in the system.

Quality Programs. In 1996 the mental health department participated with Health Partners in a NCQA survey that resulted in full accreditation. The next NCQA survey date is set for 1999. Currently, the Park Nicollet Medical Center is preparing for their next site survey by the Joint Commission on Accreditation of Healthcare Organizations (JCAHO). This will be the first time that the mental health department has joined in seeking JCAHO accreditation.

Participation in the Outcomes Management Project (see Chapter Nine) is a mainstay of the department's measurement of clinical outcomes and patient satisfaction.

Clinical improvement teams are active as a part of the Treatment Redesign Project (TRP) to create and implement special clinical programs to better serve patients and the department's capitated contracts. Several of the programs listed under services are initiatives that came from the TRP.

The Future. Through the continued efforts of the TRP, Park Nicollet envisions a mental health service with more programmatic treatment services. Cognitive behavioral groups for persons with anxiety disorders will likely be next. The department also has a vision of further integrating services with general medicine throughout the Minneapolis metropolitan area.

Of special interest is the Multiple Center Behavioral Health Outcomes Consortium. This is a project involving several medical systems in Minnesota, along with Dartmouth University and the University of North Dakota. The project is currently seeking funding to form standardized data exchanges and analyses to monitor the care and clinical outcomes of over one million individuals in both urban and rural areas.

Lovelace ParkCenter

The mental health department of Lovelace Health Systems at ParkCenter, is the exclusive mental health provider for Lovelace Health Plan (enrollment is 114,000) in the Albuquerque metropolitan area (population of 500,000 +) (see Exhibit 11.4). Most inpatient and outpatient mental health and substance abuse treatment is done in one central location using thirty full-time equivalent (FTE) clinicians (a staff model). The clinician FTEs are broken down as follows: psychiatry—7.3, psychology—4.0, nurse practitioners/physician's assistants—2.5, case managers—1.5, and psychotherapists—15.0. Assessment and treatment are also done at primary and speciality care sites where mental health clinicians colocate with medical staff. ParkCenter staff support the medical facility by offering consultation and liaison services twenty-four hours per day.

Exhibit 11.4. Lovelace ParkCenter.

Corporate Headquarters: 7801 Jefferson Street, N.E., Albuquerque, NM 87109

Year Founded: 1992

Administrators: Dennis James, M.S.W. and Jane Keeports, M.B.A.

Medical Director: Jeff Mitchell, M.D.

Doing Business In: New Mexico

Number of Credentialed Clinicians: 36 staff clinicians

NCQA Accredited: 1996

Services Offered: Managed Mental Health and Substance Abuse Treatment
State Medicaid Initiatives

Capitation Contracts:

Type of Program	Number of Contracts	Covered Lives
Commercial MH/SA	1	101,000
Commercial EAP Only	—	—
Commercial MH/SA & EAP	—	—
Medicaid Only	—	—
Utilization Management Only	—	—
Other	—	—
Total	1	101,000

Lovelace ParkCenter is unique in its relationship to a national carve-out company—MCC Behavioral Care. Both MCC and Lovelace (delivery system and health plan) are owned by Cigna, a large national insurance company. Through their shared owner, ParkCenter and MCC have forged a working relationship in which ParkCenter serves all behavioral needs of Lovelace Health Plan members in the Albuquerque area (defined by zip codes), whereas MCC provides behavioral care throughout New Mexico using a network model. They even share a common toll-free intake telephone number that is based on the caller's telephone prefix (first three digits) and automatically directs the caller to a ParkCenter or an MCC triage specialist for an intake assessment. HMO members are not required to have a PCP referral to mental health to access services.

ParkCenter is capitated for services to Lovelace Health Plan members (both commercial and Medicare) in Albuquerque, whereas MCC is capitated for services to members outside Albuquerque. Regarding management of services, ParkCenter works collaboratively with Lovelace Health Plan to administer patient referrals, intake processes, and the utilization of behavioral services in the Albuquerque area. Oversight of quality programs, staff credentialing, and claims payment for the few subcontractors used is done by Lovelace Health Plan.

Services Offered. Lovelace has many programs that integrate behavioral services with general medical needs. This is especially true for emergency services in Lovelace facilities and for the many geriatric services available. In geriatrics, ParkCenter has a distinct inpatient and partial hospital unit.

ParkCenter offers a full continuum of care, including inpatient, partial hospital, day treatment (three hours per day), and intensive outpatient services (three times per week), along with standard outpatient office services. Service teams are multidisciplinary and are designed by life stage, offering services to children, adolescents, adults, and seniors.

For substance abuse, a modular program is available in which combinations of the following components can be used for an individualized treatment plan: an individual assessment, two types of treatment groups, a full intensive outpatient program (average length of treatment is twenty-two three-hour blocks of care), a day of family intervention, and an aftercare group.

Quality Programs. In 1996 ParkCenter participated with Lovelace Health Plan in a NCQA survey, which resulted in a three-year accreditation. ParkCenter's inpatient programs are also accredited by the Joint Commission on Accreditation of Healthcare Organizations.

Since 1995 ParkCenter has been a member of the Outcomes Management Project (OMP) coordinated by the University of Cincinnati. In 1997 the OMP is central to the department's measurement of clinical outcomes and patient satisfaction. Lovelace ParkCenter also participated in 1997 as a pilot site for the OMP Inpatient Module. ParkCenter has been active in implementing the OMP and sharing other common services with their main competitor in Albuquerque—Mesa Mental Health (see next profile).

Several quality improvement teams are active at ParkCenter. The department also has a well-developed quality plan with an array of indicators and reporting mechanisms.

The Future. Increased partial hospital usage and a broader menu of programs for adolescents and families are seen as important in the near future. In-home psychiatric care is being actively considered, along with a geriatric assessment clinic. ParkCenter sees itself as likely to have growth in both Medicaid and geriatric populations to serve in the next few years.

REGIONAL CARVE-OUT COMPANIES

Across the country during the 1980s and 1990s local insurers and large employers who self-insure their employees created a niche for local or regional managed behavioral health organizations. In most cases these companies began as large group practices that legally incorporated into a single business. They then developed the management knowledge and physical infrastructure (as outlined in Chapter Three) to accept small populations (fifteen thousand to one hundred thousand) under capitation. Having successfully implemented one or two contracts, many have expanded to incorporate several contracts. A few of these groups have even become multistate in their operations.

Some regional carve outs serve as subcapitated entities for the national carve-out companies. For example, Value Behavioral Health has been especially active in contracting with these regional companies to become what VBH calls "clinical groups." However, as these regional companies have grown they are now often seen as local competitors with the national firms.

For this chapter we profile two regional companies: Mesa Mental Health (my own group) and an MBHO that developed from a department of psychiatry: Alliance Behavioral Care of Greater Cincinnati.

Mesa Mental Health

Mesa Mental Health represents the evolution of a small private practice that I started in 1984 (see Exhibit 11.5). When another psychologist and a psychiatrist joined in 1987, we believed that it was best to incorporate as a business in order to build a multidisciplinary practice. Shortly after we incorporated, a local HMO covering 30,000 people came to us with a proposal: Would we be interested in working under a capitated arrangement? We said, "What's that?" But we quickly found out and set up a network of contracted local clinicians and a crude home-grown capitation computer system to track utilization and to pay claims. Since that rough beginning we have constantly grown through additional capitation contracts (the original one turned into an eight-year arrangement). Now we have four capitation contracts covering almost 250,000 lives across the state of New Mexico and a large employee assistance division. We serve approximately 60,000 lives through administrative-services-only arrangements. The ASO contract employs Mesa to provide the clinical network including credentialing, customer service, and utilization management, while the insurer bears the financial risk for the cost of services and the payment of claims. The latest venture is a new corporation called Mesa Behavioral of Texas, which is an alliance with a west Texas psychiatric group.

Mesa's original goal with regard to clinical delivery was to provide the majority of services through our own group practice. By 1995 we had over thirty-nine full-time equivalents forming a clinical staff (psychiatrists—7.2, psychologists—7.5, and psychotherapists/EAP counselors—23) in five offices, including an office in Santa Fe. As managed care has become dominant in New Mexico (over 90 percent of all insured individuals in Albuquerque are in managed care), we have increasingly turned from a staff model focus to a network model. Today we have a clinical staff of just below fifteen FTEs (psychologists—3.4 and

Exhibit 11.5. Mesa Mental Health.

Corporate Headquarters: 6723 Academy Road, N.E., Albuquerque, NM 87109

Year Founded: 1987

CEO: Steve Sehr, M.D.

Doing Business In: New Mexico and Texas (separate corporations)

Number of Credentialed Clinicians: 371

NCQA Site Visit: Anticipated for 1999

Services Offered: Behavioral Healthcare Management and Administrative Service
Mental Health and Substance Abuse Treatment
Employee Assistance Programs

Capitation:

Type of Program	Number of Contracts	Covered Lives
Commercial MH/SA	5	245,000
Commercial EAP Only	58	135,000
Commercial MH/SA & EAP	1	4,500
Medicaid Only	—	—
Utilization Management Only	—	—
Other: Administrative Services Only	1	60,000
Total	65	444,500

psychotherapists—9.2) in three offices, but a subcontracted network exceeds three hundred facilities and clinicians.

Mesa has, since 1994, run the largest employee assistance program in New Mexico: Corporate Health Resources. With over fifty clients in three states Mesa has actively integrated standard behavioral services covered by insurance with the assessment and brief counseling strengths of EAP to form a seamless system for employers. On-site employee services, organizational consultation, and a system of employer/employee trainings are additional services of the EAP program.

Services Offered. Mesa offers a full range of inpatient, partial hospital, facility-based, intensive outpatient, and outpatient treatments to New Mexicans in the three largest cities of the state. In the highly rural areas, a strong network of inpatient and outpatient treatments are available. EAP services are also available across New Mexico.

Members of the health plans contracted to Mesa access services initially through a toll-free number. They are given a full triage and clinical risk assessment by telephone before being referred for services. Crisis triaging is available twenty-four hours per day. For EAP clients the Immediate Consultative Response program developed by the staff clinicians offers all initial callers the opportunity to begin counseling within two minutes of waiting by having a clinician conduct telephonic counseling followed by face-to-face counseling if the client so wishes. This service is especially popular with employees and their dependents who live in rural areas.

In Albuquerque, Mesa offers a special assessment and crisis program for new or existing patients with a long history of mental health or substance abuse problems or who are likely to have frequent crisis episodes. The program—Outpatients at Risk for Extended Resources (OPERA)—has been very successful in providing a full evaluation, crisis stabilization, written treatment planning, and interpretation of the evaluation and treatment plan to patients having a wide array of severe conditions. Since 1995 Mesa also has offered an extensive attention deficit/hyperactivity disorders education and assessment program with multiple treatment options, including a martial arts class designed to teach self-control.

Mesa has developed a full depression diagnostic and treatment protocol with primary care physicians. The program was designed to be deployed statewide with family physicians. Details of the depression protocol and both the OPERA and ADHD programs are available in *The Behavioral Healthcare Quality and Accountability Tool Kit* (Daniels, Zieman, Kramer, and Furgal, 1997).

Quality Programs. Mesa has been a leader among regional MBHOs in quality improvement programs. Like many smaller MBHOs, Mesa is preparing to seek its own NCQA accreditation rather than continue as a survey participant when each of the insurers who contract with Mesa have their NCQA site visits.

Jointly with the Quality Center at the University of Cincinnati College of Medicine, Mesa codeveloped the Outcomes Management Project, which measures patient functional levels, patient satisfaction, mental health symptoms, and physical health from a pretreatment assessment through six months after beginning care. Locally, both Mesa and our competitor, Lovelace ParkCenter, offer health plans and offer their members an outcomes report card in which all outcomes measures and procedures are identical. The outcomes project also provides baseline data for a variety of clinical studies of the populations we serve to help us learn to serve them more effectively.

The Future. Mesa sees its future in being a locally responsive, yet regional, MBHO throughout the greater Southwest. This growth is expected to go hand in hand with strong quality programs and measures culminating in our own NCQA accreditation. The continued development of treatment protocols for common conditions, especially protocols that include primary medical care, will remain a focus. Further integration of insured behavioral plans with employee assistance programs is a continuing goal.

Alliance Behavioral Care

The beginnings of Alliance Behavioral Care (ABC) were in 1983 when the department of psychiatry at the University of Cincinnati College of Medicine formed University Psychiatric Services (UPS) (see Exhibit 11.6). UPS is a group practice composed of university faculty and staff providers; the practice served as the provider anchor for the University Health Plan (UHP), a university-owned insurer serving commercial and Medicaid members. The initial goals of UPS were to internally serve the university HMO and to expand funding sources for psychiatric residency training. In 1985 UPS was awarded delegation to handle all behavioral triage and utilization management needs of UHP and its PPO products. In 1991 UPS negotiated a capitation arrangement with UHP to cover 12,000 lives and spun off a new corporation to manage risk-based contracts. This new entity—University Managed Care (UMC)—then expanded into the private market and accepted full-risk capitation for both HMO lives and administrative services only (ASO) contracts with MetLife for 40,000 enrollees. By 1994 University Managed Care had 35,000 lives under capitation and a well-established history of ASO contracting. UMC has expanded this base by contracting with a statewide Blue Cross organization—the successor to UHP. In addition, University Managed Care currently contracts with United Health Care and local self-insured companies to provide managed behavioral health care.

Now a nationally recognized leader in private managed care contracting among academic medical centers, UMC has sought to strengthen its position by affiliating with the Health Alliance of Greater Cincinnati. This affiliation between University Hospital and three other local hospital systems has afforded UMC a chance for growth. As the Alliance's strategic partner for managed behavioral health, UMC changed its operating name to Alliance Behavioral Care (ABC). In this new role ABC manages all of the Alliance's behavioral care, including delegation for quality improvement, utilization management, member services, credentialing, and claims.

Services Offered. In the transformation from UPS to ABC, the department of psychiatry successfully moved from a primary staff model delivery system to a full network model having community providers throughout the Greater Cincinnati area. UPS remains as one of the care network provider groups. Alliance Behavioral Care reimburses providers on a universal fee schedule that is based on CPT codes rather than the discipline of the practitioner.

A special service that ABC brings to insured populations is an advanced psychiatric emergency service. This service includes a separate and distinct psychiatric emergency room located in a university hospital, as well as a mobile crisis team. The psychiatric emergency room serves the Greater Cincinnati area and is

Exhibit 11.6. Alliance Behavioral Care.

Corporate Headquarters: Department of Psychiatry
University of Cincinnati College of Medicine
222 Piedmont Ave., Suite 8500, Cincinnati, OH 45219

Year Founded: 1983 (University Psychiatric Services)

CEO: Allen Daniels, Ed.D.

Medical Directors: Marcia Kaplan, M.D., Clinical Services
Naakesh Dewan, M.D., Quality Improvement

Doing Business In: Ohio, Kentucky, Indiana

Number of Credentialed Clinicians: 200

NCQA Site Visit: Anticipated in 1999

Services Offered: Managed Mental Health and Substance Abuse Treatment
Quality Improvement Products and Healthcare Data Analysis

Capitation:

Type of Program	Number of Contracts	Covered Lives
Commercial MH/SA	3	72,000
Commercial EAP Only	—	—
Commercial MH/SA & EAP	—	—
Medicaid Only	1	18,000
Utilization Management Only	2	28,000
Other: Medicare	1	4,000
Total	7	122,000

staffed twenty-four hours per day by behavioral health providers, including psychiatrists.

Quality Programs. Structurally, the quality improvement program reports directly through the CEO to the ABC board of directors. In preparation for an NCQA accreditation review, ABC has formed seven parallel continuous improvement teams, one each for the seven major areas of the NCQA behavioral standards:

- The Quality Program
- Accessibility, Availability, Referral and Triage
- Utilization Management
- Credentialing and Recredentialing
- Members' Rights and Responsibilities
- Preventive Health Services
- Clinical Evaluation and Treatment Records

Among the items put into place by these teams is a prevention program using a dedicated phone line; patients can call for data on and answers to a broad array of mental health and psychiatric medical questions.

ABC is a cofounder of the Outcomes Management Project (see Chapter Nine and the two previous MBHO descriptions) and is the national data center for OMP; ABC provides quarterly benchmarking data for participants. ABC has also developed an entire division for the dissemination of quality programs and the special analyses of healthcare data. This division—the Center for Quality Innovations and Research—will assist ABC in being a quality leader and will provide services for healthcare entities nationally in all areas of behavioral care. This development represents a strong commitment to academic principles in the management and advancement of behavioral health care.

The Future. For Alliance Behavioral Care, the future appears strong. With an established role in an evolving integrated delivery system, ABC is able to support all behavioral components of the Health Alliance of Greater Cincinnati. In addition, ABC has been instrumental in the creation and development, by other academic centers, of managed behavioral health programs. With a firm commitment to quality improvement and measured outcomes, ABC is poised to remain in the forefront of managed behavioral care.

CLOSING NOTE

I wish to thank the six organizations profiled here for their willingness to be included and their efforts to provide information about themselves.

Although data that would have given a wholly balanced perspective, including data from providers and health plan members related to these individual organizations, were not available, I hope that these six profiles have provided you with an instructive sample of the types of MBHOs in all their variations in size, focus, vision, and services of which they are proud.

Next, we turn to a very important topic—ethics. With all the emotional and opposing opinions about how clinical, business, and patient concerns and needs can be met—or violated—the many facets of ethical practice in a managed care world make up an essential subject. Chapter Twelve explores this critical topic.

Ethical Issues in Managed Care

In 1927, M. L. Harris, M.D., wrote an essay in the *Journal of the American Medical Association* entitled "Medical Economics." In part, Dr. Harris wrote (p. 41):

> If we recognize that the practice of medicine is a monopoly, we must admit
> that this monopoly entails on the profession a definite and distinct duty which
> cannot be delegated and this duty is the care of the sick and suffering. . . . If the
> medical profession as a body fails to grasp and to fulfill its entire duty in this
> respect, then will private and public institutions and legislatures step in and
> take the matter out of the hands of the profession?

Although it is not justified to say that the medical profession has failed in its duty to care for the sick and suffering, it is very clear that, with clinicians and consumers driving the healthcare system, the nation has not fulfilled its duty to ensure that all citizens have healthcare (see Chapters One, Two, and Ten). As predicted by Dr. Harris, private and public institutions (primarily employers) and legislatures (consider Medicaid and Medicare) have stepped in today and taken matters partly out of the hands of the consumers and practitioners.

A healthcare system with strong business and governmental influence is the reality in which we function. Therefore, our discussion of ethics must focus on professional issues in managed care that take into account business and governmental points of view.

Simultaneously, we must consider the needs and perspectives of patients, clinicians, and payers (namely, insurers as well as the purchasers of insurance: employers and government). In a very cogent chapter on ethics, R. Wyatt (1995) has referred to these three forces as the "Triumvirate," whose needs must be balanced in all healthcare decisions. Throughout this chapter I frequently refer to the Triumvirate.

ETHICS AND MANAGED CARE

Discussions of ethics and managed care often center around the debate between clinical ethics—especially those set forth by the major professional associations—and the business ethics of MCOs. The debate typically focuses on the following topics: needs of the individual patient versus the larger population, big business versus cottage industry, confidentiality, access to care, insurance exclusions, patient abandonment, and disclosure of financial incentives. I will discuss each of these.

For each area of ethical concern, I conclude by giving direct and explicit advice regarding what I believe to be the best course of action in weighing the needs of the Triumvirate. Most important, however, is not so much what I think or what I advise. Most important is that this text prepares you to evaluate my advice critically and respond within your own convictions when presented with one of these ethical dilemmas in practice.

Disclosure of Financial Incentives

Very early in any managed care and ethics discussion the controversial topics listed earlier most often break down into a comparison between practice under self-pay, indemnity insurance, and managed care. In other words, central to ethical debates is who the bill payer is and how the bill is being paid. Does the payer deserve a say in treatment planning and access to patient and treatment data? Consequently, our first topic must be the impact of basic financial arrangements on clinical ethics.

The Triumvirate generally wants to believe that treatment and ethical care are not connected to the financial aspects of care. Unfortunately, this is not true. Who pays and what limits are set in the payment system have always affected what is considered ethical care. A comparison across payment models is shown in Table 12.1.

From studying Table 12.1, two points are obvious:

1. *Financial arrangements make a considerable difference in how confidentiality, access to care, and exclusions are handled.* There is less difference, however, regarding patient abandonment, except

Table 12.1. Daily Ethical Functioning by Payment Type.

	Patient Confidentiality	Access to Care	Insurance Exclusions	Patient Abandonment	Disclosure of Financial Incentives
Self-Pay	Totally between clinician and client.	Patient may choose any available provider.	Patient chooses what treatments to receive based on clinician's recommendation.	If patient can't pay or is uncooperative, clinician decides at what point no further service will be offered. Usually not seen as abandonment if patient not in urgent need or other clinician to see patient.	Typically none. Patient to assume that whatever procedures done, clinician is to be reimbursed by the patient.
Indemnity Insurance	Clinician shares with insurer the patient's diagnosis, dates of care, and procedures.	Patient may choose any licensed provider within those types insurer accepts; e.g., non-doctoral provider.	Often exclusions for certain preexisting conditions or life time maximum $ amounts for certain diagnoses or procedures often excluded.	If insurance won't pay (preexisting condition or lifetime maximum reached) or patient cannot afford the annual deductible, same as self-pay.	Typically none. Patient to assume that for procedures the clinician is paid through a combination of annual deductible, insurance, & percentage copay due.
Managed Care (HMO)	Clinician shares with insurer the patient's diagnosis, dates of care, summary of history and treatment plan.	Patient may choose any provider listed as contracted with the insurer.	Often exclusions for certain procedures, annual limits on specialty care, & any procedure insurer believes is not medically necessary.	If insurance won't pay, or patient can't pay copayment due, same as under self-pay.	Typically none. Patient to assume that clinician is paid from insurer & copay. Patient may not know provider is paid fixed $ in advance.

that indemnity insurance and managed care have different criteria for when they will *not* pay: lifetime maximums and preexisting condition exclusions versus medically necessary definitions and annual limits on some specialty services, such as mental health.

2. *Under none of the payment arrangements is healthcare open to an active disclosure of financial incentives to patients.*

Under self-pay and indemnity insurance arrangements, providers avoid telling their patients that they are financially rewarded, at least in the short run, by providing more care and possibly overtreating. And in capitated situations, insurers and providers avoid telling patients that they are financially rewarded, at least in the short run, by providing less care and possibly undertreating. The rule in healthcare has been, *Allow patients and the general public to make their own assumptions about financial incentives and their impact on care.* The active disclosure of financial incentives has never been specifically addressed by any of the major professional associations in their ethical guidelines.

Ethical Advice. Financial arrangements between providers and insurers, and their associated incentives, should be actively disclosed to patients and general health plan members. This disclosure may be handled in a patient brochure or handbook and need not be a verbal discussion with each patient. But it must be explicit, with a balanced view that neither favors nor pans a particular payment method. Let the consumer decide what values to attach to the facts. Given that consumers will need education regarding the differences between the types of pay arrangements and incentives, it would be best to have standardized disclosure statements and educational write-ups across delivery systems as an aid in reducing confusion. The professional associations are excellent groups to produce standardized disclosure materials, especially if they will cooperate with each other.

Capitalism and Healthcare

A second area dealing with business and money is profit in healthcare. Historically, many healthcare entities have been nonprofit in their business organization. The classic national examples of this are the many church-developed healthcare delivery systems (National Jewish in Denver and Rush-Presbyterian in Chicago, for example) and the Blue Cross/Blue Shield (BCBS) plans. That is now changing. Many church-organized healthcare systems and BCBS plans are changing to for-profit. The growth of new for-profit entities in healthcare abounds.

Many consider it to be a breach of ethics that a healthcare business should make a profit—or a profit as high as that of other industries. Their view is that healthcare is a sacred area of altruism, where the motives of profit taking should not be wedded with the provision of care. They perceive profit making to be counterproductive to the best interests of patients and society at large.

The opposing view is that profit making is an excellent motivation for change and innovation at a time when the American healthcare system is struggling to handle higher costs and coverage for all citizens. Also, they point out that historically, as a cottage industry, most healthcare professionals sought personal "profit" in the form of fees and salaries higher than most other professions and that indemnity insurers generally made much larger profits than the managed care plans of today make.

Most MCOs average only a couple of percentage points of profit per year. And in 1996, 65 percent of all managed care plans lost money (Harris, 1997). The highest profits in healthcare are generally among pharmaceutical companies and some large hospital systems, not managed care insurers.

Ethical Advice. Healthcare is well along the path of industrialization and is not outside the economic forces of our broader society. Therefore, demanding or regulating that healthcare not be profit-driven is unrealistic and perpetuates the cumbersome healthcare mechanisms that have characterized Medicaid and Medicare. Although buying healthcare is more crucial than buying material items such as automobiles, to restrict or prevent profit making restricts healthcare's ability to change swiftly enough to meet societal needs. For example, without profit potential, healthcare entities are limited in their ability to access capital for the start-up or expansion of delivery systems, and they cannot easily streamline operations when governed by large, community-based boards of directors, as mandated by state and federal rules regarding nonprofit corporations.

However, consumers as patients or potential patients, the purchasers of insurance, and governmental regulators must judge whether a healthcare insurer is sacrificing quality care for profit. Merely making a substantial profit is not grounds for assuming that patients are not well cared for.

The Individual Versus the Broader Population

Here, the conflicting motivations of the Triumvirate are clearly demonstrated. A clinician treating a distressed patient values the patient and pursues whatever treatment appears, at the time, most likely to lead to improvement or a cure. A clinician is also likely to value his or her relationship with the MBHO. Most clinicians will not seek to jeopardize this relationship without believing strongly that the MBHO has made a decision that is highly detrimental to their patient.

Of course, patients are focused on what the clinician can do to make them well, whether it is one or one hundred sessions of care.

The managed care insurer, however, is most concerned with the needs of the population of insured individuals and the prevention of crisis situations. The focus of the MCO or MBHO is on the total resources available. The insurer must balance the needs of any particular individual with those of all plan members. To offer too little care can result in crisis situations among individual members that could be detrimental to the finances of the insurer and create dissatisfaction among plan members. And member dissatisfaction jeopardizes the ability of the MCO or MBHO to retain a contractual relationship with the purchaser of the insurance. So, the insurer is motivated to offer as much to the individual as they believe necessary to improve the health and satisfaction of each distressed patient, while not using so many resources that other members suffer from a shortage of resources.

Ethical Advice. As a clinician, always vigorously seek to complete a treatment plan that is most likely to remove or greatly lessen a distinct mental health or substance abuse disorder. But recognize that resources are not available from current funding levels paid to insurers to treat all distressing life conditions such as low self-esteem or romantic relationship discord. For patients with long-standing disorders, seek a maintenance therapy approach that will provide basic and ongoing stabilization.

Conversely, MBHOs and the purchasers of insurance must respect the needs of patients for care of chronic conditions. Treating only crisis conditions and refusing to pay for any care related to chronic disorders is unethical.

Parity of Behavioral and General Medical Insurance Benefits

A lengthy discussion of this topic is not necessary. There is no clinically sound or ethical business reason for not having behavioral care available to the same extent as other medical specialties. A lack of parity discriminates against the severely mentally ill and hinders the integration of physical and behavioral medicine.

Ethical Advice. All stakeholders in the Triumvirate must support parity in resources available for medical and behavioral care beyond the very limited scope of the Federal Parity Act of 1997.

Patient Confidentiality

A balance is necessary between maintaining confidentiality of patients' histories and problems while acknowledging that health plan members have purchased coverage that specifically mandates benefits only for a subset of all human problems, often with limitations on the amount of care available within a given time frame. Given these restrictions, the MBHO must have some mechanism for monitoring clinical records to ensure that resources are going toward purchased benefits. And members must be fully aware of their MBHO's access to their treatment records prior to signing up for insurance.

Ethical Advice. Each of the following is necessary:

- At the time potential insurance members are informed about their possible insurance coverage, and in future interactions, MBHOs and MCOs must be explicit that insurers will have access to their clinical records.

- MBHOs must work with their providers and members to design highly specific protocols outlining when and how records will be reviewed, as well as how the confidentiality of the records will be handled in the offices of both the clinicians and the MBHO. These protocols must be available to all members and health plan practitioners.

- Providers must keep clinical records that give enough detail to document and support the following: the diagnoses listed for the patient, an active treatment plan, risk assessments in areas such as suicidality and homicide potential, and the progress made by the patient in both symptoms and functional impairment. Process notes and extensive personal histories, except when absolutely necessary (in cases of current sexual abuse, for example), should not be retained in the clinical record. These should be kept separate and should be destroyed as soon as they are not needed.

Freedom of Choice in Providers

Health plan members, and often practitioners, desire absolute freedom for members to seek care from any clinician they wish and to have the insurer pay that clinician. Understandably, members want total choice, and providers for whom total choice is beneficial desire the same. On the opposite side, the MCO or MBHO cannot, in a total choice situation, guarantee that the clinicians it holds out to the plan membership are thoroughly screened and credentialed. Nor can the MCO or MBHO guarantee that providers are agreeable to the various MBHO requirements that protect members. An example of this would be agreeing to accept the copayment rate and not to bill the patient if a service is denied for payment by the insurer due to the actions of the provider. Additionally, attempting to contract and credential far more providers than the volume of patients dictates is very expensive (see Chapter Six) and drives up insurance premiums. Again, the needs of the Triumvirate are not in alignment, and a balance is needed.

Ethical Advice. The balance here is that the MBHO must contract with and credential a large number of providers in any geographic area but need not offer all clinicians in a given area. MBHOs must provide a network of providers that has broad clinical depth and geographic coverage, as well as specialty knowledge that exceeds the clinical needs of the covered population, while providing for quick and easy access to appointments for new and ongoing patients. Geographically, health plan members in urban and suburban areas should never be forced to travel more than thirty minutes to any provider except for very low-volume specialty care (a child neuropsychologist, for example). Reasons for not using all providers in a community must be explained clearly to health plan members.

Benefit Exclusions

Many employers and agencies sign contracts with, and in many cases demand contracts from, MCOs that have exclusions such as no payment for marital therapy or no coverage except for crisis stabilization. This is done to save dollars—in the short run. Such contracts annoy patients and providers, as well as staff in the MCOs and MBHOs who have the hassle of managing such contracts. No one in the Triumvirate is served well in the long run by these arrangements. They reward individuals for becoming so distraught or ill that they have crises, which are expensive to treat.

Unfortunately, I am all too aware of the ethical dilemma of exclusions versus long-term needs. One of my daily roles has been to clinically supervise the outpatient portion of our utilization management department. We are contracted with one insurer for whom a portion of their population has signed up for a benefit package that in no uncertain terms excludes marital or relationship therapy. Almost daily we receive calls from distraught health plan members in relationship crises. If they clearly appear to have an individual psychiatric diagnosis that goes beyond relationship distress, we authorize care and pay for it from our monthly capitation check. If their problems appear to be mostly limited to relationship issues, we swallow hard and suggest self-pay, or we give a referral to a community relationship group. Many of the callers become mad. We used to send them to care even though it was beyond their treatment benefit. But when we lost significant sums of money with that HMO insurer, and the HMO reprimanded us for not following the purchased benefit package, we stopped such referrals. No one could win. If we refused to continue the contract, we knew that another MBHO was waiting to snap up the HMO's business, with or without a relationship benefit. And many of the employers who purchased this pared-down benefit plan were clearly uninterested in paying for a better benefit plan.

Ethical Advice. We must push for a minimum standard of insurance benefits that serves the long-term nature of the population, not just the short-term budget of anyone in the Triumvirate. This is an area in which legislative action must be used to raise the bar as to minimum insurance coverage limits that include all common acute and chronic conditions.

Ethical Closure Versus Abandonment

Here, all members of the Triumvirate have a distinct responsibility. The provider, patient, and MBHO have a responsibility to be aware at all times of the likely limits on the care being provided to every individual and to plan for a gradual closure to care—not an abrupt stoppage, which in many cases is abandonment. For example, if a patient having been seen for an episode of major depression shows distinct improvement, it is incumbent on the MBHO not to demand an abrupt stop in care but to authorize a few follow-up sessions. The provider should also have advised the patient that care must end once there is substantial improvement. Neither the patient nor the provider should allow the development of a dependent relationship such that the patient will then need or demand care for an extended period of time.

Clinicians must be skilled at bringing treatment to closure and recognizing that patients may return for new episodes of care, some several times, as they progress through life. This has been called "brief intermittent psychotherapy throughout the life cycle" (Cummings, 1990, p. 169). Managed care supports this model, given that most care limits are annual, not lifetime maximums.

At Mesa Mental Health we have come up with many creative ways to offer ethical care, even to those patients who have severe and ongoing needs but who bring to their treatment a very restrictive insurance benefit. We have redefined, with our contracting MCOs' consent, the meaning of "one visit," as listed in a patient's insurance certificate, to be an hour of service, thereby allowing patients to be seen for two half-hour sessions or four fifteen-minute medication checkups while only using one hour of their benefits. Additionally, many of our network clinicians speak with their patients up front about having long-term needs and early in the treatment begin alternating between sessions under self-pay and sessions billed under the patient's insurance.

Ethical Advice. MBHOs must educate providers, members, potential members, and insurance purchasers about the common realities and expectations with regard to care and covered benefits. For example, if 90 percent of outpatient psychotherapy cases for All-American HMO conclude with less than ten treatment sessions, and relationship counseling is not covered, these data should be made available to all stakeholders both at the time they are deciding which insurance to purchase and, subsequently, in an ongoing manner.

Clinicians must design treatment plans that mirror the realities of the resources available and the clinical needs for each individual patient.

Finally, universities and professional schools have a responsibility to train clinicians in skills that truly reflect what will be needed in applied clinical settings. To train students in a clinic where the average outpatient receives more than twenty sessions for care is not training that mirrors the world into which students will enter. Carol Austad's book *Is Long-Term Psychotherapy Unethical?* (1996) must be seriously studied.

Overall, the advice given in this chapter has been designed to be practical in daily professional life, where the needs and desires of patients, practitioners, insurance purchasers, and insurers culminate in the actual provision of care.

In the next chapter I pull together information from all of the previous chapters to advise you on what to expect and how to prepare for a professional life in a managed care world.

CHAPTER THIRTEEN

A Future in
Managed Care

The preceding chapters have shown that managed care is a complete health-care system, not simply a means of payment or a type of clinical practice. Managed care is a four-way partnership among providers (facilities and practitioners), purchasers of healthcare insurance (primarily employers and government agencies), health plan members, and managed care organizations (MCOs). Although each group has specific needs and desires, each depends on the other, in the true nature of a system.

For many clinicians and facilities, however, involving MCOs and purchasers as partners in the system of care provision has been an unsettling alliance. Managed care demands that providers not only treat plan members but also engage in quality improvement activities, follow systemwide rules around such areas as timeliness and financial consciousness, and share with the payer decision making about what is efficient and necessary care.

The realities of such a partnership require clinicians with a distinctly different professional mind-set than did the indemnity model. For many clinicians these realities match well with their personalities, professional goals, and training; others may not find a match. That is why, in this chapter, I explore aspects of working with managed care plans and suggest ways to proceed if you choose not to associate yourself with managed care.

ENGAGING WITH MANAGED CARE

From reading the previous chapters, you have probably formed opinions about how well you would fit in a managed care environment. This section is designed for those of you who believe that a managed care association may be best for you. Specific "you should" and "you will need to" advice is given here to facilitate your learning how to work effectively within managed care. First, I explore the professional mind-set and general attitudes that are needed to function effectively and comfortably in a managed care environment. Next, I tackle the necessary clinician behaviors and daily operational changes. And finally, I discuss the professional opportunities in managed care for psychotherapists, psychiatrists, and psychologists.

Mind-Set and Attitudes

Whether you practice as a subcontracted provider or as an employee of a managed care system, there are beliefs and general points of view that will connect you comfortably with health plans, insurance purchasers, and patients who are members of managed care health plans. In the following sections, attributes that will improve your occupational satisfaction and maximize your effectiveness with patients within the resource and system limitations of managed care are described.

Accept and Understand Managed Care. Although this may seem obvious, coming so late in this text, it is worth repeating because if you cannot accept and understand managed care, your professional satisfaction and effectiveness will be impaired.

Every clinician in the delivery system must acknowledge that managed care has become the mainstream operational mode of healthcare and actively seek to understand in some detail the internal workings of managed care plans (which you are doing by reading this book). Accepting and understanding does not require that you believe managed care is the best system possible but that you consent to work with it and are willing to make constructive changes from within.

As we enter the next century, healthcare will be dominated by large, integrated delivery systems that are regional or national. Other service areas of the American economy have already industrialized; healthcare is in the process of industrialization. Treating patients in the context of a larger, highly structured healthcare system is the likely future for the majority of new clinicians. Work within it, and keep developing it for the better.

Welcome Accountability. Healthcare in the past assumed high quality, based on passive data collection such as the number of patients who returned to a provider or the low number of complaints. Such semi-anecdotal measures are unacceptable in a delivery system where quality improvement (QI) programs demand specific and verifiable information and where clinician practices must meet quality accreditation mandates.

Clinicians must actively welcome QI programs. Those who encourage data collection and information feedback, and who see QI as an opportunity to improve clinical and logistical practices across the delivery system, will flourish within managed care. Such practitioners consider the costs of QI activities as an investment in the future of the system to provide better care.

View Utilization Management as a Necessary Component. In a managed care organization the utilization management (UM) department has the responsibility of ensuring that the limited healthcare resources are applied as efficiently and fairly as possible. Clinicians often battle with UM staff over a member's treatment needs without considering the purchased benefit package that the patient brings to the treatment or the national need for less expenditure in healthcare. As we saw in the last chapter, clinicians have a responsibility to treat patients within the resources available, as well as with therapies providing sound clinical care.

Clinicians can best work with managed care utilization management by

- Assisting patients and families early in treatment to understand what services are covered and not covered by their insurance, and how ongoing care is authorized periodically during the course of treatment—not all at the beginning or at the end.

- Recognizing that managed care plans cannot authorize large chunks of care (for example, sixteen outpatient sessions) in one authorization and still meet the oversight criteria with which they are charged. Therefore, clinicians should expect to communicate with the UM department every two to ten sessions, or every couple of inpatient days, to assess the patient's need for continued care at the current level.

- Learning how to interact through appeals and grievances with the UM department whenever the clinician or patient disagree strongly with authorizations for care.

- Knowing how to appeal to the employer or government purchaser of the health plan, as well as to the customer service department of the MCO or MBHO, whenever the benefit package is too limited or otherwise inappropriate.

Expect to Join an Integrated, Multidisciplinary Group. The many forces described in this text foretell an ongoing trend toward multidisciplinary group practices and clinics with employed clinicians. Solo private practice is less and less viable as the payer systems push for integrated delivery systems that use organized clinics to cover metropolitan areas or entire regions of the country.

One-stop shopping clinics are encouraged. Clinical and business-savvy groups are designing offices where patients can receive medications, psychotherapy of various types, psychological testing, and prevention programs—all in one place with one clinical chart, one appointment scheduling system, and one billing statement.

Even the structure of group practice is changing. Traditionally, groups have been a collection of clinicians, often from the same discipline, who share expenses but retain for themselves the status of being an independent business within the group's walls. To meet today's market forces, though, groups are finding that the only way to obtain large segments of business is to be multidisciplinary and incorporated as a business, with the clinicians as shareholders and employees. Incorporated groups can offer a full array of integrated clinical services with greater efficiency.

Although you will experience a loss of individual autonomy in an integrated group, you will enjoy greater control over the market forces shaping your professional life. Prepare for and anticipate the high probability that your future will be as an employee in a team-functioning group or clinic.

Clinician Behaviors

Along with certain attitudes and beliefs, an array of behaviors will enhance your success in a managed care environment. Your clinical success in managed care depends heavily on adapting to and supporting these professional behaviors.

Focus on Functional Impairment, Not Symptoms. In an acute care treatment model, not symptomatology but impairment is the focus, especially in assessing the need for continued treatment.

Most managed care plans decide the need for treatment based on the definition of medical necessity, as discussed in Chapter One. A service or treatment is generally determined to be medically necessary if it meets all of the following four criteria:

1. The treatment is for a distinct mental disorder, as defined by the latest version of the *Diagnostic and Statistical Manual of Mental Disorders* published by the American Psychiatric Association.

2. The condition is likely to show sustained improvement from the proposed treatment, or crisis intervention is necessary to prevent harm.

3. The treatment is provided in the least restrictive setting appropriate.

4. The treatment meets community and national standards for appropriate care.

The functional orientation to treatment comes from the second item in the phrase, "likely to show sustained improvement." This definition assumes that the patient will function better as a result of treatment. Continued symptoms are not a primary reason for extending care, but improvement in function with the reasonable expectation of further improvement is. Under managed care, continuing symptoms with little functional change is often a reason for denying further treatment or insisting on a major change in the treatment plan (sometimes including a change of clinicians). The logic here is that unless the symptoms represent a clear and immediate danger to the patient's physical being, continued care without distinct improvement is not an efficient or appropriate use of resources.

Whether in direct treatment or in completing a treatment plan form, focus on functional status and change, not on symptoms.

Practice Brief, Problem-Focused Therapies. It almost goes without saying that there is a strong demand from MCOs, MBHOs, and insurance purchasers for brief treatments. Clinicians who are comfortable and skilled in brief therapies that address current functional impairments are highly valued.

To lend a context to the meaning of brief therapies in managed care, the initial findings of the Outcomes Management Project serve as a good benchmark (Zieman, Williams, Daniels, and Kramer, 1997). The project included over 5,100 outpatients seen from 1995 through early 1997 across seventeen managed-care-oriented group practices and clinics in twelve states. Very few Medicaid or Medicare recipients were included in the study. Most of the patients assessed in the project were covered by a managed care plan. From patient chart audits completed six months after treatment was initiated, the findings were that the average patient received 5.6 sessions of psychotherapy (standard deviation = 3.1) and 2.0 medication visits (standard deviation = 1.3). And well over 80 percent of the patients had ended care within six months. Those continuing in care were receiving primarily medication management or widely spaced maintenance psychotherapy. Clinical outcomes were tracked via patient self-reports of symptoms, functional impairment, and satisfaction with the treatment received. Success was measured by the amount that patients were significantly improved at three and six months after seeking treatment and the percentage of those expressing being satisfied or very satisfied with their care. Patients reported significant clinical improvements in a wide array of symptom and functional areas, and to most questions regarding satisfaction, including believing that care had assisted them, approximately 90 percent reported being satisfied or very satisfied. As my former hospital supervisor often lamented, "Another nail in the coffin of analytic therapy."

In managed care settings patients with chronic disorders such as personality and dissociative disorders are often managed through ongoing maintenance care that may last several years. Even in programs for the seriously mentally ill, treatments are heavily oriented toward maintenance and functional improvement through psychosocial programs rather than through frequent individual treatment sessions.

The message is clear. Master the brief treatments and use them.

Have Rapid Patient Access and Complete Emergency Coverage. The quality standards to which national accrediting bodies hold MBHOs require that routine outpatient clients must be offered an appointment within ten business days and that urgent patients must be evaluated face-to-face within seventy-two hours. Emergent patients are to receive immediate access to care, such as through an emergency room or a defined emergency triage professional.

In light of these standards, HMO, PPO, and POS plans create networks of providers who can offer reliable and speedy access to new patients and an organized after-hours system for existing patients with urgent needs. The days when a mental health clinician can have an answering machine or voice mail directing urgent situations to the local community mental health center or nearest emergency room are coming to a close.

Clinicians prepared for the managed care marketplace provide rapid access to care, make follow-up care available, and have an internal system for urgent and emergent situations after hours.

Collaborate with General Medicine. Behavioral healthcare is recognized as one of the most important specialities in the continuum of healthcare services. Large healthcare systems are actively creating programs that address the high prevalence of mental health and substance abuse disorders in the general population. On-site mental health staff at family care clinics, immediate telephone consultation services for primary care staff with mental health clinicians, and joint treatment protocols bringing behavioral medicine and primary care together are flourishing.

Clinicians are learning that active coordination of care with associated medical colleagues is an absolute requirement of today's clinical practice. In fact, most HMO member certificates contain a clause in which the subscriber has agreed that specialists must share treatment data with the patient's primary care physician (PCP) regarding any service paid for by the MCO. Mental health clinicians are expected to share the basics of any initial treatment plan or future treatment plan changes with the patient's PCP. The concept that mental health treatment is so confidential that other healthcare providers treating the patient should not know about it is quickly waning.

The advice is clear. Coordinate care and treatment protocols with medical colleagues.

Work Smarter, Not Harder. In a world of declining rates of reimbursement for clinical services, working more to increase income is not a productive response.

Managed care values efficiency—not the number of procedure codes billed. In discounted fee-for-service settings, the average length of treatment is carefully monitored for every provider and used in deciding which clinicians get new patient referrals and which will be recredentialed. And often providers are paid through case rates or capitation. Simply conducting more treatment sessions per patient under these financial arrangements will actually result in less income.

The effective response is to provide more care to more patients with less professional time expended. Such approaches are valued and frequently financially rewarded by managed care payers. Offer special treatment or evaluation programs and prevention activities that focus on a segment of the total insured population. In other words, seek to treat the population of potential patients rather than simply treating every individual patient.

Ask not how you can provide more services but how you can serve more patients with better services.

Operational Changes

Managed care has also encouraged modifications to common professional events that greatly affect the lives of clinicians. These daily operational changes are primarily focused in two areas: technological changes and professional role alterations. Adapting to them is crucial.

Incorporate Technological Changes. The emphasis that managed care places on integrated, multidisciplinary groups has not only altered the healthcare field away from solo practice but has strongly pushed for integrating advanced technology into groups and clinics. Integrated technology translates into computerized offices that facilitate the flow of data and communicate electronically with MCOs and MBHOs.

On the road to extinction are paper-based clinical records, appointment books, typed HCFA 1500 forms for billing, treatment forms that are mailed to the MBHO, and MBHO treatment authorization letters sent to you via the U.S. Post Office. In the new office, for which the software is already available today, all patient records will be kept on a computer (called a computerized patient record) with intense password protection. Appointment scheduling and insurance billing will be entirely electronic, with money transfers directly delivering payments to your bank account. Built into these systems will be e-mail or Web site connections that allow you to send treatment plans to MBHOs when you are seeking authorization to see a patient and to receive back the authorization in a similar fashion. The all-electronic office is on the horizon for behavioral care.

In designing an office, seek space for a computer terminal on every desk, not a filing room that will handle years of closed patient charts.

Accept Professional Role Changes. Integration of the different mental health disciplines into one office or clinic is no longer a situation of simply cohabitating professionally. Integration, as encouraged by managed care, means integrating assessment, psychotherapy, medication, and prevention functions through teams made up of Ph.D.'s, Psy.D.'s, M.S.W.'s, M.A.'s, R.N.C.'s (a master's-degreed nurse with a mental health clinical specialty), D.O.'s, M.D.'s, R.N.P.'s (registered nurse practitioners), and P.A.'s (physician's assistants). Close coordination and team functioning to achieve efficiency, however, require that each professional group must adjust to bring unique skills to the treatment team. The adjustment brings along with it expansions and restrictions in current professional roles. For many practitioners these role adjustments mean a loss of what they once believed was their domain. Simultaneously, however, new professional roles are opening for all professional groups. For example, they are opening for

1. *Psychotherapists.* Managed care has greatly expanded the use of licensed, master's-degreed therapists and clinical social workers for routine psychotherapy cases. Today, therapists are often called on to be front-line providers, frequently on hospital teams and in after-hours, on-call groups. The depth of independent functioning for therapists has increased greatly, bringing with it a greater need for therapists to understand legal issues, reimbursement models, outcomes management and assessment, focused treatments, and active case management (Trachta, 1997). Consequently, the training of therapists and clinical social workers is requiring simultaneously greater depth and breadth.

Along with increased clinical roles, the ability for therapists to move into supervisory roles in clinics and into managerial roles with MBHOs (as leaders of utilization management departments, for example) has greatly expanded. No group is likely to see their numbers increase more under managed behavioral care than clinical social workers and psychotherapists.

2. *Psychologists.* In a managed care environment, psychologists are sought for their skills in dealing with difficult psychotherapy cases, especially cases with chronic or forensic aspects, and in cases where psychological testing will save time or money in treatment planning. Psychologists are, however, being used less for routine psychotherapy cases. For a review of the changes occurring for psychologists, see Shaw (1997).

In several states, psychologists have gained hospital admission privileges and are joining psychiatrists as the primary attending doctor for routine mental health inpatients. In these situations the psychologist typically is teamed with a psychiatrist who follows the psychologist's initial work-up of the patient with a focused evaluation of medication needs. The degree to which this model will spread across the country remains unclear at this time, as does the prospect that psychologists will gain limited medication prescriptive authority.

Currently, psychologists are increasingly in demand for supervisory functions and clinical program development. The emphasis on clinical guidelines and protocols has also increased demand for psychologists to bring their research skills to bear on problems of quality data collection and programs for prevention and population management regarding specific problem areas or diagnostic conditions.

Administrative positions for psychologists in MCOs are increasing in number. Several MBHOs, large and small, have been founded or have major management positions occupied by psychologists.

3. *Psychiatrists.* Major changes are affecting psychiatry. What has been the profession designated to perform both psychotherapy and medication management is, under managed care, increasingly reserved for (or should we say restricted to) services that directly involve medical issues and medication management with patients.

Many MBHOs restrict psychiatrists, usually for financial reasons, from providing routine psychotherapy. And those that allow it often do so with limitations such as using thirty-minute sessions or for fees equivalent to the rates paid to psychologists. Besides generally angering the psychiatric community, these restrictions and the fact that an increasing portion of direct care is being provided by master's-degreed therapists are resulting in a reduced reliance by many psychiatrists on psychotherapy as a mainstay of their profession. Kaplan (1997) notes that in psychiatric residencies, the curriculum today is certainly more focused on medication management, brief psychotherapies, and consultation services.

Also, the medical portion of the multidisciplinary clinical team now frequently includes "mid-levels," that is, nurse practitioners and physician assistants who prescribe psychotropic medications. The responsibility of the psychiatrist in these teams often rests with the more difficult or initial medication evaluations and with supervising the mid-level providers.

Psychiatrists must train for team functioning. Supervising and leading treatment teams, especially in hospital settings, are the strongholds of psychiatry. Additionally, there is a resurgence of general medicine calling on psychiatry for consultation and liaison services. Coordinating with primary care physicians and assisting in joint projects such as the development of treatment guidelines are also areas where psychiatrists find their expertise in demand.

For business-minded M.D.'s, there are many opportunities for administrative positions in managed care systems. Although the traditional management position for physicians has been to become a medical director of a treatment program in an MBHO or an MCO, many administrative positions today extend to direct business positions such as overseeing systems of outpatient clinics or serving as a vice president of an MCO or MBHO. A large number of insurers are encouraging their physicians with leadership potential to seek direct business training as a prerequisite to advancement into management. In fact, there has been an explosion in recent years of training programs designed to train "physician executives" for the healthcare industry. Many of these programs are even designed for the physician to earn a master's degree in business accounting or other business school degree.

CHOOSING NOT TO ENGAGE WITH MANAGED CARE

Many clinicians profoundly dislike managed care and wish to have no involvement with it, most often because managed care has promoted the idea of the payer having a role in the clinical decision process and because managed care is much more stringent in fee payments than had been true in the indemnity insurance era. Other common reasons are provider networks limiting patients' access to clinicians and managed care's overall prominence in developing integrated delivery systems that do not value solo practitioners or small group practices.

For whatever the reason, many clinicians do not want to connect in any way with MCOs or MBHOs. My best psychologist friend chooses not to interact with managed care, and our different views of where healthcare is headed can be quite a lunch topic. But what are the choices if you are among this adamant group of clinicians? Luckily, there are still options. In general, the options are clinical positions that are not classified as coming under the umbrella of health insurance.

Specifically, the following opportunities remain almost totally outside of managed care:

1. *Academic teaching and/or research positions.* (Sorry, I couldn't help but list this first. There are many days when the offer of an academic appointment would be a dream come true for me. I left my Ph.D. training saying I'd never be in the private practice world; I was going to find a teaching position in the southwestern states. The rest is history.)

There are many options for academic teaching positions at universities, colleges, and professional schools. These positions are not only in counseling, social work, psychology, and medical school settings but often can be found in business schools (see the earlier discussion about business schools concerning psychiatrists), education departments, and corrections programs. In addition, clinical research remains desperately in need of fresh studies, including studies regarding managed care. I include here new-medication drug trials, which can be very lucrative for university psychiatrists and those in organized private practice. Many other research grants are also available for the resourceful clinician, especially in the areas of brief psychotherapies, biological aspects of mental disorders, and the treatment and prevention of substance abuse.

2. *A practice based on private payment.* There are and will remain a notable percentage of those needing or desiring behavioral care who have the resources and choose to seek care outside healthcare insurance. This seems to be especially true in areas with a concentration of affluence and for certain specialty services such as trauma and substance abuse clients. Additionally, there are many individuals in most cities who believe they need long-term care such as psychoanalysis and are willing to pay for it.

Although there is a commonly held belief that the percentage of individuals choosing self-pay is higher in areas with more managed care, I know of no data to confirm this. I hypothesize that the desire to seek care outside insurance rises when managed care is new to an area but decreases once managed care is well established. Among managed care clinicians and administrators, a practice based on private payment is called a boutique practice.

3. *Forensic evaluations and mediation services.* Nationally, many clinicians, especially those with doctoral degrees, have developed a speciality in court-related matters and stay very busy with lucrative incomes doing mental health evaluations and court testimony in legal cases, as well as mediation with family or civil disputes.

4. *Penal system clinicians.* Our jail and prison systems continue to need and use mental health clinicians to evaluate, treat, and provide program consultations. Recent federal and state legislative initiatives have expanded mandates to provide mental health, substance abuse, and vocational training services to prisoners and those in postrelease programs. Many governmental grant funds are available in this area for clinicians skilled in work with offenders of all types.

5. *School psychology.* Special education programs in public schools receive state and federal funds for a limited number of psychological services to be provided by doctoral or master's-degreed psychologists. Although many positions require these psychologists to have an advanced degree specifically in school psychology, many do not.

6. *Sports psychology.* For over two decades, professional teams, Olympic teams, and many university athletic programs have employed behavioral professionals with special training in performance enhancement. Sports psychology is a growth industry among recreational and serious nonprofessional athletes of all ages and all sports. Even dancers and other performing artists engage mental health professionals on a fee-for-service basis to aid them in enhancing their performance.

7. *Consultations to residential programs.* A wide array of facilities such as residential agencies for the developmentally disabled and behavior problem adolescents use consulting mental health professions to assist in program develop-

ment and staff training. Much of the direct patient care in such facilities is paid by insurance, especially Medicaid and Medicare.

8. *Business consultations.* The area of industrial and organizational (IO) psychology has grown rapidly in the last three decades. Many corporations and executives use behavioral consultants to assist them in applying psychological knowledge to personnel management, staff training, and corporate strategic planning.

Although many corporate positions require a specific degree in IO psychology, other positions are filled by mental health clinicians who are simply very good at this type of work. I have a good friend who rose from a staff psychologist position to a management role within a regional MBHO, and then quit to become a management coach. She now works with high-level corporate executives, training them in effective management and business-savvy behavior. And she hosts a radio show discussing psychological aspects of daily life. I'm impressed. She gets far more attention at conferences than I do, and I'm sure she's reporting larger annual numbers to the IRS than I am.

9. *Employee assistance professionals.* In 1994 my partners at Mesa Mental Health and I decided to acquire a local employee assistance program (EAP). It was a great move. Not only has the business grown dramatically, it has been very complementary to insurer-oriented behavioral services (employers purchase both health insurance and EAP services). And EAP counselors know a great deal about brief treatment and efficient use of resources. I have learned a lot from our EAP staff.

Nationally, EAP companies are growing and represent an excellent opportunity for mental health professions to not only engage in care but to create prevention programs and workplace training modules. Don't forget this area if managed care is not your preference.

Overall, there are many opportunities for clinicians not wishing to engage in managed care. And, of course, I assert that there are a wealth of opportunities in all areas of managed care, both administrative and clinical, for clinicians who desire them.

Whether a position within managed care is best for you or not, I hope reading this book has been a sound educational experience. Explaining the rapid business, operational, and sociological changes occurring in behavioral healthcare has been my purpose. The advice given has been offered as a catalyst to stimulate your adaption more quickly to the evolution taking place around us. I can only hope that what I have set forth leads you to a more prosperous and satisfying career journey.

My career in mental health and managed care has certainly taught me that the journey must be the reward because the endpoint is ever changing and elusive. Healthcare and behavioral services are in your hands. Forward!

APPENDIX A:
GLOSSARY OF MANAGED CARE TERMS

Accept Assignment: A term from the Medicare program meaning that a provider has agreed to accept reimbursement directly from Medicare as the total reimbursement for services provided and will not bill the patient for any difference between the clinician's usual and customary charge and the amount paid by Medicare.

Access: An individual's ability to obtain medical services on a timely and financially acceptable basis.

Accreditation: The certification by an accrediting body that a healthcare provider or plan has attained a certain level or degree of service provision, usually for quality of services.

Accrediting Body: An organization that monitors and surveys healthcare entities for the purpose of bestowing accreditation to those entities meeting the standards required for the particular accreditation.

Administrative Loading: The amount above the actual cost of healthcare services (called pure premium) in premium costs necessary to cover administration, marketing, and profit.

Administrative Service Only: A management service contracted to control a health plan's costs, conduct utilization review, and pay providers. See Third-Party Administrator and Pass Through.

Administratively Necessary Day: A day of hospital stay that is necessary, not for clinical reasons but for disposition or discharge planning and transfer.

Adverse Selection: Enrollment that disproportionately creates adverse risk, for example, a more impaired population with higher healthcare utilization.

Any Willing Provider: A provision, often legal, requiring that any provider with appropriate credentials and agreeing to the terms of a managed care contract be allowed to join the network of a managed care organization.

Appeal: The formal written process by which a health plan member or provider requests that a health plan decision (typically a utilization management decision) be reviewed and considered for a reversal or change in the decision.

At-Risk: Any financial arrangement or contract in which a provider or health plan assumes exposure for the costs of services needed by a population of enrollees.

Averaged Adjusted Per Capita Cost (AAPCC): The estimated amount it would cost to provide services through a fee-for-service model; used to determine Medicare rates to HMOs.

Average Daily Census (ADC): The mean number of patients daily in a hospital or other facility.

Average Length of Stay (ALOS): The mean length (in days) of hospital stays for a population of enrollees. Sometimes also used for the mean length of outpatient treatment (represented by mean number of treatment sessions or hours of treatment).

Balanced Budget Act of 1997: Legislation that, among other broad provisions, reduced the fees for services and treatments that Medicare pays to practitioners, treatment facilities, and HMOs offering managed care Medicare insurance plans.

Benefit Package: A contractually defined set of healthcare benefits that are covered under an insurance, HMO, or capitation plan.

Beta Risk: A form of direct financial risk, especially under capitation, resulting from the cost of catastrophic cases; often used when the number of covered lives is too small to compensate for outliers.

Biased Selection: The distribution of relatively healthy versus unhealthy individuals in an insured population. See Adverse Selection.

Boutique Practice: The managed care term for a private clinical practice that does not accept insurance but specializes in seeing patients who pay out-of-pocket.

Capitation: A method of payment for healthcare in which the provider is prepaid a fixed amount, usually monthly, for each member of a health plan, regardless of whether they access services. The fixed rate pays for all services necessary for the population, regardless of actual utilization or costs.

Capitation Rate: For the insurer, the monthly revenue requirement from premiums per member per month to cover the health plan's costs; for providers, the rate paid per month under a capitation arrangement to provide care to a fixed population. See Per Member per Month.

Carve In: When specialty health services (such as behavioral care), which could be or have been managed separately from standard medical services, are integrated into the management system along with general medical services. See Carve Out.

Carve Out: Removing specific health services to be managed separately from the standard medical coverage. For example. a carve out for mental health. See Carve In.

Case Management: The comprehensive coordination or directing of a patient's treatment as to which services are needed and how they should be provided. Often used when a patient has multiple treatment needs or is seeing many different clinicians for care.

Case Mix: The blend of diagnoses and/or treatment types (for example, inpatient and outpatient) for a particular provider, facility, group practice, or health plan.

Case Rate: A flat-rate fee schedule based on a fixed amount per patient receiving care when the length of treatment does not change the fee paid. See Fixed Rate and Diagnostic Related Group.

Civilian Health and Medical Program of the Uniformed Services (CHAMPUS): The former (prior to 1998) federal program providing healthcare coverage to military personnel, their dependents, and certain military retirees.

Closed Panel: A fixed group of clinicians from which enrollees in a health plan must choose.

Combined Provider Organization (CPO): See Hospital-Physician Organization.

Community Rate Setting: The method of setting premiums mandated for federally qualified HMOs. For a defined service area, an HMO sets a community-wide premium rate or equivalency formula based on the average family size, mix of single versus family contracts, and community standards.

Comprehensive Medical Plan (CMP): An HMO plan for Medicare only, usually employing capitation.

Concurrent Review: A form of utilization review conducted during the provision of services (for example, during an inpatient treatment period) to determine if the services meet the requirements of the insurer or third party to justify payment for the services provided.

Consolidated Omnibus Budget Reconciliation Act of 1985 (COBRA): A congressional bill passed in 1986 requiring employers to extend the option to continue healthcare insurance to employees who lose coverage due to layoffs, termination, divorce, separation, or death of the subscriber; extensions are for eighteen months if due to layoff but thirty-six months if due to divorce, separation, or death.

Coordination of Benefits (COB): An insurance provision defining, when an insured member is covered by more than one insurer, which insurer is responsible for primary payment and which is responsible for secondary payment. The coordination prevents double reimbursement.

Copayment: A cost-sharing arrangement under which the insured pays a fixed fee according to type of service at the time of service, which augments the amount paid by the health plan. The copayment does not vary with the provider's charge for the service.

Cost Sharing: A provision of a health plan that requires the insured to pay some portion of the costs for services. Deductibles and copayments are forms of cost sharing.

Covered Benefit: A service for which the insurer will reimburse the provider. For example, a member can be covered for substance abuse rehabilitation.

Credentialing: The process through which a managed care organization reviews the credentials (education, professional work history, licenses, references, and so forth) to determine if the clinician meets the standards set by the MCO for inclusion in the MCO's network of providers.

Credentials Verification Organization (CVO): An agency or company that specializes in performing credentialing tasks, especially doing primary verification of provider credentials (licensure and university degrees, for example); usually subcontracted to an MCO or MBHO.

Current Practitioner Terminology (CPT): A system from the American Medical Association, now in its fifth version, of coding healthcare services for use in billing insurers for services rendered. For example, the CPT code for forty-five to sixty minutes of an initial diagnostic interview is 90801.

Death Spiral: See Meltdown Scenario.

Deductible: In an indemnity insurance health plan, the amount an individual or family must pay (usually annually) out-of-pocket before insurance coverage begins.

Demand Risk: A form of direct financial risk, especially under capitation, resulting from enrollees demanding more treatment than is necessary.

Denial: When an insurer refuses to authorize or pay for a service.

Diagnostic Related Group (DRG): A prospective payment arrangement under which services are paid for on a case rate or fixed rate; rate is based on retrospective data about costs for treating certain diagnoses.

Discounted Fee-for-Service: A fee-for-service payment that is based on a rate fixed by the insurer, not the clinician's usual and customary charge.

Disease State Management: Any set of organized activities, such as treatment guidelines, which are designed to manage and/or treat a particular disease or condition within a population.

Disenrollment: When a health plan member voluntarily leaves membership in the health plan, or under certain criteria is involuntarily removed by the health plan.

Dual-Choice Provision (also called Dual Option): A legal mandate pre-1991 that employers with more than twenty-five insured employees had to, if requested by employees or insurers, offer both an indemnity plan and an HMO plan.

Due Diligence Review: An employer or insured's review of a provider panel to see if the panel is adequate to meet expected healthcare needs and if providers meet community standards.

Economic Credentialing: Making credentialing decisions based on a provider's effectiveness in utilization management or financial considerations.

Employee Retirement Income Security Act of 1974 (ERISA): An act that exempts self-insured employee plans from many state laws (including freedom-of-choice laws). It has been the major force stimulating large employers to self-insure their employees for healthcare coverage. Additionally, this law has provided managed care health plans with certain controversial legal protections from legal liability.

Enrollee: The individual enrolled in a health plan or a dependent of the enrolled individual who is also covered by the plan (same as Member).

Exclusion: In a healthcare benefit package, a particular service or treatment that is not covered.

Exclusive Provider Organization (EPO): A closed panel of providers contracted on a fee-for-service or capitation basis.

Exclusivity Clause: A legal provision binding a provider to contract only with a single health plan.

Experience Rate Setting: A system of setting insurance premiums reflecting the cost and utilization experience of a particular group or employer.

Explanation of Benefits (EOB): A form that explains charges, payments, and any reasons for denying payment.

Family Mental Health Practitioner (FMHP): A therapist identified for mental health treatment as the primary practitioner for an individual or family, like PCP in routine medical care.

Federal Employees Health Benefits Plan (FEHBP): The insurance program run by the federal government for all federal employees.

Federally Qualified Plan: An HMO that has met the standards defined by the HMO Act of 1974 or its many amendments; plans are no longer mandated to be federally qualified.

Fee-for-Service (FFS): An indemnity plan payment arrangement whereby a percentage of providers' billed charges (or a flat fee per service) are paid, often with a maximum based on the determination of the usual and customary charge.

Fee Schedule: A list of fees that a health plan pays for specific diagnostic or treatment procedures or services.

First Dollar Coverage: A health plan coverage that has no deductible amounts; in some cases a copayment may be required.

Fixed Rate: A payment-for-services arrangement in which the provider is paid a certain amount per case, often by diagnosis, for providing services, regardless of the actual amount of services used or needed. Also see Case Rate and Diagnostic Related Group.

Formulary: Within the pharmacy benefit of a managed care plan, the list of medications approved for coverage by the plan. Often medications off the formulary may be purchased by members at a higher copayment.

Gag Clause: A provision in a provider subcontract restricting the provider from discussing certain terms or issues with patients, such as seeking treatments that the patient's health plan does not cover.

Gatekeeper: A provider, usually a primary care physician, who pre-authorizes access to specialty treatment.

Grievance: A formal procedure following an appeal through which a health plan member or provider may file a complaint to request a reversal of a health plan decision.

Group Model: A health plan that provides healthcare services through group practices contracted to the HMO and paid on a salary, fee-for-service, or capitation basis.

High Touch: Any service with apparent high human contact from the perspective of the patient or enrollee.

Holdback: See Withhold.

Hospital-Physician Organization (HPO): A joint venture between a hospital and a group of providers to market or contract with one or more health plans.

Incurred But Not Reported (IBNR): Financial liabilities or claims for services for which a health plan or capitated provider has become responsible but which have not yet been submitted to the health plan or capitated provider for payment.

Indemnity Insurance: A type of insurance in which the covered individual is indemnified (not at any financial risk) for the cost of services. The insurer simply covers the cost of healthcare services received and does not direct the care or specify the provider in any way.

Independent Practice Association (IPA) (also called independent practice organization [IPO]): A group of healthcare providers organized together to facilitate participation in more than one healthcare plan.

Indicator: In a quality improvement program, a specific, ongoing data point collected to measure a process or outcome.

Integrated Delivery System (IDS): A business-integrated group of healthcare providers who can provide all or nearly all of the healthcare services a population will need. An example is a business that includes a hospital system and a multidisciplinary group of clinicians who can provide for the care needs of the members of a particular health plan.

IPA Model: A health plan organized to provide services through one or more independent practice associations (IPAs), which are contracted to the health plan.

Lag Factor: The percentage of claims incurred during a set time period relative to the claims processed and paid during the same period.

Last Dollar Coverage: An insurance coverage without a maximum or lifetime limit to the benefits payable.

Length of Stay (LOS): The days used in hospital or other facility treatment period. Sometimes also used to refer to the number of sessions or hours of service used in an outpatient treatment episode.

Lifetime Maximum: A maximum limit on the total costs of healthcare, either in general medical costs or within a specialty, that a health plan will cover.

Lock-In Requirement: See Closed Panel.

Managed Behavioral Healthcare Organization (MBHO): A managed care organization that is specific to managing insurance benefits for mental health and substance abuse services.

Managed Care Insurer: See Managed Care Organization.

Managed Care Organization (MCO): An insurer who implements healthcare reimbursement to members using the managed care concepts of preauthorization of services, utilization management, and a fixed network of providers.

Managed Care Payer: See Managed Care Organization.

Managed Care Plan: A healthcare insurance plan offered by a managed care organization.

Managed Indemnity Insurance: A type of indemnity insurance that has adopted some managed care features; typically, preauthorization and a fee schedule that is a discounted fee-for-service arrangement for paying clinicians.

Management Information System (MIS): A computer and data management system.

McCarran-Ferguson Act: Legislation enacted in 1945 that prohibits most antitrust actions against insurers.

Medical Loss Ratio: The percentage of the total insurance premium collected from members or of a capitation rate that is actually spent on care delivery. The remainder is spent on administrative costs, contingency funds, and profit.

Medical Necessity: Determination by a health plan as to whether a service or treatment is necessary. Generally includes the requirements that the diagnostic or treatment procedure sought is (1) a true diagnosable condition, (2) provided in the least restrictive and expensive manner appropriate, (3) a generally accepted healthcare procedure, and that (4) the patient can be reasonably expected to show sustained improvement from the procedure.

Medical Savings Account: A tax-free personal savings account funded by an individual from his or her income or by an employer to form a fund to cover personal health costs. Often individuals with an MSA purchase third-party healthcare insurance to cover catastrophic medical costs.

Medigap: The coverage difference between what Medicare pays for a service or treatment and what supplemental Medicare insurance companies will pay.

Meltdown Scenario: A phenomenon of spiraling adverse selection when high users of service repeatedly select a particular health plan, while the low users of service select another plan; also called death spiral.

Member: See Enrollee.

Moral Hazard: A form of direct financial risk to a health plan resulting from enrollee dishonesty, carelessness, or lack of judgment.

Morbidity Risk: A form of direct financial risk to a health plan, resulting from the degree or amount of psychopathology in the population.

Network: A group of providers contracted to or employed by an MCO or MBHO to provide healthcare services.

Network Model: A health plan that provides healthcare services through a network of individual practitioner or group practices that are contracted to the MCO and are paid on a fee-for-service, case rate, or capitation basis.

Omnibus Budget Reconciliation Act of 1986 (OBRA '86): A congressional act that took effect in 1991 prohibiting HMOs from making payments directly or indirectly to providers as an inducement to reduce or limit services to Medicare or Medicaid patients.

Open-Ended Plan: Opposite of closed panel; also see Open Panel.

Open Enrollment: A period of time during which new subscribers or employees of a particular employer may elect a new health plan or switch plans.

Open Panel: A broad collection of clinicians from which subscribers can choose to receive healthcare.

Outlier: An enrollee, provider, or process measurement which is distinctly distant from the average. Usually defined as ± 2 standard deviations from the mean (average) on whatever is being measured.

Out-of-Area Benefits: The benefits an insurance plan provides when members are outside the geographically defined limits of the plan; always include emergency services.

Out-of-Plan Benefits: When services are authorized to be provided by a provider or facility outside a plan's closed panel or beyond the standard limits of the plan benefit.

Out-of-Pocket: Payment for healthcare services that comes directly from the patient or his or her guardian.

Overutilization: Unnecessary or excessive offering of services by providers or demanded by enrollees.

Panel: See Network.

Pass Through: Same as Administrative Service Only and Third-Party Administrator.

Penetration Rate: In managed care plans, the percentage of subscribers enrolled in a particular plan who actually access treatment or a particular service.

Per Member per Month (PMPM): The typical fixed rate used to prepay a capitation contract monthly based on the number of enrollees.

Percentage of Premium: A fixed rate used to prepay a capitation contract based on a percentage of the total subscriber premium dollars paid to the health plan; an alternative payment arrangement under capitation to per member per month.

Pharmacy Benefit Manager (PBM): An external company hired by a health plan to manage the utilization and costs of medications paid for by the health plan.

Physician-Hospital Organization (PHO): A specific type of integrated delivery system in which a hospital and its associated physicians, or other clinicians, form a business entity for the purpose of providing healthcare services.

Point of Service (POS): A health plan where enrollees decide at the time of accessing services whether to choose HMO benefit coverage or a standard indemnity type of coverage.

Preauthorization (also called prior authorization, precertification, predetermination, and prospective review): A utilization management authorization made by an insurer immediately before the provision of services designating what services will be paid for by the insurer.

Precertification: Usually for hospital or facility-based services. See Preauthorization.

Preexisting Condition: In a health plan member, a medical condition that the member had prior to joining the specific health plan.

Preferred Provider Organization (PPO): A type of health plan in which the plan contracts with providers to provide services at a fixed discount and enrollees are given a financial incentive to use the contracted providers, but for a higher amount may seek services from noncontracted providers.

Premium: The fee, usually quoted monthly, for purchasing healthcare insurance.

Prepaid Group Practice (PGP): A group practice that is paid on a capitation basis.

Prepaid Health Plan (PHP): An insurance arrangement in which subscribers pay the insurer in advance for access to a specified set of healthcare benefits. Managed care organizations, including HMOs, are prepaid health plans.

Price Elasticity: The relationship between price and utilization of services; for example, the higher the cost of copayments the lower the use of services.

Price Responsiveness: See Price Elasticity.

Price Risk: A form of direct financial risk to insurers or capitated providers that is the variance between the insurance premium or capitation dollars received and the actual cost of providing services.

Primary Care Physician (PCP): A subscriber's designated physician for basic medical care; usually a family practitioner, pediatrician, internist, or obstetrician-gynecologist.

Primary Source Verification: In credentialing, the process of checking a provider's background using primary sources; for example, obtaining a transcript directly from a university rather than accepting a photocopy of a diploma as proof of an educational degree.

Professional Review Organization (PRO): A group of professionals, often providers, assigned to review an insurer's performance; heavily used by Medicare.

Prospective Payment System (PPS): Any payment system in which the amount to be paid to the provider is set before services commence.

Prospective Review: See Preauthorization.

Provider: A clinician or facility providing clinical care to the members of a health plan; often practitioner is used to refer to an individual clinician.

Provider Profiling: When an MCO or MBHO collects and analyzes data such as utilization patterns, cost, complaints, compliance with MCO policies, and so forth on providers; data often used in deciding which providers will be offered recredentialing and an extension of their subcontract with the particular MCO or MBHO.

Qualified: See Federally Qualified Plan.

Quality Assurance: See Quality Improvement.

Quality Improvement: A broad, very encompassing MCO or MBHO program of standards, goals, and reporting designed to monitor and improve all aspects of quality care and service delivery by the MCO or MBHO.

Quality Management: See Quality Improvement.

Recredentialing: In credentialing, a retrospective review and renewal of clinical privileges for a provider, usually done every two years.

Referral: Regarding a health plan, a written referral form requesting specialty care usually generated by a primary care physician in a gatekeeper role.

Reinsurance: Insurance carried by a health plan, insurer, or provider group under capitation to guard against excessively high costs or patient utilization.

Request for Proposal (RFP): A written document calling on potential bidders to submit a proposal addressing how they will meet the specified needs of the contracting agent, often a health plan or large employer, who let the RFP.

Resource-Based Relative Value Scale (RBRVS): A Medicare term relating to a scale that assigns a relative value and payment level to each current practitioner terminology (CPT) code.

Retrospective Review: A form of utilization review conducted after the provision of services to determine if the services meet the requirements of the insurer or third party to justify payment for the services provided.

Rider: A legal addendum or provision that modifies, either by expanding or decreasing, the agreement of a health plan to cover certain services or conditions.

Risk Adjustment: An adjustment to a provider, especially in payment amount, based on the degree of illness observed with the patient to whom services are to be rendered.

Risk Bands: Utilization strata fixing changes in capitation payments for very high or low utilization.

Risk Pool: An arrangement whereby part of a provider's payment for treatment services provided is withheld and returned to the provider in proportion to the financial well-being of the health plan. See Withhold.

Risk Sharing: Any arrangement in which business entities, such as providers of service and an insurer, share being at-risk for the costs of services to a population of enrollees.

Safe Harbors: Federal guidelines issued July 1991 for the Anti-Kickback Statutes of 1972 and 1977 regarding businesses dealing with Medicare and Medicaid; restricts provider ownership to 40 percent in a healthcare business where the provider's activities might influence financial gain.

Self-Insurance: When a group, employer, or organization assumes risk themselves for the costs of healthcare services.

Sentinel Effect: The alteration of clinical or administrative practice as a result of knowing that review or monitoring is occurring.

Service Area: The defined geographic area within which a health plan agrees to provide coverage for services.

Skimming (also called creaming): When a health plan seeks to enroll only the healthiest or lowest-risk subscribers as a means of controlling risk and costs.

Social HMO (S/HMO): An HMO serving a geriatric population with long-term care needs.

Staff Model: A health plan that employs its own providers.

Stop Loss: In a capitation contract, the maximum expense the provider can incur before the capitation rate structure changes; like a risk band, except that it only addresses the upper limit of expenses. For subscribers, the upper amount in healthcare costs after which a copayment is no longer due; the health plan assumes full coverage for the costs incurred.

Subscriber: The person in whose name an HMO or PPO insurance policy is issued.

TEFRA: Tax Equity and Fiscal Responsibility Act of 1982; allows, among other medical insurance provisions, HMOs to contract with Medicare on a capitation basis and sets payment mechanisms for reimbursing providers under Medicare.

Third-Party Administrator (TPA): Same as Pass Through and Administrative Service Only.

Treatment Guidelines: A set of standards, protocols, or recommended pathways for the evaluation and treatment of a particular condition or disease.

Triage: The assessment of a patient for medical need and assignment to appropriate care.

TriCare: The managed healthcare program implemented by the U.S. Department of Defense for insuring active duty and retired military personnel.

Triple Option: A health plan offering indemnity, PPO, and HMO plans.

Usual and Customary Charge: A fee structure for services based on assessment of prevailing fees in a particular community or region.

Utilization: The amount of services used by a patient or members of a health plan.

Utilization Management (UM): The management of patients' utilization of services by an MCO or MBHO, often for the purpose of determining need for treatment and whether a particular service will be authorized for insurance payment; may be prospective, concurrent, or retrospective.

Utilization Review Organization (URO): A business entity that provides utilization management services for insurers or self-insured employers.

Verification of Coverage: A procedure for checking an enrollee's status with a particular health plan, usually prior to beginning services, as a part of preauthorization and utilization management.

Withhold: A portion of a provider's fee retained by a health plan as part of a risk-sharing arrangement. The provider is returned all or a portion of the withhold periodically, based on the financial performance of the health plan. See Risk Pool.

APPENDIX B:
SAMPLE CAPITATION CONTRACT

CONTRACTUAL AGREEMENT
MENTAL HEALTH, SUBSTANCE ABUSE,
AND EMPLOYEE ASSISTANCE SERVICES

Preface

This Agreement is made and entered into as of the day of 199___, by and between All-American HMO (hereafter referred to as The HMO) and Behavioral Health Group (hereafter referred to as Provider).

The HMO desires that Provider furnish mental health and substance abuse services to eligible The HMO employees and dependents (hereafter collectively referred to as Members); within the terms of the Membership Certificate of each Member and the healthcare and employee assistance benefits outlined in this Agreement. For the services desired by The HMO to be furnished by the Provider, the parties agree to the following:

Article I: Definitions

1. "Membership Certificate" is any agreement between The HMO and a Member where The HMO agrees to pay for Covered Services provided to Members in accordance with the terms of the agreement.

2. "Member" is an eligible employee or eligible dependent of an employee with whom The HMO has agreed to provide healthcare and employee assistance services through a Membership Certificate.

3. "Covered Services" are those benefits as defined in the Membership Certificate which are available to Members when rendered by the Provider.

4. "Emergency" is a medical or mental condition that Provider judges to be of a severity that immediate care is necessary to prevent a life-threatening event or serious physical or mental impairment.

Article II: Obligations of The HMO

1. The HMO shall compensate Provider in a timely manner for Covered Services as set forth in Attachment A.

2. The HMO shall provide Provider with updated Member eligibility information by the fifth business day of each month and by telephone upon request.

3. The HMO shall provide identification cards to all Members which will serve as identification that the Member possesses a Membership Certificate.

4. The HMO shall identify Provider in relevant mailings, publications, and other printed material issued to Members or others.

5. The HMO shall notify Provider of any new or modified policies, procedures, or business operations within The HMO which will impact this Agreement.

6. The HMO shall cooperate with Provider in developing and maintaining a quality management program for the purpose of reviewing and enhancing the quality and cost efficiency of services provided to Members.

7. The HMO agrees to make any changes or amendments to its Plan Document to reflect the benefit structure outlined in Attachment C, Benefit Structure and Limitations.

8. The HMO agrees to educate Members regarding Covered Services and how Members may access Covered Services.

Article III: Provider Responsibilities

1. Provider shall make appropriate arrangements to ensure the prompt availability of Covered Services to Members during regular business hours and outside of regular business hours for emergencies. Members seeking services for nonemergent situations shall be regularly offered an initial appointment within five business days. Members with emergent needs shall be seen within 24 hours.

2. Provider shall adhere to applicable federal and state laws and regulations effective during the terms of this Agreement.

3. Provider shall make available and provide those Covered Services listed in Attachment A to Members who present identification representing a valid Membership Certificate.

4. Provider shall render Covered Services to Members in a manner consistent with national or local standards or best practices.

5. Provider shall possess and actively use a quality improvement program which is acceptable to The HMO.

6. Provider shall accept The HMO's payment as defined in Attachment A along with applicable copayment from Members as described in this agreement as payment in full for Covered Services. No event, including, but not limited to, nonpayment by The HMO or breach of this Agreement shall be grounds for the Provider to seek compensation from or have any recourse against Members for Covered Services rendered within the terms of this Agreement.

7. Provider shall notify The HMO in writing within thirty (30) days of any of the following: Change in ownership or business address, any legal, or governmental actions which have the potential to impede the Provider's ability to meet any of the terms of this Agreement.

8. Provider shall allow representatives of The HMO to audit, with written advance notice of at least seven days, the Provider's medical, financial, utilization review, and credentialing records and procedures that directly relate to the provision of Covered Services as defined in this agreement.

9. Provider shall permit The HMO to use Provider's name and address and identify it as a provider in mailings, publications, and other printed material issued by The HMO.

10. Provider shall submit to The HMO, on a timely basis, those data and reports specified in Attachment D and shall maintain other records as required in this Agreement.

11. Provider agrees that employed and subcontracted providers used to provide Covered Services are duly licensed, trained, competent, and credentialed to deliver the Covered Services.

Article IV: Dispute Resolution

A. The HMO and Provider shall make a good faith effort to informally resolve any disputes which might arise under this Agreement.

B. If the parties cannot resolve a dispute, the parties shall agree to binding arbitration in accordance with the commercial arbitration rules of the American Arbitration Association. Any judgment from arbitration may be entered in any court having jurisdiction.

Article V: Term and Termination

A. This Agreement will be effective from _____ , and will continue in full force and effect until terminated by either party as provided herein.

B. This Agreement may be canceled, with or without cause, by either party by giving thirty (30) days advance written notice to the other party.

Article VI: Amendments

1. No deviation from or modification of the provisions of this Agreement shall be valid or binding unless the modification or change is set forth in writing and signed by the parties.

2. Attachments to this Agreement are part of this Agreement and may be amended from time to time, or new amendments and attachments added as long as agreed to in writing by both parties.

Article VII: Governing Law

This Agreement is set forth in accordance with the laws of the State of _____ _____ .

Article VIII: Assignment

Nothing in this Agreement may be delegated or assigned to another party without the written consent of both parties.

Article IX: Notification

Any notice required to be given pursuant to the terms and provisions of this Agreement shall be sent by certified mail, return receipt requested, postage paid, to:

All-American HMO
Anywhere, USA
Behavioral Health Group
Anywhere, USA

In Witness Hereof, the parties execute this Agreement through their duly authorized officers.

All-American HMO   Behavioral Health Group

_____   _____
Signature   Date   Signature   Date

_____   _____
Title   Title

Attachment A
Method of Payment
Provider Reimbursement
1. Provider's compensation for the provision-covered health and employee assistance services shall be based on a monthly per capita fee for each Member. The monthly Member list supplied to Provider by The HMO shall be the basis upon which the number of Members is derived. The HMO will pay to Provider per member per month. Payment to Provider shall be made the tenth day of each month beginning _____ .
2. The monthly per capita fees set forth above shall be in effect through _____ . For subsequent contract years, under the terms of this Agreement, monthly per capita fees shall be reviewed no less often than annually and adjusted by mutual agreement between The HMO and Provider.
3. The HMO agrees that Provider is not responsible for payment for services to Members under the following circumstances:
   A. Members receiving services outside the State of _____ unless the referral to an out-of-state provider involved Provider.
   B. Members receiving services not authorized by Provider.

Attachment B
Covered Services
I. Mental Health and Substance Abuse Services
Provider shall render to The HMO Members all covered services relating to medically necessary psychiatric and/or substance abuse detoxification and rehabilitation as described in The HMO Membership Certificate.
1. Services performed in an inpatient or partial hospital program:
   A. All necessary professional psychiatric, psychological, and psycho-therapy services.
   B. All accommodations, meals, dietitian, nursing, history and physical examination, laboratory, X-ray, and other diagnostic services including accompanying professional fees.
   C. Intensive duty nursing when medically necessary.
   D. Medications prescribed by a physician or other provider licensed to prescribe such medications in the State of _____ .
2. Professional services performed on an outpatient basis:
   A. All necessary professional psychiatric, psychological, and psycho-therapy services.
   B. Twenty-four-hour crisis intervention and assessment, either in person or by telephone, by a licensed mental health or EAP professional.
II. Employee Assistance Program Services
Provider shall also render to The HMO Members employee assistance services. These shall include the following:

1. Availability of an employee assistance counselor in Provider's offices on business days from 8 o'clock A.M. until 6 o'clock P.M. for the provision of crisis counseling, assessment, and, if necessary, referral on to an appropriate mental health professional for ongoing treatment. All Members, including dependents, who hold a Membership Certificate may obtain up to four hours of employee assistance aid for work or personal problems during any calendar year without a copayment due.

2. Four hours per month of available organizational development and/or consultation to The HMO. Such services will be conducted in the facilities of The HMO and at the request of The HMO.

3. Six hours per month of training or education for the staff of The HMO conducted in the facilities of The HMO and at the request of The HMO. Training/education hours are to be used in the designated month unless both parties agree to carry them over to a future date.

4. All educational materials related to EAP services including pamphlets, brochures, and supervisory information.

5. Twenty-four-hour crisis intervention and assessment, either in person or by telephone, by a licensed mental health or EAP professional.

III. In delivering covered health services, either mental health/substance abuse or employee assistance, as outlined in numbers one and two above, Provider will adhere to the following guidelines:

1. Assessment and Access to Care

   A. All Members appropriate for and seeking outpatient services will be assessed initially by an employee assistance professional (EAP). If possible the EAP will complete the necessary care, but if EAP services are inadequate alone, then the EAP may make a referral for access to mental health or substance abuse services. Members in need of evaluation for hospital-based care may be directly assessed for mental health or substance abuse services.

   B. All eligible employees and dependents of The HMO will receive a thorough and complete assessment within 24 hours for emergent need and eight working days for ongoing problems that are determined to be nonemergent. Sufficient questioning and documentation should be obtained to determine the status of the client's needs.

   C. The assessment will include enough data gathered to make a sound provisional judgment of the patient's DSM IV diagnosis and a temporary treatment plan with the criteria for discharge listed.

2. Treatment Planning

   A. There should be a mutual understanding between the client, or for minors the family, and the therapist regarding the general diagnosis, recommended treatment, expected length of treatment, estimated out-of-pocket costs for the patient, and expected outcome. A written treatment plan should be agreed upon and signed by all parties concerned.

B. Members are expected to follow the treatment plan and participate in the treatment process. Members who are noncompliant may be considered for termination of treatment, except in cases where the safety of the individual or others is a strong consideration.

C. When occupational or other work related matters are the focus of treatment, the treatment plan should include a release of information to an appropriate representative of The HMO, often the employee's supervisor. The release allows for the appropriate communication between The HMO, the employee, and the therapist for the benefit of the Member.

Attachment C

Mental Health and Chemical Dependency

Benefit Structure and Limitations

I. The HMO mental health and chemical dependency benefits:

1. Short term inpatient and outpatient evaluation and treatment for acute mental health conditions or chemical dependency are a benefit when provided and authorized by Provider.

2. The benefit is limited to a maximum of 30 inpatient days and 20 outpatient hours (80 units, 1 unit = 15 minutes) per member per calendar year. Covered services are limited to crisis intervention and acute conditions only.

3. Covered services are available only through contracted providers or facilities unless a specific exception is authorized by the Provider. The Provider must be notified within two working days of any emergency admission to a mental health facility.

4. A maximum of two chemical dependency admissions for medical detoxification and/or rehabilitation per lifetime.

5. The following are not covered health services and therefore are excluded from this Agreement:

A. Services provided for the comfort or convenience of Members.

B. Hypnotherapy, assessment or remediation of learning disabilities, and treatment for sexual dysfunction.

C. Treatment of chronic mental conditions, except to the extent that stabilization is necessary for acute episodes.

D. Nonpsychiatric medical services and medical consultations when not completed as a necessary part of a psychiatric inpatient program.

E. Services provided without prior authorization from Provider.

6. Mental health/substance abuse benefit copayments due from the Member at the time service is received:
    A. Inpatient—up to 30 days per year at 100 percent coverage after a $300 deductible due from the Member.
    B. Outpatient—20 hours (80 units) per year. A copayment of $20.00 per visit of 30 or more minutes and $12.00 for visits of less than 30 min.
    C. There is no copayment for services provided in the context of employee assistance.

Attachment D

Data and Reports to be Supplied to The HMO

Provider shall submit to The HMO the following data and reports quarterly as they pertain to covered health services described in this Agreement and rendered to The HMO Members. This data and quarterly reports to The HMO shall include the following:

1. Number of employees and dependents utilizing MH, SA, and EAP services
2. Outpatient therapy hours per thousand
3. Number of hospital days per thousand
4. Number of admissions per thousand
5. Ratio of mental health to chemical dependency utilization
6. Number of EAP visits
7. General problem areas related to EAP visits
8. Number of EAP referrals arising from supervisor referrals

APPENDIX C:
SUMMARY OF THE
NCQA GUIDELINES FOR
BEHAVIORAL HEALTH

The following is a summary of the requirements from the National Committee for Quality Assurance's Standards for Behavioral Healthcare (NCQA, 1997). These are the requirements to which managed behavioral healthcare organizations are held to become accredited and maintain their NCQA accreditation status. In the NCQA manual (120 pages of standards), each of these standards has very specific substandards, as well as a rationale for the standard and its defining items.

I. QUALITY PROGRAM

QI 1   PROGRAM STRUCTURE: Organization has clearly defined QI structures and processes and assigns responsibilities to appropriate individuals.

QI 2   PROGRAM OPERATIONS: Organization's quality improvement program is comprehensive and fully operational.

QI 3   BEHAVIORAL HEALTH CONTRACTING: Contracts with individual practitioners and organizational providers specify cooperation and compliance with the organization's QI program.

QI 4   MEMBER SATISFACTION: Organization implements mechanisms to assess and ensure member satisfaction.

QI 5   CLINICAL PRACTICE GUIDELINES: Organization adopts and disseminates practice guidelines, practice parameters or consensus statements for providing behavioral healthcare services to members of its covered population.

QI 6   CONTINUITY AND COORDINATION OF CARE: Organization ensures that the behavioral services provided to the covered population are coordinated and integrated with general medical care.

QI 7   SCOPE AND CONTENT OF CLINICAL QI ACTIVITIES: Scope and content of the QI program reflect the organization's delivery system and the relevant clinical issues affecting members of its covered population.

QI 8   CLINICAL MEASUREMENT ACTIVITIES: Organization uses data collection, measurement, and analysis to track the clinical quality improvement issues identified in QI 7.

QI 9   INTERVENTION AND FOLLOW-UP: Organization improves quality by addressing opportunities identified in QI 7 and QI 8 or through other clinical activities as appropriate and then assesses the effectiveness of interventions through systematic follow-up.

QI 10   QI PROGRAM EFFECTIVENESS: Organization evaluates overall effectiveness of the QI program and demonstrates improvement in the quality of clinical care and service provided to its members.

QI 11   QI DELEGATION: If any QI activities are delegated, the organization actively monitors, evaluates, and oversees the performance of the agency to whom they have delegated.

II. ACCESSIBILITY, AVAILABILITY, REFERRAL, AND TRIAGE

AR 1   ACCESSIBILITY OF SERVICES: Organization has written standards to ensure accessibility of behavioral healthcare services, urgent and emergent services, and member services.

AR 2   AVAILABILITY OF PROVIDERS: Organization has written standards that ensure the availability of behavioral providers (including specialty practitioners, programs and services based on assessed needs, and member preferences.

AR 3   REFERRAL AND TRIAGE: Organization has written standards ensuring that referral and triage functions are appropriately implemented, monitored, and professionally managed.

AR 4   DELEGATION: Organization actively monitors, evaluates, and oversees the delegated agency's performance, if delegation of AR activities takes place.

III. UTILIZATION MANAGEMENT

UM 1   STRUCTURES AND PROCESSES: Organization has clearly defined UM structures and processes with responsibilities assigned to appropriate individuals.

UM 2   UTILIZATION CRITERIA: Organization has written utilization review criteria that are based on reasonable scientific evidence.

UM 3   CLINICAL DECISION MAKING: Licensed, experienced, behavioral practitioners assess the clinical information used to support the UM decisions.

UM 4   CLINICAL TIMELINESS: Organization makes UM decisions in a timely manner that reflects the clinical urgency of the situation.

UM 5   MEDICAL NECESSITY: Organization obtains relevant clinical information and consults with treating practitioner, PCP, member, and UM staff prior to making a determination about medical necessity.

UM 6   DENIALS: Organization clearly documents and communicates reasons for denial or approval of services.

UM 7   NEW TECHNOLOGY: Organization evaluates the inclusion of new clinical technology or the new application of existing technology into the benefit package, including clinical interventions for procedures, pharmacological treatments and devices.

UM 8   SATISFACTION SURVEYS: Organization evaluates member and practitioner satisfaction with the UM process.

UM 9   DELEGATION: Organization actively monitors, evaluates, and oversees the delegated agency's performance, if QI activities are delegated.

IV. CREDENTIALING AND RECREDENTIALING

CR 1   POLICIES AND PROCEDURES: Organization has written policies and procedures for credentialing, recredentialing, and reappointing practitioners and facilities.

CR 2   CREDENTIALS COMMITTEE: Organization establishes a credentialing committee or other peer review body to make credentialing decision recommendations.

CR 3   PRIMARY VERIFICATION: Primary source verification includes at least the following areas:

CR 3.1 Current, valid license to practice as an independent practitioner

CR 3.2 Clinical privileges in good standing at their primary admitting facility, as applicable

CR 3.3 Valid DEA or CDS certificate, as applicable

CR 3.4 Graduation from an accredited professional school and/or highest training level applicable to the academic degree, discipline, and licensure

CR 3.5 Board certification if applicable

CR 3.6 Work history

CR 3.7 Current, adequate malpractice insurance according to the organization's policy

CR 3.8 History of professional liability claims which resulted in settlements or judgments paid by or on behalf of the practitioner

CR 3.9 Specialized training for nontraditional practitioners

CR 4   APPLICATION: Applicant completes a credentialing application which includes statements addressing:

CR 4.1 Any reasons for inability to perform essential job functions with or without accommodation

CR 4.2 Lack of present illegal drug use

CR 4.3 History of loss of license and/or felony convictions

CR 4.4 History of loss of privileges or disciplinary activity

CR 4.5 Attestation as to correctness and completeness of the application

CR 5   MONITORING DATA SOURCES: Prior to making a credentialing decision, the organization receives information from recognized monitoring organizations appropriate to the practitioner's discipline and includes this information in the credentialing record.

CR 6   INITIAL SITE VISITS: Site visits of the offices of potential high-volume practitioners are conducted prior to acceptance for network inclusion and patient referrals.

CR 7   RECREDENTIALING PROCESS: Formal recredentialing takes place every two years and includes primary verification of:

CR 7.1 Valid state license to practice

CR 7.2 Current status of their clinical privileges at facilities, as appropriate

CR 7.3 Valid DEA or CDS certificate, if applicable

CR 7.4 Board certifications since last credentialing

CR 7.5 Current, adequate malpractice insurance according to the organization's policy

CR 7.6 History of professional liability claims resulting in settlements by or on behalf of the applicant

CR 7.7 Recredentialing process includes a current signed attestation statement by the practitioner which includes:

    7.7.1 Any reasons for inability to perform essential job functions, with or without accommodation

    7.7.2 Lack of present illegal drug use

CR 8 MONITORING AGENCIES: Organization uses data from monitoring agencies in making recredentialing decisions.

CR 9 RECREDENTIALING DATA: Organization includes data from the following sources in making recredentialing decisions.

    CR 9.1 Member complaints

    CR 9.2 Information from QI activities

    CR 9.3 Information from UM activities

    CR 9.4 Member satisfaction data

    CR 9.5 Medical record reviews (as required in TR 2)

    CR 9.6 Site visits (as required in CR 10)

CR 10 SITE VISITS: Organization conducts site visits on high-volume practitioners prior to recredentialing decision.

CR 11 CHANGES IN PARTICIPATION: There are policies and procedures for changing the conditions of a practitioner's participation with the organization based on quality of clinical care and service.

CR 12 PROVIDER ASSESSMENT: Organization has written policies and procedures for initial and ongoing assessment of potential providers.

CR 13 DELEGATION: Organization actively monitors, evaluates, and oversees the delegated agency's performance if any credentialing activities have been delegated.

V. MEMBERS' RIGHTS AND RESPONSIBILITIES

RR 1 FORMAL POLICIES: Organization has written policies which identify a commitment to treating members in a respectful way, as well as its expectations of members' responsibilities.

RR 2 POLICY DISTRIBUTION: Organization distributes the policy on members' rights and responsibilities to members, participating providers, and PCPs.

RR 3 COMPLAINTS AND APPEALS MECHANISMS: Organization has written policies and procedures for timely resolution of member complaints and appeals.

RR 4   COMPLAINT ADJUDICATION: Organization adjudicates members' complaints and appeals in a thorough and timely manner meeting RR 3 and has its own internal standards for handling complaints in the areas of:
RR 4.1 Clinical care
RR 4.2 Service
RR 4.3 Access to care
RR 4.4 Termination of care
RR 4.5 Appeals

RR 5   MEMBER HANDBOOK: Organization provides members with the written information needed to understand benefit coverage, how to obtain services, and how to obtain necessary care.

RR 6   CLEAR, CONCISE INFORMATION: Written information provided to members is comprehensive and well designed.

RR 7   RECORD PROTECTION: Organization protects the confidentiality of member information and records.

RR 8   DELEGATION: Organization actively monitors, evaluates, and oversees any delegated activities in the area of members' rights.

VI. PREVENTIVE HEALTH SERVICES

PH 1   PREVENTIVE PROGRAMS: Organization establishes preventive programs which decrease the incidence, prevalence and/or residual effects of behavioral health disorders in selected areas of its covered population. Programs are primary, secondary, or tertiary in nature and reflect the needs of the covered population.

PH 2   MARKETING: Organization distributes information about its preventive programs and revisions to practitioners and providers.

PH 3   MEMBER INVOLVEMENT: Organization regularly encourages members to participate in preventive programs and services.

PH 4   ACCEPTABLE PREVENTIVE PROGRAMS: Organization monitors and evaluates at least two behavioral health preventive screening and educational offerings annually. The focus needs to be primary, secondary, or tertiary prevention and based on the needs of the covered population.

VII. CLINICAL EVALUATION AND TREATMENT RECORDS

TR 1   TREATMENT RECORD EXPECTATIONS: Treatment records are maintained in a manner that is current, comprehensive, detailed, organized, and legible in order to promote effective patient care and quality reviews.

TR 2   INTERNAL MEDICAL RECORD STANDARDS: Organization establishes standards for their medical records and systematically reviews their records for conformity and institutes corrective actions when standards are not met.

TR 3   NATIONAL MEDICAL RECORDS STANDARDS: Organization monitors their medical records according to NCQA standards to demonstrate that their records adhere to national standards of practice and reflect appropriate behavioral healthcare management.

Note: In a comprehensive appendix to the standards manual, NCQA provides detailed criteria for what documentation must be in every patient record/chart.

APPENDIX D:
MANAGED CARE RESOURCES

ORGANIZATIONS

Agency for Health Care Policy Research
2101 East Jefferson Street
Rockville, MD 20852
(301) 594–1364, www.ahcpr.gov

American Association for
  Partial Hospitalization
901 North Washington Street, Suite 600
Alexandria, VA 22314–1535
(703) 836–2274

American Association of Health Plans
1129 20th St. NW, Suite 600
Washington, DC 20036–3421
(202) 778–3200, www.aahp.org

American Association of Integrated
Healthcare Delivery Systems
4435 Waterfront Drive, Suite 101
Glen Allen, VA 23060
(804) 747–5823, fax: (804) 747–5316
www.aapho-ids.org *or* www.aaihds.org

American College of Mental Health
  Administration
7625 West Hutchinson Ave.
Pittsburgh, PA 15218–1248
(412) 244–0670, fax: (412) 244–9916

American Health Information
  Management Association
919 N. Michigan Ave., Suite 1400
Chicago, IL 60611–1683
(800) 383–2973

American Managed Behavioral
  Healthcare Association
700 13th Street NW, Suite 950
Washington, DC 20005
(202) 434–4565, fax: (202) 434–4564

American Medical Association
515 North State St.
Chicago, IL 60610
(312) 464–4818, www.ama-assn.org

American Psychiatric Association
1400 K St. NW
Washington, DC 20005
(800) 343–4671 (Managed Care Hotline)
www.psych.org

American Psychological Association
 Practice Directorate
1200 17th St., N.W.
Washington, DC 20036–3090
(202) 247–7600, www.apa.org

Council for Behavioral Group Practices
Institute for Behavioral Healthcare
1110 Mar West Street, Suite E
Tiburon, CA 94920
(415) 435–9821, www.ibh.com

Computer-Based Patient Record Institute
919 N. Michigan Ave., Suite 1400
Chicago, IL 60611–1683
(800) 383–2973

Foundation for Accountability
40 Sylvan Road
Waltham, MA 02254
(617) 466–2124, fax: (617) 466–2856

Health Care Financing Administration
7500 Security Blvd.
Baltimore, MD 21244
(410) 786–3000, www.hcfa.gov

Health Insurance Association of America
555 13th St. NW
Washington, DC 20004
(202) 824–1600, www.hiaa.org

Health Outcomes Institute
2901 Metro Drive, Suite 400
Bloomington, MN 55425–1525
(612) 858–9188, fax: (612) 858–9189

Institute for Behavioral Healthcare
1110 Mar West Street, Suite E
Tiburon, CA 94920
(415) 435–9821, www.ibh.com

InterStudy
2901 Metro Drive, Suite 4000
Bloomington MN 55425
(612) 858–9291

Joint Commission on Accreditation
 of Health Care Organizations
One Renaissance Blvd.
Oakbrook Terrace, IL 60181
(708) 916–5600, fax: (708) 842–0621

Managed Health Care Association
1225 Eye Street NW, Suite 300
Washington, DC 20005
(202) 371–8232, fax: (202) 842–0621

Medical Group Management Association
104 Inverness Terrace East
Englewood, CO 80112–5306
(303) 397–7872

National Association of Managed Care
 Physicians
1601 Trapelo Rd.
Waltham, MA 02154
(617) 290–0400, www.namcp.com

National Association of Psychiatric
 Health Systems
1317 F Street NW, Suite 301
Washington, DC 20004–1154
(202) 393–6700, fax: (202) 783–6041

National Center for Managed Health Care
 Administration
University of Missouri-Kansas City
H.R. Bloch Center
5100 Rockhill Road
Kansas City, MO 64110–2499
(816) 235–1489

National Commission for Quality
 Assurance
2000 L Street NW, Suite 500
Washington, DC 20036
(202) 955–5697, fax: (202) 955–3599
www.ncqa.org

National Institutes of Health
Bethesda Campus
Bethesda, MD 20892
www.nih.gov

National Institute of Mental Health
Bethesda Campus
Bethesda, MD 20892
www.nimh.nih.gov

National Managed Health Care Congress
1601 Trapelo Rd.
Waltham, MA 02154
(617) 290–0400

Utilization Review Accreditation
  Commission
1130 Connecticut Ave. NW
Washington, DC 20036
(202) 296–0120

PERIODICALS, DIRECTORIES, DATABASES, WEBSITES

Behavioral Healthcare Tomorrow
Institute for Behavioral Healthcare
1110 Mar West Street, Suite E
Tiburon, CA 94920
(415) 435–9821

Behavioral Health Management
MEDQUEST Communications
P.O. Box 20179
Cleveland, OH 44120–0179

Behavioral Health Outcomes
208 Governor Street
Providence, RI 02906
(800) 333–7771, fax: (401) 861–6370

Business Insurance
The Crain Syndicate
740 Rush Street
Chicago, IL 60611–2590
(800) 678–9595

Capitation Management Report
National Health Information, L.L.C.
P.O. Box 670505
Marietta, GA 30066–0126
(800) 597–6300

Capitation Rates and Data
National Health Information, L.L.C.
P.O. Box 670505
Marietta, GA 30066–0126
(800) 597–6300

*Directory of Partial Hospitalization
  Programs*
American Association for Partial
  Hospitalization
 901 North Washington Street, Suite 600
Alexandria, VA 22314–1535
(703) 836–2274

Employee Benefit News
1483 Chain Bridge Rd., Suite 202
McClean, VA, 22101
(703) 448–0520

*The Executive Report on Integrated Care
  and Capitation*
Publishing Offices
3100 Highway 138
Wall Township, NJ 07719–9982
(800) 516–4343, fax: (888) 329–6242

Health Affairs
P.O. Box 148
Congers, NY 10920–9926
(800) 765–7514
www.projhope.org/HA

Inside Medicaid Managed Care
Aspen Publishers, Inc.
P.O. Box 990
Frederick, MD 21705–9727
(800) 638–8437
www.aspenpub.com

The InterStudy Competitive Edge
InterStudy
P.O. Box 4366
St. Paul, MN 55104
(612) 858-9291

The InterStudy Quality Edge
InterStudy
P.O. Box 4366
St. Paul, MN 55104
(612) 858-9291

Journal of Clinical Outcomes
  Management
Turner White Communications, Inc.
125 Strafford Ave., Suite 220
Wayne, PA 19087-3391
(610) 975-4541

Managed Behavioral Health News
Atlantic Information Services, Inc.
1100 17th Street NW, Suite 300
Washington, DC 20036
(202) 775-9008, www.alspub.com

Managed Care
301 Oxford Valley Road, Suite 1105A
Yardley, PA 19067
fax: (215) 321-6670
www.managedcaremag.com

Managed Care Quarterly
Aspen Publishers, Inc.
7201 McKinney Circle
Frederick, MD 21704
(800) 638-8437, www.aspenpub.com

Managed Care Week
Atlantic Information Services, Inc.
1050 17th Street, NW, Suite 480
Washington, DC 20036
(202) 775-9006, fax: (202) 331-9542

Managed Healthcare
7682 Old Oak Blvd.
Riverton, NJ 08077
(800) 949-6525

MedAccess Health Information Resources
www.medaccess.com

Medical Benefits
P.O. Box 3000
Denville, NJ 07834-9727

Medical Outcomes & Guidelines Alert
Faulkner & Gray
11 Penn Plaza
New York, NY 10001-2006
(800) 535-8403, fax: (212) 967-7180

Medicine on the Net
COR Healthcare Resources
P.O. Box 40959
Santa Barbara, CA 93140-9898
(805) 564-2177, fax: (805) 564-2146

Mental Health Net
www.cmhc.com

Mental Health Report
Business Publishers, Inc.
951 Pershing Drive
Silver Spring, MD 20910-4464
(301) 589-5103 or (800) 274-6737
fax: (301) 589-8493

On Managed Care
P.O. Box 3000
Denville, NJ 07834-9727

Open Minds
44 South Franklin St.
Gettysburg, PA 17325-9959
(717) 334-0538

St. Anthony's Ancillary Capitation Report
St. Anthony's Publishing
P.O. Box 96561
Washington, DC 22090
(800) 632-0123

St. Anthony's Health Care Capitation Report
St. Anthony's Publishing
P.O. Box 96561
Washington, DC 22090
(800) 632-0123

St. Anthony's Physician Capitation Report
St Anthony's Publishing
P.O. Box 96561
Washington, DC 22090
(800) 632–0123

State Health Watch
704 Stony Hill Road, Suite 154
Yardley, PA 19067–5507
(800) 891–5172
fax: (800) 842–3081

BOOKS

American Psychiatric Association, Office of Economic Affairs and Practice Management. (1997). *The psychiatrist's guide to capitation and risk-based contracting.* Washington, DC: Author.

American Psychiatric Association, Office of Economic Affairs and Practice Management. (1997). *The psychiatrist's guide to managed care contracting.* Washington, DC: Author.

American Psychological Association. (1996). *Contracting on a capitated basis: Managing risk for your practice.* Washington, DC: Author.

American Psychological Association. (1996). *Contracting with organized delivery systems: Selecting, evaluating, and negotiating contracts.* Washington, DC: Author.

Anders, G. (1996). *Health against wealth: HMO's and the breakdown of medical trust.* Washington, DC: American Psychiatric Press.

Austad, C., & Berman, W. (Eds.). (1991). *Psychotherapy in managed health care: The optimal use of time and resources.* Washington, DC: American Psychological Association.

Bloom, S. (Ed.). (1997). *The public/private partnership handbook.* Tiburon, CA: CentraLink.

Boland, P. (1997). *The Capitation Sourcebook.* Berkeley, CA: Boland Healthcare.

Carroll, J. (1996). *Measuring and managing ambulatory care outcomes.* Frederick, MD: Aspen.

Coddington, D. C., Keen, D. J., & Moore, K. D., & Clarke, R. L. (1992). *The crisis in health care: Costs, choices, and strategies.* San Francisco: Jossey-Bass.

COR Healthcare Resources. (1997). *1997 Healthcare guide for the internet: An annotated listing of internet resources for the healthcare professional.* Santa Barbara, CA: Author

Daniels, A., Dickman, N., & Zieman, G. (1995). *The comprehensive group practice tool kit: A manual for behavioral group practice development and management.* Tiburon, CA: CentraLink.

Daniels, A., Dickman, N., & Zieman, G. (1996). *The comprehensive managed care tool kit: A manual for capitated and managed behavioral healthcare delivery systems.* Tiburon, CA: CentraLink.

Daniels, A., Zieman, G., Kramer, T., & Furgal, C. (1997). *The behavioral healthcare quality and accountability tool kit.* Tiburon, CA: CentraLink.

Duhl, L. J., & Cummings, N. C. (1992). *Health services: Coping with crisis.* New York: Springer.

Feldman, J. L., & Fitzpatrick, R. J. (1992). *Managed mental healthcare: Administrative and clinical issues.* Washington, DC: American Psychiatric Association Press.

Goodman, M., Brown, J., & Deitz, P. (1992). *Managing managed care: A mental health survival guide.* Washington, DC: American Psychiatric Association Press.

Hayes, B. E. (1997). *Measuring customer satisfaction: Survey design, use and statistical analysis methods* (2nd ed.). Milwaukee: American Society for Quality.

Insider's guide to managed care: A legal and operational road map. (1990). Washington, DC: National Health Lawyers Association.

Kongstvedt, P. R. (1996). *The managed health care handbook* (3rd ed.). Frederick, MD: Aspen.

Kongstvedt, P. R. (1997). *Essentials of managed health care* (2nd ed.). Frederick, MD: Aspen.

Lazarus, A. (Ed.). (1996). *Controversies in managed mental health care.* Washington, DC: American Psychiatric Press.

Mitchell, G., & Haber, J. (Eds.). (1997). *The primary care/behavioral health integration handbook.* Tiburon, CA: CentraLink.

Moffic, H. S. (1997). *The ethical way: Challenges and solutions for managed behavioral healthcare.* San Francisco: Jossey-Bass.

National Leadership Council Task Force. (1996). *Performance indicators in behavioral healthcare: Measures of access, appropriateness, quality, outcomes, and prevention.* Tiburon, CA: CentraLink.

Poynter, W. (1994). *The preferred provider's handbook.* New York: Brunner Mazel.

Pozgar, G. D., & Smythe, N. S. (1995). *Case law in health care administration: A companion guide to legal aspects of health care administration* (6th ed.). Frederick, MD: Aspen.

Rognehaugh, R. (Ed.). (1996). *The managed health care dictionary.* Frederick, MD: Aspen.

Schreter, R. K., Sharfstein, S. S., & Schreter, C. A. (Eds.). (1997). *Managing care, not dollars: The continuum of mental health services.* Washington, DC: American Psychiatric Press.

Schuster, J. M., Lovell, M., & Trachta, A. (Eds.). (1997). *Training behavioral healthcare professionals: Higher learning in an era of managed care.* San Francisco: Jossey-Bass.

St. Anthony's capitation reference manual (Vols. 1 & 2). (1997). Reston, VA: St. Anthony Publishing.

St. Anthony's capitation utilization and rate guidebook: 1994–95 edition. (1994). Reston, VA: St. Anthony Publishing.

St. Anthony's guide to capitation contracts. (1994). Reston, VA: St. Anthony Publishing.

Trabin, T. & Freeman, M. (1995). *Managed behavioral healthcare: History, models, strategic challenges and future course.* San Francisco: Jossey-Bass.

Trabin, T., Freeman, M. A., & Pallak, M. (Eds.) (1995). *Inside outcomes: The national review of behavioral healthcare outcomes management programs.* San Francisco: Jossey-Bass.

Trabin, T., Jarvis, D., Mockler, R., & Mauer, B. (1995). *How to respond to managed behavioral healthcare: A workbook guide to your organization's success.* Tiburon, CA: CentraLink.

Winegar, N. (1992). *The clinician's guide to managed mental health care.* New York: Haworth Press.

Woody, R. H. (1991). *Quality care in mental health: Assuring the best clinical services.* San Francisco: Jossey-Bass.

Wyatt, R. (1997). *The brief therapy companion: Essential principals for the practice of time effective psychotherapy.* Durham, NH: Free Harvest Press.

Zieman, G. L. (Ed.). (1995). *The complete capitation handbook: How to design and implement at-risk contracts for behavioral healthcare.* San Francisco: Jossey-Bass.

REFERENCES

American Managed Behavioral Healthcare Association. (1995). *Performance measures for managed behavioral healthcare programs (PERMS 1.0)*. Washington, DC: Author.

American Managed Behavioral Healthcare Association. (1996, December). *Any willing provider*. Washington, DC: Author.

American Psychiatric Association. (1997). *The psychiatrist's guide to capitation and risk-based contracting*. Washington, DC: Author.

Analysis of managed care enrollment, 1993 to 1997. (1997, February 14). *Behavior Healthcare Tomorrow*, p. 14.

Austad, C. (1996). *Is long-term psychotherapy unethical?* San Francisco: Jossey-Bass.

Belkin, L. (1996, December 6). Health care: The quality half. *New York Times Magazine*, pp. 68–71, 102–106.

Block, L. (1992, June 8). Mental health expenses make employers anxious. *Business Insurance*, pp. 3, 6–9.

Butler, S. M., & Moffit, R. E. (1995). The FEHBP as a model for a new Medicare program. *Health Affairs, 14*(4), 48.

Callahan, J. J., Shepard, D. S., Beinecke, R. A., Larson, M. J., & Cavanaugh, D. (1995). Mental health/substance abuse treatment in managed care: The Massachusetts Medicaid experience. *Health Affairs, 14*(3), 174.

Church, G. J. (1997, April 14). The backlash against HMOs. *Time*, 32–39.

Ciba-Geigy. (1996). *Report on member satisfaction with managed care.* New York: Author.

Crosby, P. (1983). Quality without tears. New York: McGraw-Hill.

Cummings, N. (1990). Brief intermittent psychotherapy throughout the life cycle. In J. K. Zeig & S. G. Gilligan (Eds.), *Brief therapy: Myths, methods, and metaphors* (pp. 169–184). New York: Brunner/Mazel.

Daniels, A., Zieman, G., Kramer, T., & Furgal, C. (1997). *The behavioral healthcare quality and accountability tool kit, version one.* Tiburon, CA: CentraLink, Institute of Behavioral Healthcare.

Daniels, A., Zieman, G., & Dickman, N. (1995). *The comprehensive group practice tool kit: A manual for behavioral group practice development and management.* Tiburon, CA: CentraLink, Institute of Behavioral Healthcare.

Daniels, A., Zieman, G., & Dickman, N. (1996). *The comprehensive managed care tool kit: A manual for capitated and managed behavioral healthcare delivery systems.* Tiburon, CA: CentraLink, Institute of Behavioral Healthcare.

Data watch: Managed care enrollment up, costs down. (1997, August). *Business and Health*, p. 60.

Deming, W. E. (1986). *Out of the crisis.* Cambridge, MA: Massachusetts Institute of Technology.

Desmarais, H. R., & Hash, M. M. (1997). Financing graduate medical education: The search for new sources of support. *Health Affairs, 16*(4), 48–63.

Digital Equipment Corporation. (1997). *HMO performance standards.* Author.

Falkson, J. L. (1980). *HMOs and the politics of health system reform.* Bowie, MD: R. Brady.

Foundation for Accountability. (1996, Fall). Major depressive disorder. *In Practice*, pp. 1–8.

Gazmararian, J. A., Kaplan, J. P., Cogswell, M. E., Bailey, C. M., Davis, N. A., Cutler, C. M. (1997). Maternity experiences in a managed care organization. *Health Affairs, 16*(3), 198–208.

Geisel, J. (1993, January 11). '94 health care outlays hit $1 trillion: U.S. *Business Insurance*, p. 3.

Grobman, M. (1997, May). Managed care's last frontier. *Business & Health*, pp. 31–33.

Hamburger, T. (1997, June 15). Medicare cuts could hurt teaching hospitals. *Star Tribune Newspaper* (Twin Cities), p. 1.

Hammonds, K. H. (1997, June 2). Medicare gets an umbrella for an avalanche. *BusinessWeek*, p. 44.

Hammonds, K. H., Schiller, Z., Stodghill, R., & Harris, N. (1996, June 24). *BusinessWeek*, pp. 62–63.

Harris, G. (1997, June 2). On managed care. *Managed Healthcare, 44*, 36–39.

Harris, M. L. (1927, November 26). Medical economics. *Journal of the American Medical Association*, pp. 78–81.

Health Affairs. (1997). *16*(1), front cover.

Health Care and Finance Authority. (1997, September 10). *HCFA: The Medicare and Medicaid Agency.* (http://www.hcfa.gov/statistics/)

Holahan, J., & Liska, D. (1997). The slowdown in Medicaid spending growth: Will it continue? *Health Affairs 16*(2), 158.

Jackson, R. A. (1992, April 2). Wilson is over: Jury says UR firm and payers not liable for bad faith denial, Wilson's death. *Managed Care Law Outlook*, pp. 31–38.

Juran, J. M. (1988). *Juran on planning quality.* New York: Free Press.

Kaplan, M. (1997). Creating the new psychiatric residency. In J. M. Schuster, M. R. Lovell, & A. M. Trachta (Eds.), *Training behavioral healthcare professionals: higher learning in the era of managed care* (pp. 31–48). San Francisco, Jossey-Bass.

Lamphere, J. A., Neuman, P., Langwell, K., & Sherman, D. (1997). The surge in Medicare managed care: An update. *Health Affairs, 16*(3), 127–138.

Lancaster, H. (1997, May 20). Managing your career. *Wall Street Journal*, p. B1.

Major, M. (1994, February 24). Managed care is credited for breaking the boom-bust cycle of premium costs. *Managed Healthcare, 44*, 46–48.

Managed Care. (1997, August). *Managed Medicare's rapid expansion.* Silver Spring, MD: Business Publishers, pp. 61–64.

Mayer, T., & Mayer, G. (1985). HMOs: Origins and development. *New England Journal of Medicine, 312*(9), 590–594.

McCall, N. (1997). Lessons from Arizona's Medicaid managed care program. *Health Affairs, 16*(4), 194–199.

McCue, M. (1997, March). Managed care's shockwave. *Managed Healthcare*, 24–26.

Mesa Mental Health. (1996). Intake statistics-1996. Albuquerque, NM: Author.

National Committee for Quality Assurance. (1996). *Health plan and employer data and information set, version 3.0.* Washington, DC: Author.

National Committee for Quality Assurance. (1997, April). *Standards for accreditation of managed behavioral healthcare organizations.* Washington, DC: Author.

National Institute of Mental Health. (1989). *Data standards for mental health decision support systems: A report of the task force to revise the data content and system guidelines of the mental health statistics improvement program.* (DHHS Publication No. ADM 89-1589). Washington, DC: U.S. Government Printing Office.

Rosenbaum, S. (1997). A look inside Medicaid managed care. *Health Affairs, 16*(4), 265.

Rubin, H. R., Gendek, B., Rogers, W. H., Kosinski, M., McHorney, C. A., & Ware, J. E. (1993). Patients' ratings of outpatient visits in difference practice settings: Results from the Medical Outcomes Study. *Journal of the American Medical Association, 270*(7), 835–840.

Schuster, J. M., Lovell, M. R., & Trachta, A. M. (Eds.) (1997). *Training behavioral healthcare professionals: Higher learning in the era of managed care.* San Francisco: Jossey-Bass.

Shaw, D. B. (1997). Managed care's impact on graduate psychology training programs. In J. M. Schuster, M. R. Lovell, & A. M. Trachta (Eds.), *Training behavioral healthcare professionals: Higher learning in the era of managed care* (pp. 49–66). San Francisco: Jossey-Bass.

Shouldice, R., & Shouldice, K. (1978). *Medical group practice and health maintenance.* Washington, DC: Information Resources Press.

State Health Watch. (1997). *Medicaid behavioral health care contracts, May, 3 & 11.* Yardley, PA: Author.

Stauffer, M. (1997). Gag clauses: An overview of state activity. *Behavioral Healthcare Tomorrow, 6*(2), 19–20.

Trachta, A. M. (1997). Current training issues in social work. In J. M. Schuster, M. R. Lovell, & A. M. Trachta (Eds.), *Training behavioral healthcare professionals: Higher learning in the era of managed care* (pp. 89–102). San Francisco: Jossey-Bass.

U.S. Department of Labor, Bureau of Labor Statistics. *Employer costs for employee compensation, 1991, 1992, 1993, 1994, 1995, 1997, 1996.* Washington, DC.

Woolsey, C. (1994, July 1). New data could reshape health plans. *Business Insurance,* pp. 12–14.

Wrightson, C. W. (1990). *HMO rate setting and financial strategy.* Ann Arbor, MI: Health Administration Press Perspectives.

Wyatt, R. (1995). Grappling with ethical issues. In G. Zieman (Ed.), *The complete capitation handbook: How to design and implement at-risk contracts for behavioral healthcare* (pp. 175–188). San Francisco: Jossey-Bass.

Zieman, G. (Ed.). (1995). *The complete capitation handbook: How to design and implement at-risk contracts for behavioral healthcare.* San Francisco: Jossey-Bass.

Zieman, G., Williams, C., Daniels, A., & Kramer, T. (1997, April). *Outcomes management project-quarterly report.* University of Cincinnati, Department of Psychiatry.

ABOUT THE AUTHOR

Gayle L. Zieman received his Ph.D. in counseling psychology from Colorado State University in 1982. He completed his clinical internship at Children's Medical Center in Tulsa, Oklahoma. Prior to starting in solo private practice, Zieman was for three years an itinerant psychologist serving rural towns and Native American reservations in New Mexico.

Zieman has been a pioneer in managed care and group practice since 1988, when his own group became one of the first in the country to contract with MCOs and self-insured employers on a capitation basis. Mesa Mental Health in Albuquerque, of which he is cofounder and vice president, has transformed into a managed behavioral healthcare organization administering mental health benefits for nearly 300,000 covered members of HMOs, other managed care plans, and large employers. Since 1988, Zieman has been a national leader in training clinicians and group practices in the realities and opportunities of managed care.

Zieman has given clinical workshops in nine countries and is a frequent national presenter on managed care contracting, finances under managed care, outcomes measurement, and quality management. He is a founding member of the Council of Behavioral Group Practices and coleads the consortium's Outcomes Management Project, which since 1995 has collected clinical data on over 16,000 managed care patients in twelve states.

In addition to his consultation work, Zieman edited *The Complete Capitation Handbook* (1995) and coauthored *The Comprehensive Group Practice Tool Kit* (1997), *The Behavioral Quality and Accountability Tool Kit* (1997), and *The Comprehensive Managed Care Tool Kit* (1996).

INDEX

Independent practice associations (IPAs): defined, 7; establishment of, 16
Information services department, 40–41
Inpatient care delivery, 45–46
Intake process, 31–33, 39
Integrated behavioral departments, 138, 143–148
Integrated delivery systems (IDSs), 11, 108

J
Jackson, R. A., 23
Joint Commission for Accreditation of Healthcare Organizations (JCAHO), 26, 36, 127
Juran, J. M., 112

K
Kaiser-Permanente Health Plan, 15
Kaplan, J. P., 23, 173
Kramer, T., 46, 169

L
Lamphere, J. A., 135
Lancaster, H., 1
Langwell, K., 135
Larson, M. J., 133
Legal liability: civil suits, 23–24; emergent patient and, 64; malpractice and, 53, 73
Legislated regulations, 22–23
Liska, D., 131
Lovelace ParkCenter, 146–148
Lovell, M. R., 136

M
Major, M., 20
Malpractice policies, 53, 73
Malpractice reports, 88
Managed Behavioral Healthcare Leadership Award, 139, 141
Managed behavioral healthcare organizations (MBHOs): application, documentation needed for, 50–54; basic types of, 137–138; clinician's goals in joining, 49–50; clinician's pre-contract assessment of, 49–59; defined, 27; organizational structure, 28–41; restrictions and clinical autonomy in, 54–55; work groups, option to participate in, 58. *See also* Financial considerations
Managed care: consumer/ provider opposition to, 20–23; cost control and, 19–20; customer satisfaction with, 24–25; early contractual arrangements in, 12–17; historical conflicts in, 14–15. *See also* Health maintenance organizations (HMOs); Managed behavioral healthcare organizations (MBHOs)

Managed indemnity plans, 5
Marketing department, 40
MassHealth, 132–133
Mayer, G., 13
Mayer, T., 13
Maximum allowable fees, 63
McCall, N., 133
Medicaid: benefit structures, 130–131; discounted fee-for-service system of, 130; managed care programs, 1, 10, 23, 131–132, 137; Massachusetts state conversion (MassHealth) program, 132–133; as secondary insurance, 69; statistics, 128, 129–130; waiver system, 131–132
Medical associations, managed care and, 14, 22
Medical director, responsibilities of, 29–31
Medical emergency, defined, 63
Medical necessity: criteria, 33, 168; indemnity insurance and, 5
Medical records review, confidentiality and, 69–72, 161
Medicare: cost-cutting proposals, 135–136; managed care model, 1, 10, 134–136; reimbursement methods, 134–135; Resource Value Based Scale (RVBS), 104–105, 134–135; as secondary insurance, 69; statistics, 128, 134
Member advocacy, 31–33
Membership certificate, defined, 62
Member services department, 38
Mental Health Statistics Improvement Program (MHSIP), 125–126, 130
Mesa Mental Health, 46, 149–151, 163
Military managed care plans, 1, 129
Moffit, R. E., 129
Multidisciplinary groups, 47–48, 167–168, 172–174

N
National Association of Social Workers, 22
National carve-out companies, 137–143
National Committee for Quality Assurance (NCQA): accreditation requirements, 36, 72; Behavioral Healthcare Standards, 26, 44, 58, 125, 197–203; preventive standards, 123–124; recredentialing mandates, 37
National Community Mental Health Council, 22
National Institute of Mental Health standards, 125–126
National standards, 57, 124–126. *See also* National Committee for Quality Assurance (NCQA)